Robert Lee

The Order of Public Worship and Administration of the Sacraments

as used in the Church of the Greyfriars, Edinburgh

Robert Lee

The Order of Public Worship and Administration of the Sacraments
as used in the Church of the Greyfriars, Edinburgh

ISBN/EAN: 9783337291525

Printed in Europe, USA, Canada, Australia, Japan

Cover: Foto ©Lupo / pixelio.de

More available books at **www.hansebooks.com**

THE ORDER OF PUBLIC WORSHIP

AND

ADMINISTRATION OF THE SACRAMENTS

AS USED IN THE CHURCH OF THE
GREYFRIARS, EDINBURGH.

BY

ROBERT LEE, D.D.,

MINISTER OF GREYFRIARS,
PROFESSOR OF BIBLICAL CRITICISM, ETC., IN THE UNIVERSITY OF EDINBURGH,
SENIOR DEAN OF THE CHAPEL ROYAL,
AND ONE OF HER MAJESTY'S CHAPLAINS IN ORDINARY IN SCOTLAND.

"Let all things be done decently, and according to order."—1 COR. XIV. 40.

EDINBURGH:
PRINTED BY THOMAS AND ARCHIBALD CONSTABLE,
PRINTERS TO THE QUEEN, AND TO THE UNIVERSITY.

ADVERTISEMENT.

THE present volume is a reprint of the Third Edition, entitled, "A Presbyterian Prayer-Book," etc. (published last year), with some slight corrections and additions. This edition contains, also, Services for Baptism, Marriage, and the Burial of the Dead, all of which were wanting in the Third Edition.

In the following Morning and Evening Services the three acts of worship are arranged uniformly according to what appears the natural order—the Word, Prayer, and Praise; and the Service consists of these acts thrice repeated in the same order. The Sermon, with Prayer and Praise, constitutes a fourth repetition. If it be desired to shorten the Service, the Sermon comes in before the third Prayer, and then both lessons are read before the second Prayer. It is, however, the practice in the Greyfriars' Church to substitute in one of the Sunday Services a short exposition of each of the lessons instead of a Sermon.

It has been the aim of the author to draw his compositions rather from Scriptural than Ecclesiastical sources, however good or venerable these may appear to be. He has convinced himself by considerable study, that, while these documents may suggest useful hints, and may guard us against some errors, it is not wise to revive, or even closely copy, any of them, either those which are more ancient, or those which originated at the period of the Reformation; it being evident that both have faults which would render them unsuitable and unacceptable to us : we ought rather, as he thinks, to derive our devotional compositions more directly from the Scriptures themselves, especially the Book of Psalms, which should be regarded as the grand magazine of devotion for the Church of God in all ages. Under this impression selections from the Psalms have been largely interspersed among the other Prayers, with the view of giving to the Service greater richness and solemnity. These selections, being in the first person singular, furnish to each individual a kind of response, in the familiar and venerable language of Scripture, to those petitions which have just been uttered in the plural number in the name of the whole congregation.

This kind of composition, though it may appear at first sight extremely easy, will be found by any one who comprehends the qualities which should distinguish it, to be very difficult. Accordingly, few eminently successful examples of it have appeared in modern times— fewer probably than in any other department of religious literature.

The author of the following Prayers has done his

ADVERTISEMENT. v

best endeavour that they should not be declamatory, oratorical, or fine,—familiar, tedious, or particular,—didactic or sermonizing; and he has laboured to make them, as far as he could, simple, dignified, and devotional; suggesting as much as possible, without running into detail. He has also studied that they should assert, or rather imply Christian doctrines in a catholic spirit, avoiding all sectarian vehemence and controversial exaggeration. It has also appeared to him becoming that the Prayers of the Church should express Christian doctrines,—especially those of them which are termed *mysteries*,—as much as possible in the language of Scripture; and that they should perpetually suggest the connexion of the duties and graces of the Christian character with the great Gospel verities; aiming at the production neither of a dead morality on the one hand, nor of an equally dead and far less useful orthodoxy on the other; but seeking to combine Christian life with Christian motive and feeling—faith working by love.

The numerous works of the same class with the present, which have within the last few years been published by ministers of Presbyterian and Independent Churches, are a pleasing sign that the prejudices which have so long prevailed against composed prayers are rapidly dying away, if they be not already extinct, among all but the most ignorant; and that we are gradually returning to the wiser views and more edifying practices of the older Presbyterians in all countries, who, while averse to the rigid Ritualism of Episcopal Churches, and reasonably desirous not to exclude extemporaneous or free prayer, used habitually the Liturgies which their great divines had composed, and transmitted them, as not the least precious fruit of the Reformation, to their children and successors.

It cannot but appear wonderful that, when sermons are composed with so much care and pains, we should leave our prayers altogether to the impulse of the moment; as if it were more needful that our speeches to our fellow-men should be well ordered, than our addresses to God. In every point of view, extempore preaching is far more natural and becoming than extempore prayer; because any want of order, propriety, or solemnity, which is so difficult to be altogether avoided in unpremeditated speech, is far less offensive in a discourse to our fellow-mortals, than in those solemn appeals which we present in their name and our own to the Father of our spirits.

The second part of the present work consists of selections from the Metre Psalms and from the Paraphrases, with the addition of a few Hymns from the collection published by the General Assembly's Committee. These selections comprehend all those portions of the Psalms and Paraphrases which appear suitable for public worship; those Psalms and portions of Psalms being omitted which are *didactic*, or belong in their spirit and tone to the *Jewish* dispensation, or are strictly *prayers*, and should be used as such (as many of them are in the following compositions), or which appear for some other reason to be less proper for use as Psalms in Christian congregations. These selections are arranged in convenient lengths for singing; and appended to each of them is the name of an appropriate tune. This is designed to promote the practice (the propriety of which will be obvious to any one who considers the subject) of each Psalm being always sung with the same tune. I am indebted for the selection of tunes here given to the Leader of the Music in the Greyfriars' Church, Mr. Joseph Geoghegan, whose judgment and taste as a musician are well known.

Upon the whole, I am not without hopes that this selection and arrangement of Psalms and Paraphrases may be found convenient and useful both to ministers and precentors, and perhaps also to those congregations which are honourably distinguished by the desire that our Public Worship should be more systematic, refined, and solemn than it now generally is.

ROBERT LEE.

EDINBURGH, *Nov.* 14, 1864.

NOTE.—*The Fourth Edition of the Prayer Book having been for some time out of print, the Executors of Dr. Lee issue the present edition in order to meet the continued demand for the book.*

EDINBURGH, *December* 1873.

First Sunday of the Month.

Forenoon Service.

[*The congregation being assembled, the Minister may recite one or more of the following sentences.*]

Seek ye the Lord while he may be found; call upon him while he is near. Let the wicked forsake his way, and the unrighteous man his thoughts; and let him return unto the Lord, and he will have mercy upon him, and to our God, for he will abundantly pardon. *Isa.* lv.

Let all the earth fear the Lord; let all the inhabitants of the world stand in awe of him: for he spake, and it was done; he commanded, and it stood fast.

Blessed is the nation whose God is the Lord; and the people whom he hath chosen for his own inheritance.

Behold, the eye of the Lord is upon them that fear him, upon them that hope in his mercy. *Ps.* xxxiii.

Having these promises, dearly beloved, let us draw near to the throne of grace with true hearts, in full assurance of faith. Let us pray.

The First Prayer.

I.

O God, whom heaven and the heaven of heavens cannot contain, but who dwellest with humble and contrite hearts, Look in thy mercy upon us who are here assembled according to thine ordinance to offer up our sacrifices of prayer and praise before thy Divine Majesty.

Grant us thy Holy Spirit, we entreat thee, O Lord, to guide and sanctify us, that we may be acceptable in thy sight, and may obtain our petitions; for we come before thee not in our own name, but in the name of our great High Priest and Advocate Jesus Christ. —Amen.

Hear my cry, O God:
—Attend unto my prayer.
From the end of the earth will I cry unto thee when my heart is overwhelmed:
—Lead me to the Rock that is higher than I.
For thou hast been a shelter for me:
—And a strong tower from the enemy.
I will abide in thy tabernacle for ever:
—I will trust in the covert of thy wings. *Ps.* lxi.

II.

We humble ourselves before thee, O God; for we have transgressed thy holy laws in thought, word, and deed; and we are miserable sinners in thy sight. Thou hast revealed unto us the way of righteousness and peace; but we have refused to walk in it, and have gone astray from thee; and we have received in ourselves that recompence of our error which is meet.

We acknowledge our sin and misery before thee, O God our heavenly Father, who searchest our hearts, and art acquainted with all our ways. Look down upon us in thy tender mercy, and forgive us all our iniquities; through Jesus Christ thy Son, who is the propitiation for our sins, and not for ours only, but also for the sins of the whole world.—Amen.

FORENOON SERVICE.

O Lord, rebuke me not in thine anger :
—Neither chasten me in thy hot displeasure.
Have mercy upon me, O Lord, for I am weak :
—O Lord, heal me, for my bones are vexed.
My soul is also sore vexed; but thou, O Lord, how long ?
—Return, O Lord, deliver my soul ; oh, save me for thy mercy's sake.
Depart from me, all ye workers of iniquity :
—For the Lord hath heard the voice of my weeping.
The Lord hath heard my supplication :
—The Lord will receive my prayer. *Ps.* vi.

In this was manifested the love of God toward us, because that God sent his only-begotten Son into the world, that we might live through him. Herein is love, not that we loved God, but that he loved us, and sent his Son to be the propitiation for our sins. 1 *John* iv.

The Lord is merciful and gracious, slow to anger, and plenteous in mercy. *Ps.* ciii.

III.

We thank thee, O God our heavenly Father, for that message of grace and mercy which thou hast sent unto us in the gospel of thy Son Jesus Christ. Dispose and enable us, we pray thee, to receive the same in faith and love, and to walk worthy of our high calling, not turning the grace of God into licentiousness, but bringing forth continually the fruits of holy obedience, to the praise of thy name ; through Jesus Christ our Lord, who taught us thus to pray—

Our Father which art in Heaven, Hallowed be thy name. Thy kingdom come. Thy will be done on earth, as it is in heaven. Give us this day our daily bread. And forgive us our debts, as we forgive our debtors. And lead us not into temptation ; but deliver us from evil.—Amen.

Bless the Lord, O my soul :
—And all that is within me, bless his holy namè.

[*Then may be said or sung one or both of these Psalms.*]

PSALM VIII.

O | Lord our | Lord, ‖ how excellent is thy | name in | all the | earth !
Who | hast... | set ‖ thy | glory a- | bove the | heavens.
Out of the mouth of | babes and | sucklings ‖ hast | thou or- | dained | strength
Be- | cause of thine | enemies, ‖ that thou mightest still the | enemy | and the a- | venger.
When I consider thy heavens, the | work of thy | fingers, ‖ the moon and the | stars, which | thou hast or- | dained ;
What is man, that thou art | mindful | of him ? ‖ and the son of | man, that thou | visitest | him ?
For thou hast made him a little | lower than the | angels, ‖ and hast | crowned him with | glory and | honour.
Thou madest him to have dominion over the | works of thy | hands ; ‖ thou hast put | all things | under his | feet ;
All | sheep and | oxen, ‖ yea, | and the | beasts of the | field ;
The fowl of the air, and the | fish of the | sea, ‖ and whatsoever passeth | through the | paths of the | seas.
O | Lord our | Lord, ‖ how excellent is thy | name in | all the | earth !

PSALM XCVIII.

O sing unto the | Lord a new | song ; || for | he hath done | marvellous | things :

His right hand, and his | holy | arm, || hath | gotten | him the | victory.

The Lord hath made known | his sal- | vation : || his righteousness hath he openly | shewed in the | sight of the | heathen.

He hath remembered his | mercy and his | truth || to- | ward the | house of | Israel :

All the ends of the | earth || have seen the sal- | vation | of our | God.

Make a joyful noise unto the Lord, | all the | earth : || make a loud noise, and re- | joice, and | sing... | praise.

Sing unto the | Lord with the | harp ; || with the | harp, and the | voice of a | psalm.

With trumpets and | sound of | cornet || make a joyful noise be- | fore the | Lord, the | King.

Let the sea roar, and the | fulness there- | of ; || the world, and | they that | dwell there- | in.

Let the floods | clap their | hands : || let the hills be joyful to- | gether be- | fore the | Lord ;

For | he... | cometh, || he | cometh to | judge the | earth :

With righteousness shall he | judge the | world, || and the | people with | equi- | ty.

[*Then may be read the Lesson from the Old Testament : after which follows*]

The Second Prayer.

I.

O Lord, who hast given thy holy Word to be a light unto our feet and a lamp unto our path, Guide our steps at all times in the way of thy precepts. Suffer us not to go astray from thee, or to err from thy truth. Acknowledging our own ignorance and the deceitfulness of our hearts, we call upon thee, O God, for help and deliverance, who savest all them that put their trust in thee.—Amen.

II.

O Lord our merciful Father, Be pleased to guide and defend us in all our ways, that we may be delivered in all dangers and temptations of this day; and may so follow the example and pattern which thy dear Son hath left us, both in joyfully bearing and constantly performing thy holy will, that we may glorify thy name, and may abide in thy love; even as he kept thy commandments and abode in thy love.—Amen.

III.

O Lord God Almighty, who makest all things work together for good to them that love thee, We pray that thou wouldst so order the course of thy providence respecting us, and so enlighten and purify our souls, that all the events of this life may be made conducive to our eternal salvation; through Jesus Christ our Lord.—Amen.

IV.

Almighty and most merciful Father, who workest in thy children both to desire and to perform those things that please thee, Grant us grace that we may pursue our several callings and duties in the world, with a devout, holy, and heavenly mind, considering that we are ever in thy presence and under thine eye; that in all our works and labours, working the work of God, and labouring for the meat that endureth unto everlasting life, we may be found good and faithful servants, and may finally, with all thine elect, enter into the joy of our Lord.—Amen.

V.

O God, everlasting and almighty, who art the Creator and Preserver of all men, and who willest not that any should perish, but that all should come to repentance, Send forth thy light and thy truth among all nations.

Guide all thy flock in the paths of truth, righteousness, and peace; and make them to be numbered with thy saints in glory everlasting.

Comfort the afflicted: send consolation and joy to those that are in trouble and sorrow: hear the groaning of the prisoners: deliver the oppressed from him that spoileth him: relieve the wants of the poor; and save the afflicted people. Arise, O God, for judgment, and save all the meek of the earth.—Amen.

I will extol thee, my God, O King:
—And I will bless thy name for ever and ever.
Every day will I bless thee:
—And I will praise thy name for ever and ever.

[*Here a Psalm may be sung: after which is read the Lesson from the New Testament. Then follows*]

The Third Prayer.

I.

O God, who hast revealed to us the light of thy gospel, and called us into the fellowship of thy Son, Grant that we may put away all the works of darkness, and may walk in purity, uprightness, and truth, that we may have fellowship with thee, for thou art light, and in thee there is no darkness at all; that so, when the shadows of this mortal life are passed away, we may behold those things which the eye of man hath not seen, and be made partakers of everlasting glory; through Christ our Lord.—Amen.

II.

Grant, we pray thee, O Lord, that we, who have believed in the name of thy Son Jesus Christ, may die daily through his death, and also may be quickened through the power of his resurrection. Being crucified with Christ, may we live to thee, through faith of the Son of God, who loved us and gave himself for us; that when he shall appear in glory, we also may be manifested as thy sons, and may inherit the kingdom which thou hast prepared for them that love thee.—Amen.

III.

Almighty and most gracious God, Look in thy compassion upon our manifold infirmities, and uphold us by thy mighty power. Let us not faint or be weary in running the race that is set before us; but, animated by thy promises, may we be strong both to do and to endure thy holy will, looking unto our merciful High Priest, Jesus Christ, who himself suffered and was tempted, and is able to succour us when we are tempted.—Amen.

IV.

Almighty God, the Creator of all things, who hast so loved the world as to give thy Son, that they who were far off might be brought near unto thee, Send forth thy gospel into all lands, and hasten the time when all the kindreds of the nations shall turn unto the Lord, and Jew and Gentile shall be one flock, under one Shepherd—Jesus Christ.—Amen.

V.

O God, merciful Father, Look upon all thy family which thy Son Jesus Christ hath purchased with his own blood. Deliver them from ignorance and sin, and from the power of Death; and grant unto them all a portion in thy kingdom of heaven, the hope of which thou hast inspired in the hearts of thy chosen; through Him who was dead and liveth for ever, and who sitteth at thy right hand, till Death, the last enemy, be destroyed, and all things be put under his feet.—Amen.

VI.

God of all grace and consolation, Send forth thy Holy Spirit, the Comforter, into the hearts of all those who, under thy wise and holy providence, are called to endure any sickness, trouble, or adversity. Let thy fatherly chastisement, though for the present it be not joyous but grievous, work the peaceable fruit of righteousness in them that are exercised thereby. Enrich their souls with faith and hope, with patience and fortitude; and, while they look at those things which are not seen, may their present affliction work for them a far more exceeding, even an eternal weight of glory. —Amen.

VII.

We beseech thee, O Lord, by whom kings reign and princes decree justice, to regard with thy favour Victoria, our Queen and Governor. Enrich her with thy blessing: sanctify her by thy grace: defend her from all evil. May she reign in righteousness, peace, and prosperity all the days of her life upon earth; and finally may she receive that crown of glory which fadeth not away.

Be very gracious, we entreat thee, O Lord, to the Prince and Princess of Wales; and to all the members of the Royal Family.

We pray that thou wouldst grant a spirit of wisdom and judgment to the Ministers and Counsellors of the Crown; to the Nobles and Representatives of the people in Parliament; to Magistrates, Judges, and all that are invested with authority; that we under them may lead a quiet and peaceable life in godliness and honesty, adorning the doctrine of God our Saviour.

And bestow thy blessing upon all ranks and conditions of men among us. Bless them in the work of their hands; prosper their honest industry; grant unto them the things that are needful for the body and the life that now is; above all, make them rich toward God and heirs of thine everlasting kingdom.

We pray for our kindred, our friends, and all whom thou hast made the instruments of thy grace and bounty to us, that thou wouldst reward and bless them abundantly; and also for our enemies, slanderers, and persecutors, that thou wouldst grant them repentance, and enable us to forgive them from the heart.—Amen.

VIII.

O God, whose blessing is upon them that fear thee from generation to generation, We desire to commit ourselves to thee as a faithful Creator, who hast said, "I will never leave thee nor forsake thee." Strengthen us that we may seek first thy kingdom and righteousness, trusting in thy promise that all things needful shall be added unto us. And seeing we brought nothing into this world, and can carry nothing out, may we, having food and raiment, be therewith content. —Amen.

Lord, have mercy upon us, and grant us thy peace:
—Have mercy upon us, O Lord, and grant us thy salvation.
Through Jesus Christ, the Lamb of God, which taketh away the sin of the world, receive our prayer.
—O Lord, hear us, of thy great mercy, through the same Jesus Christ our Lord.

Now unto him that is able to keep us from falling, and to present us faultless before the presence of his glory with exceeding joy; to the only wise God, our Saviour, be glory and majesty, dominion and power, both now and ever.—Amen.

[*Then a Psalm or Doxology may be sung.*]

The Benediction.

The grace of the Lord Jesus Christ, and the love of God, and the communion of the Holy Spirit, be with you all.—Amen.

First Sunday of the Month.

AFTERNOON SERVICE.

[*The congregation being assembled, the Minister may recite one or more of the following sentences.*]

Look unto me and be ye saved, all the ends of the earth; for I am God, and there is none else. *Isa.* xlv.

The Lord is nigh unto them that call upon him; to all that call upon him in truth.

He will fulfil the desire of them that fear him: he also will hear their cry, and will save them. *Ps.* cxlv.

[*Or the following.*]

The Lord reigneth; let the people tremble: he sitteth between the cherubim; let the earth be moved.

The Lord is great in Zion; and he is high above all the people.

Exalt ye the Lord our God, and worship at his footstool; for he is holy. *Ps.* xcix.

Brethren, let us with humble and contrite hearts draw near to the throne of grace, in the name of our great High Priest and Advocate Jesus Christ.

First Prayer.

I.

O Lord our heavenly Father, who hast commanded us not to forsake the assembling of ourselves together,

AFTERNOON SERVICE. 13

Be pleased to sanctify and bless our meeting together at this time: and grant that, by thy Word and Spirit, our minds may be enlightened, our hearts cleansed, and our wills directed to keep thy holy commandments; through Jesus Christ our Redeemer.—Amen.

My soul cleaveth unto the dust:
—Quicken thou me according to thy word.
Teach me the way of thy statutes:
—And I shall keep it unto the end.
Give me understanding, and I shall keep thy law:
—Yea, I shall observe it with my whole heart.
Turn away mine eyes from beholding vanity:
—And quicken thou me in thy way. *Ps.* cxix. 25.

II.

We confess our sins before thee, O God, thou righteous Judge, to whom all things are naked and open. We have done evil in thy sight, transgressing thy law, which is holy, just, and good; and we are verily guilty before thee.

We praise thy name that when we were enemies we were reconciled unto thee by the death of thy Son, and for the comfortable assurance that if we confess our sins, thou art faithful and just to forgive us our sins, and to cleanse us from all unrighteousness. Be it unto us, O Lord, according to thy word.

Justify us freely by thy grace, through the redemption that is in Christ Jesus; that, having our hearts sprinkled from an evil conscience, and our bodies washed with pure water, we may serve thee in holiness and righteousness all our days, rejoicing in the hope of thy glory, and waiting for the appearing and kingdom of our Lord and Saviour Jesus Christ.—Amen.

Unto thee, O Lord, do I lift up my soul. O my God, I trust in thee:
—Let me not be ashamed; let not mine enemies triumph over me.
Lead me in thy truth, and teach me:
—For thou art the God of my salvation; on thee do I wait all the day.
Remember, O Lord, thy tender mercies and thy loving-kindnesses:
—For they have been ever of old.
Remember not the sins of my youth, nor my transgressions:
—According to thy mercy remember thou me, for thy goodness' sake, O Lord.
Good and upright is the Lord:
—Therefore will he teach sinners in the way.
The meek will he guide in judgment:
—And the meek will he teach his way.
All the paths of the Lord are mercy and truth:
—Unto such as keep his covenant and his testimonies.
For thy name's sake, O Lord, pardon mine iniquity:
—For it is great.
O keep my soul, and deliver me:
—Let me not be ashamed; for I put my trust in thee. *Ps.* xxv.

III.

O God, thou Father of lights and Fountain of all wisdom and knowledge, We thank thee that thou hast sent thy Son Jesus Christ into the world to enlighten our darkness, and to guide our steps in the ways of truth and righteousness.

May we hear his voice: may we know and embrace the doctrine which he hath taught us: may we follow

AFTERNOON SERVICE.

his example: and finally may we receive those exceeding great and precious promises which he hath given us. And these things we ask in his name who taught us, when we pray, thus to say—

Our Father which art in Heaven, Hallowed be thy name. Thy kingdom come. Thy will be done on earth, as it is in heaven. Give us day by day our daily bread. And forgive us our debts, as we forgive our debtors. And lead us not into temptation; but deliver us from evil.—Amen.

My mouth shall speak the praise of the Lord:
—And let all flesh bless his holy name for ever and ever.

[*Then may be said or sung one or both of these Psalms.*]

PSALM XCIII.

The Lord reigneth, he is | clothed with | majesty; ‖ the Lord is clothed with strength, where- | with he hath | girded him- | self:

The world | also is | stablished, ‖ that | it can- not be | moved.

Thy throne is e- | stablished of | old: ‖ thou | art from | ever- | lasting.

The floods have lifted up, O Lord, the floods have lifted | up their | voice; ‖ the | floods lift | up their | waves.

The Lord on high is mightier than the noise of | many | waters, ‖ yea, than the | mighty | waves of the | sea.

Thy testimonies are | very | sure: ‖ holiness becometh thine | house, O | Lord, for | ever.

PSALM LXXXIV.

How amiable | are thy | tabernacles, ‖ O | Lord... of... | hosts!

My soul longeth, | yea, even | fainteth || for the | courts... | of the | Lord :
My | heart and my | flesh || cry | out for the | living | God.
Blessed are they that | dwell in thy | house : || they | will be still | praising | thee.
Blessed is the man whose | strength is in | thee ; || in whose | heart... | are thy | ways.
O Lord God of hosts, | hear my | prayer : || give | ear, O | God of | Jacob.
Behold, O | God our | shield, || and look upon the | face of | thine a- | nointed.
For the Lord God is a | sun and | shield : || the | Lord will give | grace and | glory :
No good thing will | he with- | hold || from | them that | walk up- | rightly.
O | Lord of | hosts, || blessed is the | man that | trusteth in | thee.

[*Then may be read the Lesson from the Old Testament: after which follows*]

The Second Prayer.

I.

O God, whose word is quick and powerful and sharper than a two-edged sword, Grant unto us who are here before thee, and to all thy people everywhere, that we may receive thy truth into our hearts, in faith and love. By it may we be taught and guided, upheld and comforted ; that we be no longer children in understanding, but grow in grace unto the stature of a perfect man in Christ Jesus, and so be prepared for every good word and work, to the honour of thy name ; through Jesus Christ our Lord.—Amen.

II.

Be pleased, almighty and most gracious God, to increase our faith, hope, and charity, our patience, fortitude, and meekness, our zeal and diligence in thy service. May we, through thy grace, mortify all sinful affections, resist and subdue all evil habits, and abound in every good work. Let our good resolutions be ripened into acts and habits of holiness and virtue, that we may be as epistles of Christ, thy laws being written in our hearts and upon our whole lives; that so we may walk worthy of our high vocation and adorn the doctrine of God our Saviour.—Amen.

III.

Dwell in our hearts, we pray thee, O Lord God, and make us temples of thy Holy Spirit; that whereas in ourselves we are weak, corrupt, and mortal, we may through thee be strengthened and sanctified, and finally having obtained the victory over death, may reign in immortal life; through Him who died for our sins and rose again for our justification, and liveth and reigneth with thee the Father in the unity of the Spirit, world without end.—Amen.

IV.

Gracious God, Father of mercies, who hast sent thy Son into the world, that whosoever followeth him might not walk in darkness, Grant, we beseech thee, that thy gospel may speedily be preached among all nations for the obedience of faith, that all flesh may see the salvation of God.

Let the kingdoms of this world at length become

the kingdoms of our Lord and of his Christ. Take the veil from the heart of the Jew, that he may see the end of that law which was commanded unto the fathers; and let all the kindreds of the nations turn unto the Lord; through the one Mediator Jesus Christ, who hath broken down the partition between Jew and Gentile, by one Spirit reconciling both unto thee.—Amen.

O praise the Lord, all ye nations :
—Praise him, all ye people.
For his merciful kindness is great toward us :
—And the truth of the Lord endureth for ever.
Praise ye the Lord :
—Amen. *Ps.* cxvii.

[*Then a Psalm may be sung: after which is read the Lesson from the New Testament. Then follows*]

The Third Prayer.

I.

O God, everlasting and almighty, whose grace hath appeared, bringing salvation to all men, Teach us to deny ungodliness and worldly lusts, and to live soberly, righteously, and godly in this present world, looking for that blessed hope, even the glorious appearing of the great God, and our Saviour Jesus Christ; who gave himself for us that he might redeem us from all iniquity, and purify us unto himself, a peculiar people, zealous of good works.—Amen.

II.

Eternal God, who quickenest all things, and by

whose Spirit the Church, which is the body of thy Son, is governed and sanctified, We pray that all who profess his religion may adorn his doctrine by walking as Christ walked; that they and we may at length obtain that incorruptible crown which thou hast promised to them that love thee.

And we beseech thee, O Lord, who hast built thy Church upon the foundation of the apostles and prophets, Jesus Christ himself being the chief cornerstone, to grant a spirit of wisdom and power to thy servants who are appointed to labour in the ministry of the word; that by their doctrine and example thy saints may be built up in their holy faith, and sinners may be converted unto thee. And everywhere let thy word have free course and be glorified; through Him who is the Apostle and High Priest of our profession, Christ Jesus.—Amen.

III.

Father of mercies, Look down in compassion upon the sick and afflicted, upon the poor, the miserable, and the dying, upon the friendless, the despairing, and the tempted, and upon all who are in danger, necessity, or tribulation.

Send them comfort and deliverance, O God: and do thou, who makest all things work together for good to them that love thee, sanctify their pains and sorrows to the health and salvation of their souls in the day of our Lord Jesus Christ.—Amen.

IV.

We beseech thee, O God, to bless all men: bring them to the knowledge and obedience of the truth.

Break thou the arm of the oppressor everywhere; and scatter the people that delight in war:

And in all the earth let thy kingdom come, which is righteousness and peace and joy in the Holy Ghost.—Amen.

[*Then a Psalm or Doxology may be sung.*]

The Benediction.

Now the God of peace, that brought again from the dead our Lord Jesus, that Great Shepherd of the sheep, through the blood of the everlasting covenant, make you perfect in every good work to do his will, working in you that which is well pleasing in his sight, through Jesus Christ; to whom be glory for ever and ever.—Amen. *Heb.* xiii.

Prayer before Sermon.

Let thy good Spirit of Grace and wisdom dwell in our hearts, and guide us in all our words and works, we humbly entreat thee, O Lord; that our speaking and hearing at this time may be unto our edification and profit, and to the glory of thy great name; through Jesus Christ our Redeemer.—Amen.

Prayer after Sermon.

O Lord, have mercy upon us. Grant that we may receive thy word into good and honest hearts, and may bring forth the fruit of good living, to the honour of thy great name.—Amen.

Evening Prayer.

O God, who hast given the day to man for labour

and the night for rest, Protect us by thy watchful providence during the coming night and all the nights and days of our pilgrimage.

Cover all our sins with thy mercy, as thou coverest the earth with darkness during the night watches. And when our work is finished and our days are ended in this world, may we depart hence in the blessed assurance of thy favour, and in the joyful hope of the resurrection to immortal life, which thou hast given us in our Lord and Saviour Jesus Christ.—Amen.

Second Sunday of the Month.

FORENOON SERVICE.

[*The congregation being assembled, the Minister may recite the following sentences.*]

Draw nigh unto God, and he will draw nigh unto you. *James* iv.

Cast away from you all your transgressions, whereby ye have transgressed; and make you a new heart and a right spirit: for why will ye die, O house of Israel? For I have no pleasure in the death of him that dieth, saith the Lord God: wherefore turn yourselves, and live ye. *Ezek.* xviii.

Dearly beloved brethren, we are here assembled in obedience to the command that we forsake not the assembling of ourselves together, and in hope of that promise which our Lord Jesus Christ hath given to his disciples, that wherever two or three shall meet together in his name, he will be in the midst of them. Let us, therefore, with reverence and godly fear draw nigh to the throne of grace, that we may obtain mercy and find grace to help in time of need.

First Prayer.

I.

Almighty God, the Maker of all things, visible and invisible, our Creator and Preserver, who hast sent thy Son to bring us near who by our sins were far off, and to make us sons of God and heirs of eternal life, Grant unto us thy grace and blessing as we are here assembled to offer up our common supplications before thy Divine Majesty, to confess our sins and iniquities, and to render thanks for thy great goodness and mercy.

May we put away all heedlessness and levity, all vain thoughts and distracting cares; and may we draw near to thy presence with earnest, humble, and faithful hearts, in holiness and truth.

And let our worship and service, being offered in the name and spirit of thy Son, be acceptable unto thee and profitable unto us; through him who is our Mediator and Advocate Jesus Christ.—Amen.

Give ear to my words, O Lord:
—Consider my meditation.
Hearken unto the voice of my cry, my King and my God:
—For unto thee will I pray.
My voice shalt thou hear in the morning, O Lord:
—In the morning will I direct my prayer unto thee, and will look up.
For thou art not a God that hath pleasure in wickedness:
—Neither shall evil dwell with thee.
The foolish shall not stand in thy sight:
—Thou hatest all workers of iniquity.
But as for me, I will come into thy house in the multitude of thy mercy:
—And in thy fear will I worship toward thy holy temple. *Ps.* v.

II.

We confess before thee, O God our heavenly Father, that we are miserable sinners; for we have transgressed thy holy laws times innumerable, in thought, word, and deed.

We have not loved thee with all our hearts; neither have we loved our neighbour as ourselves.

We have not glorified thee with our bodies and our spirits; but we have lived in ungodliness, pride, and vanity; in envy and uncharitableness; in covetousness and discontent; and we have made provision for the flesh to fulfil its lusts.

We have loved the world and the things that are of the world; and have not set our affection on things above, or laid up treasure in heaven, where Christ our risen Lord sitteth at thy right hand.—Amen.

If our heart condemn us, God is greater than our hearts, and knoweth all things.

Enter not into judgment with thy servants, O Lord:
—For in thy sight shall no man living be justified.

Have mercy upon me, O God, according to thy loving-kindness:
—According to the multitude of thy tender mercies, blot out my transgressions.

Wash me thoroughly from mine iniquity, and cleanse me from my sin:
—For I acknowledge my transgressions, and my sin is ever before me.

Create in me a clean heart, O God:
—And renew a right spirit within me.

Cast me not away from thy presence:
—And take not thy Holy Spirit from me.

Restore unto me the joy of thy salvation:
—And uphold me with thy free Spirit.

O Lord, open thou my lips:
—And my mouth shall shew forth thy praise.

For thou desirest not sacrifice:
—Thou delightest not in burnt-offering.

The sacrifices of God are a broken spirit:
—A broken and a contrite heart, O God, thou wilt not despise. *Ps.* li.

God so loved the world that he gave his only-begotten Son, that whosoever believeth in him should not perish, but have everlasting life. For God sent not his Son into the world to condemn the world, but that the world through him might be saved. *John* iii.

Like as a father pitieth his children, so the Lord pitieth them that fear him. *Ps.* ciii.

III.

Almighty God, Father of our Lord Jesus Christ, who hast in thy gospel proclaimed remission of sins to all them that believe in the name of thy Son, and repent of their transgressions against thee, Confirm us, we beseech thee, in the faith and hope of this thy promise: and for this end so work in us by thy Holy Spirit, that we may embrace and hold fast thy truth in a pure conscience unto the end, and also may bring forth fruits meet for repentance; that being justified freely by thy grace, and walking continually in the way of thy commandments, we may glorify thy holy name, and may know that we are indeed thy children and heirs of the kingdom which thou hast promised to them that love thee.—Amen.

Our Father which art in heaven, Hallowed be thy name. Thy kingdom come. Thy will be done on earth, as it is in heaven. Give us this day our daily bread. And forgive us our debts, as we forgive our debtors. And lead us not into temptation; but deliver us from evil.—Amen.

It is a good thing to give thanks unto the Lord:
—And to sing praises unto thy name, O most High;

To shew forth thy loving-kindness in the morning :
—And thy faithfulness every night. *Ps.* xcii.

[*Then may be said or sung one or more of these Psalms following.*]

PSALM XCVII.

The Lord reigneth ; let the | earth re- | joice ; || let the multitude of | isles be | glad there- | of.

Clouds and darkness are | round a- | bout him : || righteousness and judgment are the habi- | tation | of his | throne.

A fire | goeth be- | fore him, || and burneth up his | enemies | round a- | bout.

The heavens de- | clare his | righteousness, || and all the | people | see his | glory.

Zion | heard, and was | glad ; || and the daughters of Judah rejoiced be- | cause of thy | judgments, O | Lord.

For thou, Lord, art high above | all the | earth : || thou art ex- | alted a- | bove all | gods.

Ye that love the | Lord, hate | evil : || he preserveth the | souls... | of his | saints ;

He de- | livereth | them || out of the | hand... | of the | wicked.

Light is | sown for the | righteous, || and | gladness for the | upright in | heart.

Rejoice in the | Lord, ye | righteous ; || and give thanks at the re- | membrance | of his | holiness.

PSALM XXXVI. 5.

Thy mercy, O Lord, is | in the | heavens ; || thy faithfulness | reacheth | unto the | clouds.

Thy righteousness is | like the great | mountains ; || thy | judgments | are a great | deep :

O Lord, thou preservest | man and | beast. || How excellent is thy | loving- | kindness, O | God !

Therefore the children of men | put their | trust ||
in the | shadow | of thy | wings.

They shall be a- | bundantly | satisfied || with the |
plenteousness | of thy | house ;

And thou shalt | make them | drink || of the | river |
of thy | pleasures.

For with thee is the | fountain of | life : || in thy |
light shall | we see | light.

O continue thy loving-kindness unto | them that |
know thee ; || and thy righteousness | to the | upright
in | heart.

PSALM LXVII.

God be merciful unto | us, and | bless us ; || and
make his | face to | shine up- | on us ;

That thy way may be | known upon | earth, || thy
saving | health a- | mong all | nations.

Let the people | praise thee, O | Lord ; || let | all
the | people | praise thee.

O let the nations be glad and | shout for | joy : ||
for thou shalt judge the people righteously, and govern
the | nations | upon | earth.

Let the people | praise thee, O | God ; || let | all
the | people | praise thee.

The earth shall | yield her | increase : || God, | our
own | God, shall | bless us.

God | shall... | bless us ; || and all the | ends of the |
earth shall | fear him.

[*Here the Lesson from the Old Testament may be read: after which follows*]

The Second Prayer.

I.

O God, who desirest not sacrifice and hast no delight

in burnt-offering, but hast shewed us what is good, and requirest of us to do justly, to love mercy, and to walk humbly with thee, Grant us, we pray thee, true repentance of our sins and godly sorrow, and so direct and govern our hearts and lives that we may render a constant and unfeigned obedience to thy holy laws; that, offering to thee the sacrifices of righteousness, we may be acceptable in thy sight, and may obtain our petitions; through Jesus Christ, who is our High Priest and sacrifice, and the altar that sanctifieth our gift.— Amen.

II.

O God, thou King eternal, immortal, invisible, the blessed and only Potentate, May we who cannot see thee with the eye of flesh, behold thee steadfastly with the eye of faith, that we faint not under the manifold temptations and afflictions of this mortal life, but endure as seeing thee who art invisible; that after we have done and suffered thy will upon the earth, we may behold the vision of God in heaven, and be made partakers of those joys unspeakable which thou hast promised to them that love thee.—Amen.

III.

O God, our bountiful Benefactor, We thank thee for the bread that perisheth and for all the good things of this present life. May we receive them with gratitude, and enjoy them with temperance and charity. But man liveth not by bread alone. Make us to hunger and thirst after righteousness; that our souls may at length be satisfied with the fulness of thy truth and grace; through Him who is the bread of God and giveth life unto the world, Jesus Christ our Lord.— Amen.

IV.

O Lord, who knowest our necessities before we ask, and our ignorance in asking, Bestow upon us, we entreat thee, such a measure of grace and strength that we may both resist and subdue the sins that do more easily beset us, and may faithfully and truly follow thy blessed Son Jesus Christ, who was holy, harmless, and undefiled, and who suffered for us in the flesh, leaving us an example that we might follow his steps.—Amen.

[*Here a Psalm may be sung : after which is read the Lesson from the New Testament. Then follows*]

The Third Prayer.

I.

Let thy truth, O God, be received into our hearts in faith and love ; and by it may we be made wise unto salvation; through Jesus Christ, who is the way, the truth, and the life.—Amen.

II.

Most gracious God, who didst send thy well-beloved Son to die for our sins and to rise again for our justification, Grant that we, who have been baptized into his death, may put away all the pollutions of the old man, all evil thoughts, unholy desires, and malignant passions : and may we rise with Christ to newness of life; abounding in godliness, justice, charity, and meekness, in purity and temperance, in patience and fortitude ; that we may indeed be followers of him in all the steps of his holy and blessed life, and may walk worthy of our high vocation ; through the same Jesus Christ our Redeemer.—Amen.

III.

God of all grace and consolation, whose Son Jesus Christ hath ascended on high, leading captivity captive and receiving gifts for men, Leave not us thy family comfortless, but send forth into our hearts thy Holy Spirit to abide with us for ever; that we, being taught and quickened, purified and strengthened by thy heavenly grace, may faithfully and joyfully serve thee all our days; through Christ our Lord.—Amen.

IV.

Blessed Lord, whose will it is that all men should be saved, and who hast commanded us to make intercessions and prayers for all men, We offer up before thee our supplications for the whole human race, that they may be brought to the knowledge and obedience of the truth:

For all thy people upon earth, that they may fight the good fight and lay hold on eternal life; and may so run the race that is set before them that in due time they may obtain the prize:

For all afflicted persons, that it may please thee to sanctify, uphold, and comfort them, and to redeem their souls from all evil.

Look down from the height of thy sanctuary, O merciful Father, upon the sick, the sorrowful, and the dying; upon widows and orphans, upon the despairing and the tempted; and upon those who have not God in all their thoughts. Lord, have mercy upon them, and upon us also, for we are men of like passions, and compassed about with infirmity. Grant unto us to be humble, sober, and watchful, that we may stand in the evil day.

We pray for our kindred, friends, and benefactors,

that thou wouldst enrich them with thy favour, and make them heirs of the kingdom which cannot be moved:

And in obedience to the command of thy dear Son we pray also for our enemies, that thou wouldst forgive them, and enable us to forgive them from the heart; that, rendering good for evil, we may be thy children, and perfect, as thou our Father in heaven art perfect.—Amen.

V.

O God, thou King of glory, who rulest all the nations of the world, and to whom pertain all might, majesty, and dominion in heaven and earth, We beseech thee to regard with thy favour our Sovereign Queen Victoria. Endow her with thy Holy Spirit: may she reign in wisdom and righteousness, in peace and prosperity, all the days of her life; and may she afterwards inherit that crown of righteousness which the Lord hath promised to them that love him.

Be gracious, O Lord, to the Prince and Princess of Wales, and to all the members of the Royal Family.

We pray for the Queen's Ministers; for the Members of both Houses of Parliament; for Magistrates, Judges, and all persons invested with authority. Be pleased to grant unto them a spirit of wisdom and of the fear of the Lord; and may we, and all under them, lead a quiet and peaceable life in godliness and honesty, shewing forth thy praise, who hast called us out of darkness into the marvellous light of thy gospel. —Amen.

VI.

O God, by whose gracious providence we enjoy the good things of this present life, and also all things pertaining to godliness and the life everlasting, We unite with one heart in rendering thanks and praise unto thy great name.

Enable us, we entreat thee, O Lord, to manifest our gratitude by a willing and constant obedience to thy righteous commands, and by walking at all times after the example of Him whom thou didst send into the world to take away its sin, and to make us sons of God and heirs of eternal life, Jesus Christ our Redeemer.—Amen.

Lord, have mercy upon us, and grant us thy peace;
—Have mercy upon us, O Lord, and grant us thy salvation.

Through Jesus Christ, the Lamb of God, which taketh away the sin of the world, receive our prayer.

—O Lord, hear us, of thy great mercy, through the same Jesus Christ our Lord.

Now unto Him that is able to keep us from falling, and to present us faultless before the presence of his glory with exceeding joy; to the only wise God, our Saviour, be glory and majesty, dominion and power, both now and ever.—Amen.

[*Then a Psalm or Doxology may be sung.*]

The Benediction.

The grace of the Lord Jesus Christ, and the love of God, and the communion of the Holy Spirit, be with you all.—Amen.

Second Sunday of the Month.

Afternoon Service.

[*The congregation being assembled, the Minister may recite the following sentences.*]

The eyes of the Lord are upon the righteous; and his ears are open to their cry.

The Lord is nigh unto them that are of a broken heart; and saveth such as be of a contrite spirit. *Ps.* xxxiv.

Ask, and it shall be given you; seek, and ye shall find; knock, and it shall be opened unto you: for every one that asketh receiveth; and he that seeketh findeth; and to him that knocketh it shall be opened. *Matt.* vii.

Brethren beloved in the Lord, let us draw near to the throne of grace with reverence and godly fear, in the name of our Lord and Saviour Jesus Christ. Let us pray.

The First Prayer.

I.

Almighty and everlasting God, who hast promised that in all places where thou dost record thy name thou wilt meet with thy servants and bless them, Fulfil to us at this time thy promise, we beseech thee, and make us joyful in thy house of prayer.

Solemnize and purify our minds: raise our hearts to thee: endow us with wisdom and understanding: may we know, believe, and love thy truth: and let the words of our mouth and the meditation of our heart be acceptable in thy sight, O Lord, our strength and our Redeemer.—Amen.

II.

Lord, have mercy upon us; for we daily sin against thee, transgressing thy holy laws, failing of the duty thou requirest of us, and grieving thy Spirit of grace. Through Jesus Christ thy Son, who is the propitiation for our sins, and who ever liveth in thy presence in heaven, our High Priest and Mediator, Be pleased, O Lord, merciful Father, to blot out all our offences, our ignorances and negligences, our unfaithfulness in thy service, our sloth and pride, our carnality and love of the world, and all our secret faults and presumptuous sins, by which we have been disobedient unto thy heavenly calling, and have merited thy just displeasure. If thou shouldst enter into judgment, we could not stand; but there is mercy with thee that thou mayest be feared.

O God, who despisest not the sighing of a contrite heart nor the desire of such as be sorrowful, Grant unto us true repentance and godly reformation of life; that, being redeemed from our sins and vanities, we may henceforth walk in the way of thy precepts in all things, and abound in good works; that so we may adorn the doctrine of God our Saviour, and make our calling and election sure.—Amen.

Judge me, O Lord, for I have walked in mine integrity:
—I have trusted also in the Lord; therefore I shall not slide.
Examine me, O Lord, and prove me:
—Try my reins and my heart.

For thy loving-kindness is before mine eyes :
—And I have walked in thy truth.
I have not sat with vain persons :
—Neither will I go in with dissemblers.
I have hated the congregation of evil-doers :
—And will not sit with the wicked.
I will wash mine hands in innocency :
—So will I compass thine altar, O Lord :
That I may publish with the voice of thanksgiving :
—And tell of all thy wondrous works.
Lord, I have loved the habitation of thy house :
—And the place where thine honour dwelleth.

Ps. xxvi.

III.

O Lord our heavenly Father, who hast made thy Christ to be wisdom and righteousness, sanctification and redemption to them that follow him and obey his voice, Vouchsafe unto us thy good and holy Spirit, we beseech thee; that we may be wise unto salvation; may be just, upright, sincere, doing unto others as we would they should do unto us; may be purified from all base, unholy, and malignant passions; may be liberated and made free from bondage to the world, the flesh, and the devil; and finally may obtain the adoption, even the redemption of our bodies, that death may be swallowed up of victory. And these things we ask in His name who is the author and finisher of the faith, Jesus Christ our Saviour; who also hath taught us thus to pray—

Our Father which art in heaven, Hallowed be thy name. Thy kingdom come. Thy will be done on earth, as it is in heaven. Give us day by day our daily bread. And forgive us our debts, as we forgive our debtors. And lead us not into temptation; but deliver us from evil.—Amen.

I will bless the Lord at all times :
—His praise shall continually be in my mouth.
O magnify the Lord with me :
—And let us exalt his name together.   *Ps.* xxxiv.

[*Then may be said or sung one or both of these Psalms.*]

PSALM XIX.

The heavens declare the | glory of | God ; || and the firmament | sheweth his | handy- | work.

Day unto day | uttereth | speech, || and night unto | night... | sheweth | knowledge.

There is no | speech nor | language, || their | voice... | is not | heard.

Yet their instruction is gone out through | all the | earth, || and their | words to the | end of the | world.

The law of the Lord is perfect, con- | verting the | soul : || the testimony of the Lord is | sure, making | wise the | simple :

The statutes of the Lord are right, re- | joicing the | heart : || the commandment of the Lord is | pure, en- | lightening the | eyes :

More to be desired are | they than | gold, || yea, than | much... | fine... | gold ;

Sweeter | also than | honey, || e- | ven the | honey- | comb.

Moreover, by them is thy | servant | warned : || and in keeping of | them is | great re- | ward.

Who can under- | stand his | errors ? || cleanse thou | me from | secret | faults.

Keep back thy servant also from pre- | sumptuous | sins ; || let them not have do- | minion | over | me :

Then shall | I be | upright, || and I shall be innocent | from the | great trans- | gression.

Let the | words of my | mouth, || and the medi- | tation | of my | heart,

Be acceptable in thy | sight, O | Lord, || my | strength, and | my Re- | deemer.

PSALM XXIV.

The earth is the Lord's, and the | fulness there- | of; || the world, and | they that | dwell there- | in :

For he hath founded it up- | on the | seas, || and established | it up- | on the | floods.

Who shall ascend into the | hill of the | Lord? || or who shall | stand in his | holy | place?

He that hath clean hands, and a | pure... | heart; || who hath not lifted up his soul unto | vanity, nor | sworn de- | ceitfully.

He shall receive the | blessing from the | Lord, || and righteousness from the | God of | his sal- | vation.

Lift up your heads, O ye gates; and be ye lift up, ye ever- | lasting doors; || and the King of | glory | shall come | in.

Who is this | King of | glory? || The Lord strong and mighty, the | Lord... | mighty in | battle.

Lift up your heads, O ye gates; even lift them up, ye ever- | lasting | doors; || and the King of | glory | shall come | in.

Who is this | King of | glory? || The Lord of hosts, | he is the | King of | glory.

[*Then may be read the Lesson from the Old Testament; after which follows*]

The Second Prayer.

I.

O God, who didst speak in times past unto the fathers by the prophets, and hast, in these last days, spoken unto us by thy Son, Give us, we pray thee, humble, teachable, and obedient hearts, that we may lend a willing ear to the doctrine which he hath taught us, and may embrace the same and hold it fast, to thy honour and praise.

Deliver us, O Lord, from the instruction that causeth to err. Let not us receive for doctrines the commandments of men; seeing one is our Master, even Christ, and all we are brethren. May we know the truth, and so be made free from all darkness and unbelief, from all error and sin.

And for this end give us, O Lord, the love of the truth: purify our souls from heedlessness and vanity, from hypocrisy and hardness of heart, from covetousness and love of the world, and from fleshly lusts which war against the soul; and endow us with seriousness and earnestness of spirit, that we may fight the good fight of faith, and lay hold of eternal life.—Amen.

II.

Blessed Lord, who hast sent forth thy Son Jesus Christ to die for our sins, and also, by his heavenly doctrine and holy life, to lead us in the paths of truth and righteousness, Grant us thy Holy Spirit to dwell in our hearts, to guide our lives, and to sanctify us wholly in spirit, soul, and body; that having glorified thee upon the earth and finished the work thou hast given us to do, we may obtain the victory over all our enemies, and reign in immortal life; through Him who is thy Word made flesh, Jesus Christ.—Amen.

Behold, bless ye the Lord, all ye servants of the Lord:

—Ye who stand in the house of the Lord.

Lift up your hands in the sanctuary, and bless the Lord.

—The Lord that made heaven and earth bless thee out of Zion. *Ps.* cxxxiv.

[*Here a Psalm may be sung: after which is read the Lesson from the New Testament. Then follows*]

The Third Prayer.

I.

O thou great Master and Lord, who art calling us to serve thee that we may be free, and art intrusting thy talents to our keeping for a season, Grant us mercy to be wise and faithful stewards even in that which is least. May we not abuse or bury thy gift, but improve it to thy glory; that when the Lord shall reckon with us, we may be found of him in peace, and may enter, with all thine elect, into the joy of our Lord.—Amen.

II.

O God, who hast given us the promise of thy heavenly rest, May we labour earnestly to enter into it. For this end quicken, we pray thee, our drowsy faith and hope. Teach us to mortify whatever in us is earthly, carnal, and corrupt. Putting off the works of darkness, which cannot abide the light of thy countenance, may we be clothed with truth, righteousness, and purity, and walk as Christ walked; that we may have confidence and not be ashamed before him at his coming.—Amen.

III.

Almighty and most merciful God, thou Father of lights and Fountain of all goodness, who didst send forth thy Son to be the light of the world, that whoso followeth him should not walk in darkness, Be pleased so to illuminate and guide all pastors and teachers that they may fully know and faithfully declare thy holy gospel; that the whole body of the Church may grow in faith and charity and patience, and may abound in every good word and work.

And we humbly entreat thee, most merciful God, to receive graciously the sacrifices of praise and prayer which thy holy and spiritual priesthood have this day throughout the world offered unto thee.

Let the cry of thy family enter into thine ears, O Father; and send unto thy children an answer in peace; through our Elder Brother Jesus Christ, who is also our High Priest and Sacrifice, and the altar which sanctifieth our gift.—Amen.

IV.

O Lord, who art from everlasting to everlasting, who knowest the end from the beginning, and callest the things which are not as though they were, and who hast given to thy Son the heathen for his inheritance, Hasten, we entreat thee, the coming and kingdom of thy Christ. Our eyes fail, waiting for thy salvation.

Let all the ends of the earth remember and turn to the Lord; let all the kindreds of the nations worship before thee. And do thou, who holdest the hearts of all men in thy hand, open a great door and effectual for the preaching of thy servants everywhere, that their sound may go into all the earth, and their words to the ends of the world.—Amen.

V.

O Lord, who art very pitiful and of tender mercy, who art the Father of the fatherless and the husband of the widow, and dost not willingly afflict or grieve the children of men, We who are ourselves in the body, lift up our hearts unto thee on behalf of all our brethren who are in any affliction or distress.

Look down from thy holy habitation upon the poor and destitute; upon the bereaved and the sorrowful, the sick and the dying; upon those that are in pain and anguish; upon such as are unjustly held in bondage; and upon all that are desolate, wronged, and oppressed.

Send them speedy help and deliverance, O thou Judge of the earth: and so enrich the souls of thy afflicted servants with patience and hope, that their present trouble may conduce to their eternal salvation: and may they and we receive, in due time, the end of our faith; through our merciful High Priest Jesus Christ, who suffered and was tempted, and is able to succour us when we are tempted.—Amen.

VI.

Lord of all power and might, We call upon thee whose mercies are from everlasting. We are ignorant, weak, and perverse: leave us not, O God, neither forsake us. Guide us with thy counsel: uphold us by thy power. Suffer us not to go astray from thy ways: let us not be weary in well-doing. May we live in thy fear all the days of our life; may we die in thy favour; and let our portion be among thy saints at the second and glorious appearing of our Lord and Saviour Jesus Christ.—Amen.

[*Then a Psalm or Doxology may be sung.*]

Benediction.

The peace of God, which passeth all understanding,

keep your hearts and minds through Christ Jesus. And the grace of the Lord Jesus Christ, and the love of God, and the fellowship of the Holy Ghost, be with you all.—Amen.

Prayer before Sermon.

Let not thy word, O God, return unto thee void; but let it prosper in the thing whereunto thou hast sent it; that we and all thy servants may be edified and built up in our holy faith, and through patience and comfort of the Scriptures may have hope.—Amen.

Prayer after Sermon.

O God our heavenly Father, Suffer not the good seed of thy word to be caught away by the wicked one out of our hearts : neither let it be scorched of tribulation or persecution ; or be choked with cares and pleasures of this life : but being received into good and honest hearts, may it bring forth abundantly, in us and in all Christians, the fruits of faith and good works, to the glory of thy grace.—Amen.

An Evening Prayer.

O Lord God, in whose presence there is no darkness, for thou dwellest for ever in unapproachable light, Keep and defend us and all thy saints, in soul and body, during the coming night, and in all the darkness of this mortal life.

May we rest in the assurance of thy favour ; in the peace of a good conscience ; in the hope of a better life ; in the faith of thy providence and protection ; and in the love of thy Spirit.

May we rise up again to be diligent in our several callings, working the work of God while the day lasts, remembering that the night cometh in which no man can work. And whether we wake or sleep, may we live together with Christ.—Amen.

Third Sunday of the Month.

FORENOON SERVICE.

[*The congregation being assembled, the Minister may recite one or more of the following sentences.*]

O give thanks unto the Lord ; call upon his name ; make known his deeds among the people. Sing unto him ; sing psalms unto him : talk ye of all his wondrous works. Glory ye in his holy name ; and let the hearts of them rejoice that seek the Lord. *Ps.* cv.

There is no difference between the Jew and the Greek ; for the same Lord over all is rich in mercy to all them that call upon him. For whosoever shall call upon the name of the Lord shall be saved. *Rom.* x.

Dearly beloved brethren, seeing that we have a great High Priest, that is passed into the heavens, Jesus the Son of God, let us come boldly unto the throne of grace, that we may obtain mercy and find grace to help in time of need. *Heb.* iv. Let us pray.

The First Prayer.

I.

O God, who art greatly to be feared in the assembly of thy saints, Accept, we entreat thee, our sacrifices of praise and prayer : and though we are not worthy to approach thy presence, or to ask anything of thee, do thou receive us graciously, and answer us ; through our great High Priest and Advocate Jesus Christ.— Amen.

II.

Almighty God, We render thanks unto thy great name that we have been preserved to see another of the days of the Son of man upon earth. For the sun and the shining light; for the succession of night and day, and summer and winter, and seed-time and harvest, and the ordinances of heaven; for thy fatherly care and goodness to us the children of men; for thy watchful providence and unspeakable mercy, we magnify thy name, O God.

Thou art worthy, O Lord, to receive glory and honour and blessing; for thou hast created all things, and thou dost sustain them all by the word of thy power: and when sin had disturbed the order and repose of thy works, and caused the whole creation to groan and travail in pain, thou didst send thy Son to redeem it from the bondage of corruption and the load of vanity, and to make peace by the blood of his cross; whereby he hath reconciled all things in heaven and earth.

O God, Maker and Governor of the world, who on the seventh day didst rest from all thy works, and hast promised an everlasting rest to all thy faithful servants, Make us to rest from our works, as thou didst from thine; that we who are weary with our vanities, and heavy laden with our sins and sorrows, may take up the yoke and burden of Jesus Christ, and so find rest unto our souls; for his yoke is easy, and his burden is light.—Amen.

III.

We confess that we are miserable sinners before thee, O God; for we have transgressed thy holy laws, and done despite to thy good Spirit, and walked in counsels of our own.

O Lord, we acknowledge that we have not loved thee with all our heart, or believed thy faithful word, or hoped for thy promises, but have been disobedient and rebellious.

Neither have we loved our neighbour as ourselves: we have lived in selfishness and pride, in envy and uncharitableness, and have judged and condemned our brethren, forgetting that thou, Lord, judgest both us and them.

We have debased our souls with vain and earthly passions, setting our affection on things below, loving the world and laying up treasure upon earth; so that the love of the Father hath not been in us.

Neither have we been sober and watchful, nor mortified the deeds of the body: but our hearts have been overcharged with cares and pleasures of this life; and we have been conformed to the world, and have not waited for the second coming of Christ our Lord.

Our own hearts condemn us, and thou art greater than our hearts, and knowest all things.

Save me, O God:
—For the waters are come in unto my soul.
I sink in deep mire where there is no standing:
—I am come into deep waters, where the floods overflow me.
I am weary of my crying:
—Mine eyes fail while I wait for my God.
O God, thou knowest my foolishness:
—And my sins are not hid from thee.
But as for me, my prayer is unto thee in an acceptable time:
—O God, in the multitude of thy mercy hear me, in the truth of thy salvation.
Let not the waterflood overflow me, neither let the deep swallow me up:

FORENOON SERVICE.   47

—And let not the pit shut her mouth upon me.
Hear me, O Lord, for thy loving-kindness is good :
—Turn unto me according to the multitude of thy tender mercies.
Draw nigh unto my soul, and redeem it :
—Deliver me because of mine enemies.
I am poor and sorrowful :
—Let thy salvation, O God, set me on high.
Ps. lxix.

This is a faithful saying, and worthy of all acceptation, that Christ Jesus came into the world to save sinners, even the chief. 1 *Tim.* i. 15.
Behold the Lamb of God, which taketh away the sin of the world. *John* i. 29.

IV.

Almighty God, Father of mercies, We render thanks and praise unto thee for sending thy Son into the world, that he might redeem us from our sins and miseries, and make us heirs, according to the hope of everlasting life.
Being justified by faith, may we have peace with thee, through our Lord Jesus Christ: and grant us thy grace, we beseech thee, O Lord, that we may depart from all iniquity, and may be a peculiar people, zealous of good works, shewing forth thy praise, who hast called us out of darkness into thy marvellous light.
God of all grace, be pleased to receive our prayer, through thy well-beloved Son, who commanded us in the spirit of adoption thus to say—
Our Father which art in heaven, Hallowed be thy name. Thy kingdom come. Thy will be done on earth, as it is in heaven. Give us this day our daily

bread. And forgive us our debts, as we forgive our debtors. And lead us not into temptation; but deliver us from evil.—Amen.

Praise ye the Lord:
—Praise him, O ye servants of the Lord.
Praise the Lord; for the Lord is good:
—Sing praises unto his name; for it is pleasant.
          Ps. cxxxv.

[*Then may be said or sung one of these Psalms.*]

PSALM LXV.

Praise waiteth for thee, O | God, in | Sion : ‖ and unto | thee shall the | vow be per- | formed.

O thou that | hearest | prayer, ‖ unto | thee shall | all flesh | come.

Blessed is the man | whom thou | choosest, ‖ and causest to approach unto thee, that | he may | dwell in thy | courts :

We shall be satisfied with the | goodness of thy | house, ‖ even | of thy | holy | temple.

By terrible things in righteousness | wilt thou | answer us, ‖ O | God of | our sal- | vation ;

Who art the confidence of all the | ends of the | earth, ‖ and of them that are afar | off up- | on the | sea :

Who by his strength setteth | fast the | mountains ; ‖ being | gird-... | ed with | power :

Who stilleth the | noise of the | seas, ‖ the noise of their waves, and the | tumult | of the | people.

They also that dwell in the | uttermost | parts ‖ are a- | fraid... | at thy | tokens :

Thou makest the outgoings | of the | morning ‖ and | evening | to re- | joice.

FORENOON SERVICE.

Thou visitest the | earth, and | waterest it : ‖ thou greatly enrichest it with the river of | God, which is | full of | water :

Thou pre- | parest them | corn, ‖ when thou hast | so pro- | vided | for it.

Thou waterest the ridges there- | of a- | bundantly : ‖ thou | settlest the | furrows there- | of :

Thou makest it | soft with | showers : ‖ thou | blessest the | springing there- | of.

Thou crownest the | year with thy | goodness ; ‖ and thy | paths... | drop... | fatness.

They drop upon the | pastures of the | wilderness : ‖ and the little | hills re- | joice on | every side.

The pastures are | clothed with | flocks ; ‖ the valleys also are | covered | over with | corn ;

They | shout for | joy, ‖ for | joy they | also | sing.

PSALM CXLV.

I will extol thee, my | God, O | King ; ‖ and I will bless thy | name for | ever and | ever.

Every day | will I | bless thee ; ‖ and I will praise thy | name for | ever and | ever.

Great is the Lord, and greatly | to be | praised ; ‖ and his | greatness | is un- | searchable.

One generation shall praise thy | works to an- | other, ‖ and shall de- | clare thy | mighty | acts.

I will speak of the glorious honour | of thy | majesty, ‖ and | of thy | wondrous | works.

And men shall speak of the might of thy | terrible | acts ; ‖ and | I will de- | clare thy | greatness.

They shall abundantly utter the memory of | thy great | goodness, ‖ and shall | sing of thy | righteous- | ness.

The Lord is gracious, and | full of com- | passion ; ‖ slow to | anger, and | of great | mercy.

The Lord is | good to | all : || and his tender mercies are | over | all his | works.

All thy works shall | praise thee, O | Lord ; || and thy | saints shall | bless... | thee.

They shall speak of the glory | of thy | kingdom, || and | talk of | thy... | power ;

To make known to the sons of men his | mighty | acts, || and the glorious | majesty | of his | kingdom.

Thy kingdom is an ever- | lasting | kingdom, || and thy dominion is through- | out all | gener- | ations.

The Lord upholdeth | all that | fall, || and raiseth up all | those that be | bowed | down.

The eyes of all | wait upon | thee ; || and thou givest them their | meat in | due... | season.

Thou | openest thine | hand, || and satisfiest the desire of | every | living | thing.

The Lord is righteous in | all his | ways, || and | holy in | all his | works.

The Lord is nigh unto all them that | call up- | on him, || to all that | call up- | on him in | truth.

He | will ful- | fil || the de- | sire of | them that | fear him :

He also will | hear their | cry, || and | will... | save... | them.

The Lord preserveth all | them that | love him : || but all the | wicked will | he de- | stroy.

My mouth shall speak the | praise of the | Lord :|| and let all flesh bless his holy | name for | ever and | ever.

[*Then may be read the Lesson from the Old Testament: after which follows*]

The Second Prayer.

I.

O God, who in the beginning didst cause the light

FORENOON SERVICE.   51

to shine out of darkness, and hast made thy sun to rise again upon the world, scattering all the shades of night, Shine in our hearts, we pray thee, and deliver us from ignorance and error, from doubt and fear; and so cleanse us by thy Holy Spirit, that we, renouncing the hidden things of dishonesty, and all the unfruitful works of darkness, may walk before thee in sincerity, purity, and righteousness; that we may have fellowship with thee, and may be followers of Him whom thou didst send to be the light of the world, Jesus Christ our Lord.—Amen.

II.

Almighty and most merciful God, who didst feed thy people of old with manna in the wilderness, teaching us that man liveth not by bread alone, We thank thee for the supply of our daily wants, for the bounties of thy good providence, for life, and breath, and all things:

Especially for Jesus Christ, thine unspeakable gift, who is the bread of God, coming down from heaven, and giving life unto the world. May we eat of this bread, and live for ever.

Guide and strengthen us, O God, with thy truth; refresh our fainting souls with thy promises; animate our hearts, and purify them with thy love; that we may walk with constancy in the way of thy precepts: and having finished our earthly pilgrimage in faith and patience, may we at length be delivered from the toils and dangers of the wilderness, and enjoy for ever thy heavenly rest; through Him who is the author and finisher of the faith, Jesus Christ our Lord.—Amen.

III.

O God, omnipotent and everlasting, who art the

Saviour of all men, specially of them that believe, and whose eternal providence is over all thy works, so that a sparrow falleth not on the ground without thee, and even the hairs of our head are numbered, We beseech thee to help and deliver us, thy servants, in all time of our trouble and adversity, and also in all time of our prosperity and wealth; that we be not overwhelmed with despondency and fear, or lifted up with presumption and pride; but enjoying thy bounties with humility and thankfulness, and bearing thy chastening with faith and hope, we may endure unto the end, and having finished the work thou hast given us to do, may through thy mercy enter into the joy of our Lord.—Amen.

The Lord hear thee in the day of trouble :
—The name of the God of Jacob defend thee ;
Send thee help from the sanctuary :
—And strengthen thee out of Zion ;
Remember all thy offerings :
—And accept thy sacrifice.
Grant thee according to thine own heart :
—And fulfil all thy counsel.
We will rejoice in thy salvation, and in the name of our God we will set up our banners :
—The Lord fulfil all thy petitions.
Some trust in chariots, and some in horses :
—But we will remember the name of the Lord our God.—Amen. *Ps.* xx.

I will praise thee, O Lord, among the people :
—I will sing unto thee among the nations.
For thy mercy is great unto the heavens :
—And thy truth unto the clouds.
Be thou exalted, O God, above the heavens :
—Let thy glory be above all the earth. *Ps.* lvii.

FORENOON SERVICE. 53

[*Here a Psalm may be sung: after which, the Lesson from the New Testament is read. Then follows*]

The Third Prayer.

I.

O eternal God, who didst speak unto thine ancient Israel, out of the midst of thick darkness, with thunderings and lightnings and terrible majesty, We bless thee that thy grace and truth are now revealed unto us by Jesus Christ thy Son; whom thou hast sent forth, in the fulness of time, to redeem us; that we might no more be servants, in bondage under the elements of the world, but might be sons and heirs of God, through him.

Send forth into our hearts, we entreat thee, O Lord, the Spirit of thy Son, crying Abba, Father. Inspire us with perfect love, which casteth out fear; that we may draw nigh to thy throne of grace, at all times, with true hearts in full assurance of faith; and having served thee in peace and joy all the days of our life upon earth, may at length be made partakers of thy heavenly inheritance; through our great High Priest, who is passed into the heavens, Jesus the Son of God.—Amen.

II.

Grant unto us grace, we beseech thee, Almighty God, that as thou hast taught us thy will, so we may at all times choose and obey thy holy laws; making our light shine before men, to the glory of thy name; through Jesus Christ our Lord.—Amen.

III.

Almighty God, who hast made of one blood all

nations, and whose will it is that all men should come to the knowledge of the truth and be saved, Send forth the light of thy gospel into all lands, and pour out thy Spirit upon all flesh; that thy name may be hallowed everywhere, and thy kingdom may come, which is righteousness, peace, and joy in the Holy Ghost.

Take the veil from the heart of the Jew, that he may see the end of that which was commanded to his fathers; and let all the kindreds of the nations turn unto the Lord; through him who hath broken down the partition between Jew and Gentile, and hath reconciled both unto thee.—Amen.

IV.

O God, Father of our Lord Jesus Christ, Look down in thy favour and compassion upon the whole body of thy faithful servants, whom thou hast called into the fellowship of thy Son.

Grant unto them a spirit of knowledge and understanding in thy truth; endow them plenteously with faith, hope, and charity, and with all heavenly gifts; and may they abound in good works, that they may adorn the doctrine of God our Saviour.

Being perfectly joined together in the same mind and in the same judgment, may they live together in unity, peace, and love, bearing each other's burdens, and so fulfilling the law of Christ.

Build up thy holy temple in the earth, O God, and fill it with thy glory. Adorn and beautify thy Church with the graces of thy Spirit; that every member of the same may be unto honour and praise at the appearing of our Lord Jesus Christ. And this we ask in His name who is exalted Head over all things, and is the Saviour of the Church which is his body. —Amen.

V.

Relieve the sick and the destitute; comfort the sorrowful; draw nigh, in thy mercy and grace, to the dying; and let all the miserable find consolation and redemption in thee, O God.—Amen.

VI.

Defend and prosper our native land. May it be governed with wisdom and justice. Grant success to all its righteous enterprises. Let the people be obedient to thy holy laws, living godly, righteous, and sober lives, to the glory of thy name.

God save the Queen. Be gracious to the Prince and Princess of Wales, and to all the members of the Royal Family. Counsel and guide the Queen's Ministers, and the High Court of Parliament. Give grace to all Magistrates, Judges, and Rulers, and to all ranks and conditions of men; that we may, each one of us, fulfil our appointed tasks as under the eye of the Great Master, and may in due time enter into the joy of our Lord.—Amen.

VII.

Almighty and most merciful Father, We, thy unworthy creatures, unite in giving thanks and praise unto thy name for thy great goodness and mercy to us and to all men. Thou loadest us with benefits: all that we have is thine: we ourselves are thine. We acknowledge thee, O Lord, as the bountiful giver of all the good things of this present life, but especially of that blessed hope of an everlasting inheritance, which thou hast given us in Christ Jesus our Lord. From this time henceforth may we consecrate ourselves to thy service in all things; living as those who are not their own, being bought with a price.—Amen.

Accept our prayers and praises, we humbly entreat thee, O Lord, and send us an answer in peace ; through thy well-beloved Son, our Lord, who liveth and reigneth with thee the Father, in the unity of the eternal Spirit, world without end.—Amen.

Sing praises to God, sing praises :
—Sing praises unto our King, sing praises.
For God is King of all the earth :
—Sing ye praises with understanding.   *Ps.* xlvii.

[*Then a Psalm or Doxology may be sung.*]

The Benediction.

The grace of the Lord Jesus Christ, and the love of God, and the communion of the Holy Ghost, be with you all.—Amen.

Third Sunday of the Month.

Afternoon Service.

[*The congregation being assembled, the Minister may recite the following sentences.*]

Humble yourselves in the sight of the Lord, and he shall lift you up. *James* iv.

Blessed are the undefiled in the way, who walk in the law of the Lord.

Blessed are they that keep his testimonies, and that seek him with the whole heart. *Ps.* cxix.

I will hear what God the Lord will speak; for he will speak peace unto his people, and to his saints: but let them not turn again to foolishness. *Ps.* lxxxv.

Having these promises, dearly beloved, let us draw near to the throne of grace with true hearts, in full assurance of faith. Let us pray.

First Prayer.

I.

Almighty and most merciful Father, We bless thee that we are permitted to approach thy throne of grace through Jesus Christ, the great High Priest of our profession; assured that thou hearest prayer, and wilt bestow upon us all things needful, whether for the body or the soul, for the life that now is, and that which is to come.

Blot out all our sins, we beseech thee, O Lord: cleanse us from all our iniquities. Give us a heart to fear and love thee. So teach us that we may know thy will; so strengthen us that we may perform it constantly, and may grow in grace, in wisdom, and in all goodness; to the glory of thy name; through Jesus Christ our Lord.—Amen.

Blessed is he whose transgression is forgiven:
—Whose sin is covered.
Blessed is the man unto whom the Lord imputeth not iniquity:
—And in whose spirit there is no guile.
I acknowledged my sin unto thee:
—And mine iniquity have I not hid.
I said, I will confess my transgressions unto the Lord:
—And thou forgavest the iniquity of my sin.
Thou art my hiding-place; thou shalt preserve me from trouble:
—Thou shalt compass me about with songs of deliverance.
Many sorrows shall be to the wicked:
—But he that trusteth in the Lord, mercy shall compass him about. *Ps.* xxxii.

II.

Lord of all power and might, who workest effectually in them that believe, and givest thy Holy Spirit unto them that obey thee, Look in mercy upon our ignorance and our manifold infirmities; and so guide and strengthen us, that we may take up our cross and follow Christ our Master; committing ourselves in faith and patience to thee, the righteous Judge; that so losing our life, we may keep it unto life eternal.

Fill us with godly fear lest we fail of the grace of

God, and make shipwreck of faith and a good conscience. Deliver us from unbelief, and hardness of heart, and a seared conscience: from selfishness and pride, from hypocrisy and love of the world, and from all fleshly lusts and debasing passions. Let our hands be clean from violence and wrong; let our hearts be pure from evil thoughts and corrupt desires; that we may be sincere and without rebuke, and, our heart not condemning us, we may have confidence toward thee.

Deliver us not, O God, into the hand of our enemies; keep us from the snares of the wicked. By well-doing may we put to silence the ignorance of foolish men; as free, and not using our liberty as a cloak of maliciousness, but as the servants of God.

O Lord, enrich us with the graces of thy Spirit; clothe our souls with the robes of righteousness, and beautify them with the garments of salvation, that we may be accepted guests at the marriage supper of the heavenly King.—Amen.

In thee, O Lord, do I put my trust; let me never be ashamed:
—Deliver me in thy righteousness.
Bow down thine ear to me; deliver me speedily.
—Be thou my strong rock, for an house of defence to save me.
Into thy hand I commit my spirit:
—Thou hast redeemed me, O Lord God of truth.
How great is thy goodness, which thou hast laid up for them that fear thee:
—Which thou hast wrought for them that trust in thee before the sons of men! *Ps.* xxxi.

III.

O Lord, who knowest that we have no power to help

or deliver us in those dangers which beset us in this our earthly pilgrimage, We beseech thee that thou wouldest be our defence and deliverer, and our high tower to save us. Let our faith and hope be in thee; and do thou make us perfect in every good word and work, to the glory of thy grace, through Jesus Christ our Lord : in whose name and words we say—

Our Father which art in heaven, Hallowed be thy name. Thy kingdom come. Thy will be done on earth, as it is in heaven. Give us day by day our daily bread. And forgive us our debts, as we forgive our debtors. And lead us not into temptation ; but deliver us from evil.—Amen.

O give thanks unto the Lord, for he is good :
—Because his mercy endureth for ever. *Ps.* cvii.

[*Then may be said or sung one or both of these Psalms.*]

PSALM LXVI.

Make a joyful noise unto God, | all ye | lands : || sing forth the | honour | of his | name ;

Make his | praise... | glorious. || Say unto God, how | terrible art | thou in thy | works !

Through the greatness | of thy | power || shall thine enemies sub- | mit themselves | unto | thee.

All the earth shall | worship | thee : || they shall | sing un- | to thy | name.

Come and see the | works of | God : || he is marvellous in his doing to- | ward the | children of | men.

He ruleth by his | power for | ever ; || his | eyes be- | hold the | nations :

Let not the rebellious ex- | alt them- | selves. || O | bless our | God, ye | people,

And make the voice of his | praise to be | heard : ||

AFTERNOON SERVICE. 61

who holdeth our soul in life, and | suffereth not our , feet to be | moved.

Come and hear, all | ye that fear | God, || and I will declare what | he hath done | for my | soul.

I cried unto him | with my | mouth, || and he was ex- | tolled | of my | tongue.

If I regard iniquity in my heart, the | Lord will not | hear : || verily God hath heard; he hath at- | tended to the | voice of my | prayer.

Bless- | ed be | God, || who hath not turned away my prayer, | nor his | mercy | from me.

PSALM CXXXVIII.

I will praise thee | with my whole | heart : || before the gods | will I sing | praise unto | thee.

I will worship towards thy | holy | temple, || and praise thy | name for thy | loving- | kindness,

And | for thy | truth : || for thou hast magnified thy | word above | all thy | name.

In the day when I cried | thou didst | answer me, || and didst | strengthen me with | strength in my | soul.

Though the | Lord be | high, || yet hath he re- | spect un- | to the | lowly.

But | the... | proud || he | knoweth a- | far... | off.

Though I walk in the | midst of | trouble, || thou wilt re- | vive... | me :

Thou shalt stretch forth thine hand against the wrath of mine | enemies, || and | thy right | hand shall | save me.

The | Lord will | perfect || that | which con- | cern- eth | me :

Thy mercy, O Lord, en- | dureth for | ever : || forsake not the | works of | thine own | hands.

[*Then may be read the Lesson from the Old Testament: after which follows*]

The Second Prayer.

I.

O Lord, omnipotent and eternal God, who didst proclaim thy law from Mount Sinai in terrible majesty, We give thee thanks that the thunder, and the earthquake, and the fire are now past, and we are permitted to hear the still small voice of thy grace speaking to us in the gospel.

Deliver us, O Lord, from the spirit of bondage and fear, and shed thy love abroad in our hearts by the Holy Ghost; that we may serve thee in peace and joy, hoping for thy glorious promises, through Jesus Christ our Saviour.—Amen.

For ever, O Lord, thy word is settled in heaven :
—Thy faithfulness is unto all generations.
Thou hast established the earth and it abideth :
—They continue this day according to thine ordinances ; for all are thy servants.
Unless thy law had been my delight, I should have perished in mine affliction :
—I will never forget thy precepts; for with them thou hast quickened me. *Ps.* cxix.

II.

Grant, we beseech thee, O gracious God, that through faith in thy Son Jesus Christ, who, at his first coming, died in the flesh to take away the sin of the world, our souls may be redeemed from their pollution and guilt; that when he shall appear the second time in glory, our corruptible bodies may put on incorruption, and

AFTERNOON SERVICE.

our mortal flesh be clothed with immortality; that as we have borne the image of the earthly, we may also bear the image of the heavenly, and be made partakers of that kingdom which flesh and blood shall not inherit. And this we ask in His name, who was dead, and liveth for evermore, Christ Jesus our Lord.—Amen.

Rejoice in the Lord, O ye righteous:
—For praise is comely for the upright.
Sing unto him a new song:
—Play skilfully with a loud noise. *Ps.* xxxiii.

[Here a Psalm may be sung: after which is read the Lesson from the New Testament. Then follows]

The Third Prayer.

I.

We praise and bless thy holy name, Father of mercies, and God of all grace, that thou hast had compassion upon us, miserable sinners:

That thou didst send thy Son to seek and save us:

That he took on him the form of a servant, and the likeness of sinful flesh, and fulfilled thy law, and was obedient to all thy will even unto death:

That he made propitiation for our sins; and when he had overcome the sharpness of death, he opened the kingdom of heaven to all believers:

That he sitteth at thy right hand in glory everlasting:

That he will come again in glory and majesty to judge the quick and the dead; and will reign till all enemies are put under his feet:

That he is our Advocate with thee; the Captain of our salvation; the author and finisher of the faith:

That he is not untouched with the feeling of our infirmities; having been, in all points, tempted as we are:

That he ever liveth to make intercession; and saveth to the uttermost them that come unto thee by him:

That thou hast sent unto us the gospel of thy grace; and hast permitted us to unite with thy Church militant in calling upon thy name, and learning the way of eternal life.

II.

O God, who dwellest from eternity in light that is inaccessible and full of glory, We thank thee that, by the manifestation of thy Son in the flesh, thou hast revealed thyself unto us, so dispelling our ignorance, and guiding our steps in the ways of righteousness and peace.

Incline our hearts, we beseech thee, to hear His voice who speaketh to us from heaven; to obey and follow Him who is the light of the world; that, being translated out of the kingdom of darkness, and redeemed from all the power of sin and death, we may at length receive thy promises, and be made partakers of glory, honour, and immortality, through our Lord and Redeemer, Jesus Christ.—Amen.

III.

Almighty God, the Creator and Preserver of all mankind, We pray thee to send forth into all lands the light of thy truth; and grant that all men may receive it in faith and love, that their spirits may be saved in the day of the Lord.

More especially we pray for the whole estate of Christ's Church upon earth; that all who make profession of his religion may be fully instructed in the

AFTERNOON SERVICE. 65

doctrine which is according to godliness; and, being delivered from superstition and impiety, from heresies and schisms, from love of the world, from slavery to the flesh and the devil, may they be united in the bonds of peace and love, and, by all righteous and holy living, make their calling and election sure, to thy glory and praise.—Amen.

IV.

We commit ourselves and all that are dear to us, our kindred, friends, and benefactors, and those who have desired to be remembered in our prayers, to thy mercy and grace, and to the keeping of thy good providence, O Lord our God.

Grant unto them and us that which is needful for the present life, and with it bestow thy blessing. Enrich us with patience and resignation, with cheerfulness and fortitude; and teach us, in whatever state we are, therewith to be content.

Cleanse our souls with the presence of thy good and holy Spirit: adorn them with the ornaments of thy grace: sanctify us wholly, in spirit, and soul, and body; and preserve us blameless to the coming and kingdom of our Lord.—Amen.

Thou shalt guide me with thy counsel:
—And afterward receive me to glory.
Whom have I in heaven but thee?
—And there is none upon earth that I desire beside thee.
My flesh and my heart fail:
—But God is the strength of my heart, and my portion for ever.—Amen. *Ps.* lxxiii.

Thou art my God, and I will praise thee:
—My God, I will exalt thee.

O give thanks unto the Lord, for he is good :
—For his mercy endureth for ever. *Ps.* cxviii.

[*Then a Psalm or Doxology may be sung.*]

Benediction.

The peace of God, which passeth all understanding, keep your hearts and minds through Christ Jesus. And the grace of the Lord Jesus Christ, and the love of God, and the fellowship of the Holy Ghost, be with you all.—Amen.

Prayer before Sermon.

O God, whose inspiration giveth to man understanding, and who didst bestow upon thy servants of old gifts of wisdom and knowledge and utterance, Vouchsafe thy grace to us who are here assembled before thee, that our speaking and hearing may be unto edification and profit, to the increase of our knowledge and faith and obedience, to our comfort and growth in grace ; through Jesus Christ our Lord.—Amen.

Prayer after Sermon.

Let thy gospel, O Lord, come to us not in word only but in power, and in the Holy Ghost ; that we may be guided into all the truth, and also may be strengthened unto all obedience and enduring of thy will with joyfulness ; that we may abound in the work of faith, and the labour of love, and the patience of hope, and so may be made meet to be partakers of thy heavenly inheritance ; through Jesus Christ our Lord.—Amen.

Evening Prayer.

O God, who dost not slumber or sleep, Guard us all, in soul and body, during the night.

May we rest under the shield of thy providence, in the peace of a good conscience, and in the hope of a better life when the night and sleep of death are past.

Raise us up again, if it please thee, O Father of our spirits, that we may still serve thee, and see the goodness of the Lord in the land of the living. And so may we spend all the days of our life, that we may have hope in our death, and may rise again to the life immortal; through Him who died for our sins, and rose again for our justification, Jesus Christ our Redeemer.—Amen.

Fourth Sunday of the Month.

FORENOON SERVICE.

[*The congregation being assembled, the Minister may recite one or more of the following sentences.*]

God is greatly to be feared in the assembly of the saints, and to be had in reverence of all them that are about him. *Ps.* lxxxix.

O worship the Lord in the beauty of holiness: fear before him, all the earth. *Ps.* xcvi.

I will hear what God the Lord will speak; for he will speak peace unto his people and to his saints; but let them not turn again to foolishness. *Ps.* lxxxv.

Open to me the gates of righteousness: I will go into them; and I will praise the Lord. *Ps.* cxviii.

Let us pray.

The First Prayer.

I.

O God, almighty and everlasting, We would draw near unto thee with reverence and godly fear, in the name of thy Son, our Mediator and Advocate, Jesus Christ; beseeching thee to fulfil to us that promise which he gave to his disciples, that wherever two or three are gathered together in his name, he will be in the midst of them.

Let our sacrifices of prayer and praise be acceptable in thy sight, O Lord, through him who is the great High Priest of our profession, and who hath consecrated for us a new and living way into the Holiest; that coming boldly unto the throne of grace, we might obtain mercy, and find grace to help in time of need.—Amen.

Truly my soul waiteth upon God :
—From him cometh my salvation.
He only is my rock and my salvation :
—He is my defence, I shall not be greatly moved.
My soul, wait thou only upon God :
—For my expectation is from him.
In God is my salvation and my glory :
—The rock of my strength, and my refuge, is in God.
Trust in him at all times, ye people :
—Pour out your heart before him; God is a refuge for us. *Ps.* lxii.

If we say that we have no sin, we deceive ourselves, and the truth is not in us: If we confess our sins, he is faithful and just to forgive us our sins, and to cleanse us from all unrighteousness. 1 *John* i.

II.

We have grievously offended thee, O Lord our heavenly Father, by our manifold sins and iniquities, transgressing thy righteous laws and resisting thy Holy Spirit. We acknowledge our guilt and misery in thy sight; entreating thee to pardon all our offences, and to create in us clean and contrite hearts; that henceforth, being redeemed from all iniquity, we may serve thee in holiness and righteousness, to the glory of thy name; through our only Saviour Jesus Christ. —Amen.

Hear my prayer, O Lord : give ear to my supplications :

—In thy faithfulness answer me, and in thy righteousness.
And enter not into judgment with thy servant :
—For in thy sight shall no man living be justified.
I stretch forth my hands unto thee :
—My soul thirsteth after thee, as a thirsty land.
Hear me speedily, O Lord :
—My spirit faileth.
Hide not thy face from me :
—Lest I be like unto them that go down into the pit.
Cause me to hear thy loving-kindness in the morning :
—For in thee do I trust.
Cause me to know the way wherein I should walk :
—For I lift up my soul unto thee.
Deliver me, O Lord, from mine enemies :
—I flee unto thee to hide me.
Teach me to do thy will; for thou art my God :
—Thy spirit is good; lead me into the land of uprightness.
Quicken me, O Lord, for thy name's sake :
—For thy righteousness' sake bring my soul out of trouble. *Ps.* cxliii.

If any man sin, we have an advocate with the Father, Jesus Christ the righteous : and he is the propitiation for our sins. 1 *John* ii.

As the heaven is high above the earth, so great is his mercy toward them that fear him. *Ps.* ciii.

Who is a God like unto thee, who pardoneth iniquity, and retaineth not his anger for ever; because he delighteth in mercy! *Micah* vii.

III.

We rejoice in thy promises, O God : we hope in thy

word. Being justified freely by thy grace, may we be made heirs, according to the hope of everlasting life. And having this hope in us, may we cleanse ourselves from all filthiness both of the flesh and of the spirit, and perfect holiness in thy fear; that the peace of God, which passeth all understanding, may keep our hearts and minds; through Christ Jesus.—Amen.

IV.

From the night early awaketh our soul unto thee, O God; for the light of thy commandments is upon the earth.

Knowing it is high time to awake out of sleep, for the day of thy judgment slumbereth not, let us cast off the works of darkness, and put on us the armour of light, and walk as those who have renounced the hidden things of dishonesty, and all the unfruitful works of darkness.

Lead us in thy truth, O God: teach us to do thy will: guide our steps in the ways of righteousness and peace: defend us from all snares and dangers, and deliver us from the powers of darkness; that we may walk before God in the light of the living. O Lord, enlighten our eyes, lest we sleep the sleep of death.

These things we ask in His name who is the resurrection and the life; who also taught us when we pray thus to say—

Our Father which art in heaven, Hallowed be thy name. Thy kingdom come. Thy will be done on earth, as it is in heaven. Give us this day our daily bread. And forgive us our debts, as we forgive our debtors. And lead us not into temptation; but deliver us from evil.—Amen.

I will praise the Lord with my whole heart:

—In the assembly of the upright, and in the congregation. *Ps.* cxi.

[*Then may be said or sung one or more of these Psalms following.*]

PSALM LXIII.

O God, | thou art my | God ; || early | will... | I... | seek thee :

My soul thirsteth for thee, my flesh | longeth for | thee || in a dry and thirsty | land, where no | water | is.

To see thy | power and thy | glory, || so as I have | seen thee | in the | sanctuary.

Because thy loving-kindness is | better than | life, || my | lips shall | praise... | thee.

Thus will I bless thee | while I | live : || I will | lift up my | hands in thy | name.

My soul shall be satisfied as with | marrow and | fatness ; || and my mouth shall | praise thee with | joyful | lips :

When I remember thee up- | on my | bed, || and meditate on | thee in the | night... | watches.

Because thou hast | been my | help, || therefore in the shadow of thy | wings will | I re- | joice.

My soul followeth | hard after | thee : || thy | right hand up- | holdeth | me.

LUKE I. 68.

Blessed be the Lord | God of | Israel ; || for he hath visited | and re- | deemed his | people,

And hath raised up a horn of sal- | vation | for us || in the | house of his | servant | David ;

As he spake by the mouth of his | holy | prophets, || which have | been since the | world be- | gan :

FORENOON SERVICE. 73

That we should be saved | from our | enemies, and from the | hand of | all that | hate us ;
To perform the mercy | promised to our | fathers, | and to re- | member his | holy | covenant ;
The oath which he sware to our | father | Abraham, | that | he would | grant unto | us,
That we being delivered out of the | hand of our | enemies might | serve him | without | fear,
In holiness and | righteousness be- | fore him, all the | days... | of our | life.
And thou, | child, shalt be | called the | prophet | of the | Highest:
For thou shalt go before the | face of the | Lord | to pre- | pare... | his... | ways;
To give knowledge of salvation | unto his | people | by the re- | mission | of their | sins,
Through the tender mercy | of our | God ; | whereby the dayspring from on | high hath | visited | us,
To give light to them that | sit in | darkness and in the | shadow of | death,
To | guide our | feet in- | to the | way of | peace.

[Then may be read the Lesson from the Old Testament: after which follows]

The Second Prayer.

I.

O Lord our heavenly Father, who hast revealed thine eternal power and Godhead in the creation of the world, and dost continually display thy glory in upholding and governing the same, We thank thee for that more perfect revelation of thy character and will, which thou hast given us in thy Word.

Grant, we beseech thee, O Lord, that we, upon whom

thou hast made the beams of thy grace and truth to shine, may walk worthy of our high vocation, and adorn the doctrine of God our Saviour, living soberly, righteously, and godly in this present world; not being weary in well-doing, or fainting when we are chastened of thee; that when Christ, who is our life, shall appear, we may be found worthy to stand before the Son of Man, and be made partakers of glory, honour, and immortality.—Amen.

Righteous art thou, O Lord:
—And upright are thy judgments.
Thy testimonies that thou hast commanded are righteous and very faithful.
—Thy word is very pure; therefore thy servant loveth it.
Great peace have they that love thy law:
—And nothing shall offend them.
Let my cry come near before thee, O Lord:
—Give me understanding according to thy word.

Ps. cxix.

II.

O eternal God, who didst in the beginning create man in thine own image, and who, when we were dead in sins, didst send forth thy Son into the world that we might live through him, We magnify thy great name that, by faith of thy Christ, we are born again to a lively hope, and are made heirs of thy incorruptible inheritance.

Do thou, who art the inexhaustible fountain of light and life, and who, as on this day, didst bring again from the dead the Lord Jesus, grant that we, who have been baptized into his death, may be quickened and raised up through the mighty power of thy Spirit; that being made free from sin, we may serve thee continually in newness of life, and may present our bodies living sacrifices, holy and acceptable, which is our reasonable service; through the same Christ Jesus, who, in the power of the eternal Spirit, offered himself without spot unto thee, and is our great High Priest and Advocate in the heavenly temple.—Amen.

Unto thee will I cry, O Lord my rock: be not silent to me:
—Lest, if thou be silent to me, I become like them that go down into the pit.
Hear the voice of my supplications when I cry unto thee:
—When I lift up my hands toward thy holy oracle.
Draw me not away with the wicked, and with the workers of iniquity;
—Which speak peace to their neighbour, but mischief is in their hearts.
Blessed be the Lord;
—Because he hath heard the voice of my supplications.
The Lord is my strength and my shield:
—My heart trusted in him, and I am helped:
Therefore my heart greatly rejoiceth:
—And with my song will I praise him.
Save thy people, and bless thine inheritance:
—Feed them also, and lift them up for ever.

Ps. xxviii.

III.

O God, who sustainest our life from day to day, from moment to moment, opening thy bountiful hand to supply all our wants, We acknowledge with gratitude thy unmerited goodness.

May we use thy bounties with humility, temperance, and charity; may we eat and drink, may we do all things and enjoy all, to thy glory ; that our bodies may be strengthened for thy service upon earth, and we may be prepared for that heavenly life, when thou wilt feed our souls with the bread of thine eternal truth, and refresh them for ever from the fountain of thine inexhaustible love ; through Christ our Lord.—Amen.

Sing unto the Lord a new song :
—And his praise in the congregation of saints.
Let Israel rejoice in him that made him :
—Let the children of Zion be joyful in their King.
Ps. cxlix.

[*Here a Psalm may be sung : after which, the Lesson from the New Testament is read. Then follows*]

The Third Prayer.

I.

Grant, O Lord, that we, whom thou hast made rational creatures, may, through thy grace, be delivered from the carnal mind, which is death, and from all the deeds of the flesh, and may serve thee, the living God, in righteousness and purity all the days of our life upon earth ; that in due time we may reign with Christ in that kingdom which flesh and blood shall not inherit ; through Him who is our only Lord and Saviour.— Amen.

II.

O thou great Master and Lord, whose are all things in heaven and earth, and who givest to every one as it seemeth meet unto thy godly wisdom, Grant us grace, we pray thee, that we may diligently and faithfully employ the talents, whatever they are, which thou hast committed to us for a season; that when the Lord shall come and reckon with his servants, we may render our account with joy, and not with grief.

Vouchsafe unto those that are rich in this world that they be not high-minded, or trust in uncertain riches, but in the living God, who giveth us all things richly to enjoy; that they be rich in good works, laying up a good foundation against the time to come, that they may lay hold on eternal life:

And unto thy servants that are poor in this world, that they be poor in spirit, but rich in faith, and heirs of that kingdom which thou hast promised to them that love thee.

By thy grace working in us, may we daily perform better the part thou hast assigned us in the world, growing and increasing continually in faith and patience, in love to God and charity to men, in contentment, in resignation and submission to thy will, in meekness, gentleness, and all holy dispositions and Christian graces; that when our last day upon the earth shall come, we may be found perfect and complete in all the will of God.

In all the work of our hands may we work thy work; and in all our labours for the meat that perisheth, may we labour for that meat which endureth to eternal life, and so use this world as not abusing it, for the fashion of this world passeth away.—Amen.

III.

O God our Saviour, who willest that all men be saved through the knowledge and obedience of the truth, and hast given us commandment to make prayers and intercessions for all men, through thy Son, the one Mediator between God and men, who gave himself a ransom for all, We entreat thee to look down in thy tender mercy upon all the kindreds of the nations, and to deliver them from ignorance and superstition, from idolatry and wickedness, from injustice, oppression, and cruelty, and from all their sins and miseries.

Cause the light of thy truth to shine in all the dark places of the earth, and hasten thy kingdom; that the glory of the Lord may be revealed, and all flesh may see it together.—Amen.

IV.

We pray for kings, and for all that are in authority, that they may govern the people committed to them in wisdom and justice, and in thy fear, who art the King of kings, and the Lord of lords:

Especially for thy servant, our Sovereign, Queen Victoria; that she may be upheld and guided by thy Holy Spirit, and may at all times enjoy thy favour and blessing; that her reign may be long and prosperous; and that she may inherit thy heavenly kingdom:

For the Prince and Princess of Wales, and all the members of the Royal Family:

For the Queen's Ministers and Counsellors; for the High Court of Parliament; and for all Magistrates, Judges, and Rulers; that we may lead a quiet and peaceable life in godliness and honesty, adorning the doctrine of God our Saviour.—Amen.

V.

Look down, O merciful Father, upon all thy creatures who are in sorrow, pain, sickness, or any other adversity. Sanctify and strengthen the living for thy service on earth: sanctify and comfort the dying; that being washed from the stains of sin, and eased of the load of guilt and fear, they may be made ready for the joys of thy presence in heaven. Let their cry enter into thine ears, O Lord of Sabaoth. Send into their hearts thy Holy Spirit the Comforter, that they may rejoice in tribulation, and be made perfect in that love which casteth out fear; through Christ our Lord, who suffered and was tempted, and is able to succour us when we are tempted; who died for us, and hath taken away the sting of death, and the victory of the king of terrors, and is gone before to prepare mansions for us in heaven, that where he is there we may be also.—Amen.

I will praise thee, O Lord, for thou hast heard me:—And art become my salvation. *Ps.* cxviii.

[*Then a Psalm or Doxology may be sung.*]

The Benediction.

The grace of the Lord Jesus Christ, and the love of God, and the communion of the Holy Ghost, be with you all.—Amen.

Fourth Sunday of the Month.

AFTERNOON SERVICE.

[*The congregation being assembled, the Minister may recite the following sentences.*]

Our help is in the name of the Lord, who made heaven and earth. *Ps.* cxxiv.

Thus saith the high and lofty One that inhabiteth eternity, whose name is Holy; I dwell in the high and holy place, with him also that is of a contrite and humble spirit, to revive the spirit of the humble, and the heart of the contrite. *Isa.* lvii.

Blessed are the people that know the joyful sound: they shall walk, O Lord, in the light of thy countenance. *Ps.* lxxxix. Let us pray.

First Prayer.

I.

O God, who lovest the gates of Zion more than all the dwellings of Jacob, and hast commanded us not to forsake the assembling of ourselves together, Be merciful to us, we beseech thee, and make us joyful in thy house of prayer.

Grant us thy grace, without which we cannot worship thee acceptably. Deliver us from unbelief, and hardness of heart, from hypocrisy and love of the world, from the dominion of the flesh, and from the powers of darkness; and endow us with faith, hope, and charity, that we may worship thee in spirit and truth; for such thou seekest to worship thee.—Amen.

II.

O God, merciful Father, who despisest not the sacrifice of a broken and contrite heart, and hast no pleasure in the death of a sinner, but rather that he should turn unto thee and live, Look upon us in thy compassion, we humbly entreat thee; for we have sinned against heaven and before thee, and are not worthy to be called thy children.

Grant unto us repentance and remission of our sins, through thy Son Jesus Christ; who was delivered for our offences, and was raised again for our justification, and is exalted at thy right hand, a Prince and a Saviour.—Amen.

Lord, I cry unto thee : make haste unto me :
—Give ear unto my voice, when I cry unto thee.
Let my prayer be set forth before thee as incense :
—And the lifting up of my hands as the evening sacrifice.
Set a watch, O Lord, before my mouth :
—Keep the door of my lips.
Incline not my heart to any evil thing :
—To practise wicked works with men that work iniquity.
Let the righteous smite me, it shall be a kindness :
—And let him reprove me, it shall be an excellent oil, which shall not break my head.
But mine eyes are unto thee, O God the Lord :
—In thee is my trust; leave not my soul destitute.

Ps. cxli:

III.

O God, who thyself workest in us, and hast commanded us to work out our own salvation with fear and trembling, We bless thee for that day of grace which thou dost afford us, in which we may learn the lessons of holy obedience, and may be exercised in the work of faith, the labour of love, the patience of hope, and in all the discipline of temperance, justice, and godliness.

May we be diligent in every good work, doing with our might what our hand findeth to do. Give us grace to be faithful in that trust which the Lord hath committed to us; that when he shall come, we may receive that sentence, Well done, good and faithful servants, enter ye into the joy of your Lord.—Amen.

IV.

Father of mercies and God of all comfort, who didst, in the fulness of time, send thy Son to be the consolation of Israel, and hast promised another Comforter to abide with us for ever, Send forth, we pray thee, thy Holy Spirit into our hearts, to enlighten, sanctify, and guide us; to strengthen us in every good word and work; to uphold us in all temptations and trials; to comfort us in all our sorrows and afflictions; to fill us with joy and peace in believing, that we may abound in hope through the power of the Holy Ghost.

In the name of Jesus Christ we present these our petitions: saying in the words which he hath taught us—

Our Father which art in heaven, Hallowed be thy name. Thy kingdom come. Thy will be done on earth, as it is in heaven. Give us day by day our daily bread. And forgive us our debts, as we forgive our debtors. And lead us not into temptation; but deliver us from evil.—Amen.

Let them praise the name of the Lord; for his name alone is excellent:

—His glory is above the earth and the heaven.
Ps. cxlviii.

[*Then may be said or sung one or both of these Psalms.*]

PSALM XCV.

O come, let us sing | unto the | Lord : || let us make a joyful noise to the | rock of | our sal- | vation.

Let us come before his | presence with | thanksgiving, | and make a joyful | noise unto | him with | psalms.

For the Lord is a | great... | God, || and a great | King a- | bove all | gods.

In his hand are the deep places | of the | earth : || the strength of the | hills is | his... | also.

The sea is | his, and he | made it : || and his hands | formed the | dry... | land.

O come, let us worship and | bow... | down : || let us kneel be- | fore the | Lord our | maker.

For | he is our | God ; || and we are the people of his pasture, and the | sheep... | of his | hand.

To day if ye will | hear his | voice, || har- | den... | not your | heart,

As in the | provo- | cation, || and as in the day of temp- | tation | in the | wilderness :

When your | fathers | tempted me, || proved | me, and | saw my | work.

Forty | years... | long || was I | grieved with | this genera- | tion,

And said, It is a people that do | err in their | heart, || and they | have not | known my | ways :

Unto whom I | sware in my | wrath || that they should not | enter | into my | rest.

PSALM CXLVI.

Praise | ye the | Lord. || Praise the | Lord,... | O my | soul.

While I live will I | praise the | Lord ; || I will sing praises unto my | God while I | have any | being.

Put not your | trust in | princes, || nor in the son of man, in | whom there | is no | help.

His breath goeth forth, he returneth | to his | earth ; || in that very | day his | thoughts... | perish.

Happy | is... | he || that hath the God of | Jacob | for his | help,

Whose hope is in the | Lord his | God : || who | made... | heaven, and | earth,

The sea, and all that | therein | is ; || who | keepeth | truth for | ever :

Who executeth judgment | for the op- | pressed : || who | giveth | food to the | hungry.

The Lord | looseth the | prisoners : || the Lord | openeth the | eyes of the | blind :

The Lord raiseth them that are | bowed | down : || the | Lord... | loveth the | righteous :

The Lord pre- | serveth the | strangers ; || he re- | lieveth the | fatherless and | widow :

But the | way of the | wicked || he | turneth | upside | down.

The Lord shall | reign for | ever, || e- | ven thy | God, O | Zion,

Unto all | gene- | rations. || Praise | ye the | Lord. A- | men.

[*Here the Lesson from the Old Testament may be read : after which follows*]

The Second Prayer.

I.

O God Almighty, who quickenest the dead, and who, as on this day, didst raise up our Lord Jesus Christ and give him glory, Bestow upon us thy grace, that, as we have been baptized into his body, we may also be made partakers of his Spirit, and may walk in newness of life.

And as Christ, being raised from the dead, dieth no more, neither hath death any more dominion over him, may we, being made free from sin, serve thee, the living God, continually, having our fruit unto holiness, and the end everlasting life; through our Redeemer and Lord, Jesus Christ.—Amen.

II.

Bestow upon us, we pray thee, O Lord, thy enlightening, purifying, and strengthening grace; that we may grow in wisdom, in holiness, and in all goodness, setting thee before us in all things, and doing thy work as wise and faithful servants.

Let not any iniquity have dominion over us; neither suffer our hearts to be hardened through the deceitfulness of sin; but do thou lead us in thy truth and guide us, for thou art the God of our salvation.

And knowing that the night cometh in which no man can work, and that after death is the judgment, when each one of us shall give account of himself unto thee, may we lay aside every weight, and run without fainting the course of faith and obedience, which is set before us; that in the end we may be found worthy to stand before the Son of man, and may receive that crown of righteousness which the Lord hath promised to them that love him.—Amen.

III.

Have mercy, we entreat thee, O Lord, upon all thy creatures, and, of thy great goodness, deliver them from those miseries and evils by which any of them are oppressed, especially from the shades of ignorance, error, and unbelief, and from the chains of sin. Them that are dead in trespasses do thou awaken unto repentance and newness of life; and let all who make profession of Christ's religion adorn his doctrine by a conversation becoming the gospel. And let thy kingdom come; let thy will be done, from the rising to the setting of the sun.—Amen.

IV.

We entreat thee, O Father, mercifully to receive the prayers of thy servants everywhere that call upon thee for help and deliverance. And for this end, grant unto them the Spirit of thy Son; that, lifting up holy hands without wrath and doubting, they may be heard in that they fear; and having learned obedience by the things they suffer, may they in due time be made partakers of thy salvation; through our merciful High Priest, Jesus Christ, who himself suffered and was tempted, and is able to succour us when we are tempted.—Amen.

How long wilt thou forget me, O Lord? for ever?
—How long wilt thou hide thy face from me?
How long shall I take counsel in my soul, having sorrow in my heart daily?
—How long shall mine enemy be exalted over me?
Consider and hear me, O Lord my God:
—Lighten mine eyes, lest I sleep the sleep of death:
Lest mine enemy say, I have prevailed against him:
—And those that trouble me rejoice when I am moved.
But I have trusted in thy mercy:
—My heart shall rejoice in thy salvation.
I will sing unto the Lord:
—Because he hath dealt bountifully with me.—
Amen. *Ps.* xiii.

AFTERNOON SERVICE. 87

[*Here a Psalm may be sung: after which is read the Lesson from the New Testament.   Then follows*]

The Third Prayer.

I.

Grant, we beseech thee, O Lord, that we may so receive thy word into our hearts, that it may be unto us a savour of life unto life. By it may we be made wise unto salvation, and be thoroughly furnished unto all good works.—Amen.

II.

O Lord God Almighty, who art the framer of our bodies, and the Father of our spirits, and hast sent thy Son Jesus Christ to redeem us from sin and death, Give us thy grace, we entreat thee; that, being purified from all filthiness both of the flesh and of the spirit, we may perfect holiness in thy fear, yielding our members instruments of righteousness unto thee, as those that are alive from the dead; that when this earthly tabernacle is dissolved, we may be received into everlasting habitations, and be clothed upon with our house from heaven, according to that working whereby Christ is able to subdue all things unto himself.—Amen.

I have set the Lord always before me:
—Because he is at my right hand, I shall not be moved.
Therefore my heart is glad, and my glory rejoiceth:
—My flesh also shall rest in hope.
For thou wilt not leave my soul in hell:
—Neither wilt thou suffer thy Holy One to see corruption.

Thou wilt shew me the path of life : in thy presence is fulness of joy :
—At thy right hand there are pleasures for evermore. *Ps.* xvi.

III.

Bless our native country, and make it prosperous in all good things. Forgive us all our sins; and turn from us all those evils which we have deserved. Thou hast not dealt with us as we have sinned, nor rewarded us according to our transgressions.

God save the Queen. Be gracious to the Prince and Princess of Wales; and to all the members of the Royal Family.

Guide and counsel the Queen's Ministers, and all persons invested with public authority, that they may discharge their several duties as the ministers of God.

We beseech thee, O Father, look in compassion upon thy universal Church; and as thou hast knit together thine elect in one communion and fellowship, grant us grace to follow thy blessed saints in all virtuous and godly living; that we may finally be united with them in thy kingdom of glory.—Amen.

IV.

O God, whose counsels are of old, even from everlasting, and all whose ways are righteousness and truth, We adore thy unfathomable wisdom, thy boundless goodness, thy judgments, which are unsearchable. Known unto thee are all thy works from the beginning; and thou bringest good out of evil, and light out of darkness, and makest even the wrath of man to praise thee.

We thank thee that, in the fulness of time, thy Son hath been manifested to destroy the works of the devil; that the darkness is past, and the true light now shineth. Let the beams of thy grace, which bringeth salvation, illuminate all the nations of the world. Let thy truth, O God, make all the peoples free.

Hasten, we pray thee, the coming and kingdom of thy Christ; that the whole creation, which sigheth and groaneth under the bondage of corruption, may be delivered, and we, with all thy saints departed, may receive the adoption, even the redemption of our bodies; that the saying which is written may be fulfilled, Death is swallowed up of Victory. Oh, the depth of the riches, both of the wisdom and knowledge of God! How unsearchable are his judgments, and his ways past finding out! For of him, and through him, and to him are all things; to whom be glory for ever.—Amen.

Praise God in his sanctuary:
—Praise him in the firmament of his power.
Let everything that hath breath praise the Lord:
—Praise ye the Lord. *Ps.* cl.

[*Then a Psalm or Doxology may be sung.*]

The Benediction.

Now the God of peace, that brought again from the dead our Lord Jesus, that great Shepherd of the sheep, through the blood of the everlasting covenant, make you perfect in every good work to do his will, working in you that which is well-pleasing in his sight, through Jesus Christ; to whom be glory for ever and ever.—Amen. *Heb.* xiii.

Prayer before or after Sermon.

God of all grace, and fountain of all wisdom, We humbly beseech thee to illuminate our minds and purify our hearts, that we may know thy truth and approve the things that are excellent.

Let us no longer be children in understanding, or be carried about with diverse and strange doctrines, ever learning, yet never able to come to the knowledge of the truth. Grant that we may be perfect men in Christ Jesus, thy word dwelling in us richly in all wisdom and spiritual understanding.

O Lord, heavenly Father, be pleased to establish our hearts with grace, according to the faith of God's elect and the truth that is after godliness—even as he hath taught us, who is thy Word made flesh, Jesus Christ, the same yesterday, to-day, and for ever.—Amen.

An Evening Prayer.

O thou that dwellest in unapproachable light, Keep us thy servants during the darkness and silence of the night, from all evil, whether of the body or the soul; for we know not what enemies and dangers encompass us about: and, when the night and darkness of this dying life are passed away, grant that we may awake to behold the light of thine eternal glory in the kingdom of heaven, with all thy saints; through him that loved us, and hath redeemed us with his precious blood, Jesus Christ our Lord.—Amen.

Fifth Sunday of the Month.

Forenoon Service.

[*The congregation being assembled, the Minister may recite the following sentences.*]

Let all the earth fear the Lord : let all the inhabitants of the world stand in awe of him.

For he spake and it was done; he commanded and it stood fast. The eye of the Lord is upon them that fear him; upon them that hope in his mercy. *Ps.* xxxiii.

The Lord is nigh unto all them that call upon him : to all that call upon him in truth.

He will fulfil the desire of them that fear him : he also will hear their cry, and will save them. *Ps.* cxlv.

Dearly beloved brethren, Let us with humble and contrite hearts draw nigh to the throne of the heavenly grace, confessing our sins, acknowledging the great goodness and mercy of our God, and asking in faith those things that are good for us; in the name of our great High Priest and Advocate, Jesus Christ. Let us pray.

First Prayer.

I.

We bow down before the footstool of thy divine Majesty, O God, adoring thee, the Lord of heaven and earth; of whom, and through whom, and to whom are all things; to whom be ascribed all might, majesty, and dominion, world without end.

All things are full of thee. The heavens declare thy glory: the earth is full of thy riches: so also is the great and wide sea. The day is thine; the night also is thine: thou hast prepared the light and the sun: thou hast set all the borders of the earth: thou hast made summer and winter. Who would not fear thee, O Lord, and glorify thy name? for thou only art holy!
—Amen.

In thee, O Lord, do I put my trust; let me never be ashamed:
—Deliver me in thy righteousness.
Bow down thine ear to me; deliver me speedily:
—Be thou my strong rock; for an house of defence to save me.
Into thy hand I commit my spirit:
—Thou hast redeemed me, O Lord God of truth.
I will be glad and rejoice in thy mercy; for thou hast considered my trouble:
—Thou hast known my soul in adversities;
And hast not shut me up into the hand of the enemy:
—Thou hast set my feet in a large room.
Make thy face to shine upon thy servant:
—Save me for thy mercies' sake.
How great is thy goodness which thou hast laid up for them that fear thee:
—Which thou hast wrought for them that trust in thee, before the sons of men! *Ps.* xxxi.

II.

O God, who art exalted above all blessing and praise, and needest not our service, for all things in heaven and earth are thine, Grant that we, and all our brethren throughout the world, may worship thee this day in spirit and truth, and may find acceptance with thee, through our Advocate and Mediator Jesus Christ.

And vouchsafe unto us, in the comfort of thy worship here, a foretaste of heavenly joy; that while we drink together of the cup of thy grace and consolation, we may be prepared to drink it new with Christ in his kingdom.—Amen.

The meek shall eat and be satisfied:
—They shall praise the Lord that seek him: your heart shall live for ever.
All the ends of the earth shall remember and turn unto the Lord:
—And all the kindreds of the nations shall worship before thee.
For the kingdom is the Lord's:
—And he is the governor among the nations.
A seed shall serve him:
—It shall be accounted to the Lord for a generation.
Ps. xxii.

Now is Christ risen from the dead, the first-fruits of them that are fallen asleep; for as by man is death, by man also is the resurrection of the dead.   1 *Cor.* xv.

III.

Almighty God, Father of our Lord Jesus Christ, We thank and praise thee that thou didst raise up, as on this day, thy Son from the dead, that the darkness of death might be dispelled, and life and immortality be brought to light; whereby we are born again to a new and lively hope.

Being risen with Christ, may we set our affection on

things above, where he is exalted and reigneth at thy right hand; from whence also we look for his second and glorious appearing.

Quicken us, O Lord, by thy Spirit, unto unfeigned repentance, to faith, hope, charity, and all holy dispositions and Christian virtues; that having in us the mind that was in Christ, we may worship thee with our hearts, as well as with our lips, offering to thy divine Majesty the sacrifices of righteousness, acceptable through Jesus Christ our Lord.—Amen.

Our Father which art in heaven, Hallowed be thy name. Thy kingdom come. Thy will be done on earth, as it is in heaven. Give us this day our daily bread. And forgive us our debts, as we forgive our debtors. And lead us not into temptation; but deliver us from evil.—Amen.

Ye that fear the Lord, praise him; all ye the seed of Jacob, glorify him:
—And fear him, all ye the seed of Israel.
For he hath not despised nor abhorred the affliction of the afflicted:
—Neither hath he hid his face from him; but when he cried unto him, he heard.
My praise shall be of thee in the great congregation:
—I will pay my vows before them that fear him.
Ps. xxii.

[*Then may be said or sung one or both of these Psalms.*]

PSALM C.

Make a | joyful | noise || unto the | Lord,... | all ye | lands.

Serve the | Lord with | gladness : || come be- | fore his | presence with | singing.

Know that the Lord | he is | God : it is he that hath | made us, and | not we our- | selves ;
We | are his | people, and the | sheep... | of his | pasture.
Enter into his | gates with | thanksgiving, and into his | courts with ' praise :
Be thankful | unto | him, and | bless his ' holy | name.
For the | Lord is | good ; his | mercy is | ever- | lasting ;
And his | truth en- | dureth to | all... | gener- | ations.

PSALM XCVI.

O sing unto the | Lord a new | song : | sing unto the | Lord,... | all the | earth.
Sing unto the Lord, | bless his | name ; shew forth his sal- | vation from | day to | day.
Declare his glory a- | mong the | heathen, | his | wonders a- | mong all | people.
For the Lord is great, and | greatly to be | praised : he is to be | feared a- | bove all | gods.
For all the gods of the | nations are | idols : || but the | Lord... | made the | heavens.
Honour and majesty | are be- | fore him : strength and | beauty are | in his | sanctuary.
Give unto the Lord, O ye | kindreds of the | people, give unto the | Lord... | glory and | strength.
Give unto the Lord the glory due | unto his | name : bring an offering, and | come in- | to his | courts.
O worship the Lord in the | beauty of | holiness : fear be- | fore him, | all the | earth.
Say among the heathen that the | Lord... | reigneth : | he shall | judge the | people | righteously.
Let the heavens rejoice, and let the | earth be glad ; let the sea | roar, and the | fulness there- | of.

Let the field be .joyful, and all that | is there- | in : ‖ then shall all the trees of the wood re- | joice be- | fore the | Lord :
For | he... | cometh, ‖ for he | cometh to | judge the | earth :
He shall judge the | world with | righteousness, ‖ and the | people | with his | truth.

[*Then may be read the Lesson from the Old Testament : after which follows*]

The Second Prayer.

I.

We humble ourselves in the dust before thee, O Lord, confessing our daily offences against thy divine Majesty. Our hearts and lives are polluted with innumerable sins. Thy fear hath not been at all times before our eyes; neither have we loved thee with all our hearts, or studied to serve and glorify thee.

We have not fulfilled that royal law which requires us to love our neighbour as ourselves, or followed after charity, and the things whereby one may edify another.

We have set our affection on things below, and have laid up treasure upon the earth, contemning that incorruptible inheritance which is reserved in heaven for the sons of God.

Hide thy face from our sins, and blot out all our iniquities. If thou shouldest mark iniquities, O Lord, who could stand ? But there is forgiveness with thee that thou mayest be feared, and plenteous redemption.

Hear, O Lord, when I cry with my voice :
—Have mercy also upon me, and answer me.
When thou saidst, Seek ye my face :

—My heart said unto thee, Thy face, Lord, will I seek.
Hide not thy face from me :
—Put not thy servant away in anger.
Thou hast been my help :
—Leave me not, neither forsake me, O God of my salvation.
Teach me thy way, O Lord :
—And lead me in a plain path, because of mine enemies.
I had fainted unless I had believed,
—To see the goodness of the Lord in the land of the living.
Wait on the Lord; be of good courage, and he shall strengthen thine heart :
—Wait, I say, on the Lord. *Ps.* xxvii.

II.

Almighty God, who art more ready to hear than we are to pray, and art wont to give more than either we deserve or desire, Pour down upon us the abundance of thy mercy; forgiving us those things of which our conscience is afraid, and giving us those good things which we are not worthy to ask, but for thy mercy's sake, through Christ our Lord.—Amen.

III.

O Almighty Father, God of all the world, in the light of whose presence there is perpetual day, We thy servants bless and praise thee, who holdest our souls in life, and makest the outgoings of the morning and evening to rejoice.

As we live by thy power, so we desire to walk according to thy laws, to be defended by thy providence, to be sanctified by thy grace. Let this day, and all the days of our life, be holy and peaceable. Send thy Holy Spirit, the Spirit of peace, to be the guide of our way, the guard of our souls and bodies; that we may spend the remaining portion of our life in blessing, and peace, and holiness.

Deliver us from all the temptations of the world, the flesh, and the devil. Take not thy grace from us; let us never want thy help in our need, or thy comforts in the day of our danger and calamity. Try us not beyond our strength, nor afflict us beyond our patience, nor smite us but with a Father's rod. Thou art our rock and our strong salvation. Deliver us, O God, from the miseries of this world, and save us from the wrath to come. Rescue us from the evils we have done, and preserve us from the evil we have deserved.

Receive thy servants who approach to the throne of thy grace, in the name of Jesus Christ. Give unto each of us that which is best for us: cast out all evil from within us: work in us a fulness of holiness, of wisdom, and spiritual understanding; and make us fruitful in every good work; that, living before thee with undefiled bodies and sanctified spirits, we may be presented without spot and blameless at the coming of our Lord Jesus Christ with all his saints.—Amen.

IV.

O Lord, whose blessed Son hath ascended into the heavens, Leave not us thy family comfortless, but send thy Holy Spirit into our hearts; that, being taught and quickened, purified and strengthened, by thy heavenly grace, we may faithfully and joyfully serve thee, both in doing and suffering thy will; through Him who suffered for us, and hath left us an example that we might follow his steps.—Amen.

V.

O God, who hast commanded us to watch and pray that we enter not into temptation, Endue us, we beseech thee, with sobriety, vigilance, and godly fear. Leave us not to our own weak and deceitful hearts; neither let us be seduced by the power of evil example; but may we put on the whole armour of God, that we may stand in the evil day. Succour us, O heavenly Father, in our time of trial and temptation, through the Spirit, by which thy Son our Lord was led into the wilderness to be tempted of the devil; that, our conflict ended, angels may be sent to minister unto us, as heirs of that salvation which thou hast promised to as many as obey and follow him.—Amen.

O magnify the Lord with me,
—And let us exalt his name together. *Ps.* xxxiv.

[*Here a Psalm may be sung: after which the Lesson from the New Testament is read. Then follows*]

The Third Prayer.

I.

O God, Father of mercies, We thy unworthy servants unite with one heart and voice in giving thanks and praise unto thee for all the goodness and grace which thou hast shewed unto us and to all men. Thou didst create us in thine own image; thou hast preserved us by thy good providence; thou hast delivered us from dangers and from death; thou hast kept our feet from falling, and our eyes from tears; thou hast bountifully supplied our wants, and loaded us with benefits: above all, we magnify and laud thy great name in that thou didst send thy Son into the world, that we might not perish by reason of our sins, but be made heirs according to the hope of everlasting life.

Let thy love, O Lord, constrain us henceforth to live as those who are not their own, that we may glorify thee with our bodies and spirits, which are thine.—Amen.

II.

O God, who art a Spirit, and with whom no sacrifices are accepted but such as are spiritual and holy, Grant unto us thy heavenly grace, that we may present our bodies a living sacrifice, holy and acceptable; offering unto thy divine Majesty day by day the reasonable service of Faith, Hope, Love, Patience, Submission, Zeal, and all the works of piety, righteousness, and sobriety; that at length we may be exalted to serve thee as kings and priests in the heavenly temple; through thy Son, who, in the eternal Spirit, offered himself without spot unto thee, and is exalted and reigneth at thy right hand, the High Priest of our profession, Christ Jesus.—Amen.

III.

Sovereign Master and Lord of the world, We commend to thy protection and favour the powers that be established to rule among the nations; especially thy servant our Sovereign Queen Victoria, the Prince and Princess of Wales, and all the Royal Family.

Grant thy grace to the Ministers of State, and to all that bear rule over us. Qualify and dispose them to govern in wisdom and righteousness; and may their administration be so blessed of thee, that, under it, the whole body of the people may have peace and prosperity; and may they enjoy thy bounties with thankful hearts.—Amen.

IV.

O Lord, our gracious God, We implore thy mercy for all who may be in peril by sea or land; for widows and orphans; for the poor; for prisoners; for the bereaved, the sick, and the dying, and for all the afflicted and sorrowful. May it please thee, merciful Father, to look upon them in thy compassion, to strengthen, comfort, and deliver them; or, if it be thy will that they now finish their course upon earth, receive their spirits into thy rest, and crown them with heavenly glory.—Amen.

V.

Thou art the Maker and Saviour of all men; and thou art rich in mercy unto all that call upon thee. Extend, O Lord, the light of thy gospel to all the nations of the earth; reclaim them from their errors and sins; abolish all doctrines and worships that are contrary to thy truth; and let all men acknowledge thee, the only true God, and Jesus Christ whom thou hast sent; that, the darkness being past, the true light may shine for ever.—Amen.

VI.

Finally, O Lord, we beseech thee to pour out thy blessing upon us, our persons, our families, our occupations, and all our concerns and interests. Give us whatever is needful for this present life, and also for that which is to come; and deliver us from vain regrets, needless anxieties, and unbelieving fears. We are in thy hand; we commit ourselves to thee; thou wilt not leave us or forsake us. May we be diligent and prudent in our several callings; and may they yield fruits to the supply of our need, to the comfort of our brethren, and to thy glory. Let not us place our good in riches, pleasures, honours, or any of the things of this perishing world, but in thy favour, in the peace and joy of thy Spirit, and in the hope of everlasting life, which thou hast promised to them that love thee.

Mercifully receive our prayers, and send us an answer in peace, through thy well-beloved Son, our Lord and Saviour Jesus Christ.—Amen.

My mouth shall speak the praise of the Lord :
—And let all flesh bless his holy name for ever and ever. *Ps.* cxlv.

[*Then a Psalm or Doxology may be sung.*]

The Benediction.

The grace of the Lord Jesus Christ, and the love of God, and the communion of the Holy Ghost, be with you all.—Amen.

Fifth Sunday of the Month.

Afternoon Service.

[The congregation being assembled, the Minister may recite the following sentences.]

The sacrifices of God are a broken spirit : a broken and a contrite heart, O God, thou wilt not despise. *Ps.* li.

I will arise, and go to my father, and will say unto him, Father, I have sinned against heaven, and before thee, and am no more worthy to be called thy son. *Luke* xv.

Dearly beloved brethren, Let us search and try our ways, and turn again to the Lord. Let us lift up our heart with our hands to God in the heavens. *Lam.* iii.

Let us pray.

The First Prayer.

I.

O God, Father of our Lord Jesus Christ, of whom the whole family in heaven and earth is named, Vouchsafe unto us who now draw near to thy presence the aids of thy heavenly grace, that we may worship thee with contrite, faithful, and obedient hearts ; and grant that we may be acceptable in thy sight, and may receive our petitions ; for we present our supplications before thee in his name, who is the great High Priest of our profession, our Mediator and Advocate, Jesus Christ.—Amen.

Make haste, O God, to deliver me:
—Make haste to help me, O Lord.
Let all those that seek thee rejoice and be glad in thee:
—Let such as love thy salvation say continually, Let God be magnified.
But I am poor and needy; make haste unto me, O God:
—Thou art my help and my deliverer; O Lord, make no tarrying. *Ps.* lxx.

II.

Almighty and everlasting God, Creator of the world, Father of angels and men;—Have mercy upon us.

Thou blessed and only Potentate, who dwellest in thick darkness, though thou thyself art light without darkness; incomprehensible, inscrutable; who seest all things, thyself unseen; who knowest all, though thou canst not be known;—Have mercy upon us.

Lord God, merciful and gracious, who daily loadest us with benefits, and art good even to the unthankful and the evil;—Have mercy upon us.

Thou didst breathe into us thy Spirit: thou didst create us in the image of God, making us only a little lower than the angels, and putting all things under our feet; but the crown is fallen from our head, for we have rebelled against thee;—Have mercy upon us.

Thou knowest our frame; thou rememberest that we are dust;—O Lord, have mercy upon us.

We have sinned, we have done very wickedly, departing from the living God; transgressing in thought, word, and deed thy most righteous laws, and resisting thy Holy Spirit: therefore we cry unto thee;

—Lord, have mercy upon us.

Before thee, the Judge of the world, and the Searcher of hearts, whose eyes behold the evil and the good, and to whom all things are naked and open, we do confess our sins, and acknowledge our great iniquity ;—O Lord, we entreat thee, have mercy upon us.

Our heavenly Father, who didst send forth thy Son, in the fulness of time, to bring near thy salvation, Grant unto us repentance and remission of sins, according to the riches of thy grace; and bless us by turning every one of us away from our iniquities :

—Have mercy upon us.

Through Christ, thy well-beloved Son, whom thou didst deliver up for us all, that he, by the grace of God, should taste death for every man ;—Have mercy upon us, and put away all our offences.

By his sufferings, death, and burial, let our old man be crucified, that, being redeemed from the power of the flesh and of the carnal mind, we may no longer live in death, or be slaves to sin in the lusts thereof :

—Lord, have mercy upon us, and for thy name's sake take away all our sin.

God, who quickenest all things, Lord and Giver of life, who didst bring again from the dead our Lord Jesus, that great Shepherd of the sheep, Quicken us thy people and sheep of thy pasture, with divine and heavenly life ; inspiring us with faith, hope, charity, patience, and all the fruits of the Spirit, that we may glorify thee upon the earth, may edify and strengthen our brethren, may work out our own salvation, may grow in grace, and be faithful unto death ; that in due time we may be presented faultless before the presence of thy glory with exceeding joy, and receive that crown of righteousness which thou hast promised to them that love thee :

—Lord, have mercy upon us, and grant us thy peace : have mercy upon us, and grant us thy salvation.

In all time of our adversity ; in our sickness, pain,

and fear; in perplexity and distress; when we suffer wrongfully, and in all time of our trial and temptation:
—Have mercy upon us.

In our health and wealth; in our ease, prosperity, and honour; and when all men speak well of us:
—Lord, have mercy upon us.

In the joys and sorrows, and in all the changes and chances of this mortal life; at the hour of our death, and in the great day of thy judgment:
—Have mercy upon us.

Out of the depths have I cried unto thee, O Lord. Lord, hear my voice:
—Let thine ears be attentive to the voice of my supplications.

If thou, Lord, shouldest mark iniquities, O Lord, who shall stand?
—But there is forgiveness with thee, that thou mayest be feared.

I wait for the Lord, my soul doth wait:
—And in his word do I hope.

Let Israel hope in the Lord:
—For with the Lord there is mercy,
And with him is plenteous redemption:
—And he will redeem Israel from all his iniquities.

Ps. cxxx.

III.

O God, who dwellest not in temples made with hands, for thou inhabitest eternity; heaven is thy throne and the earth thy footstool, and both earth and heaven are full of thy glory, We bless thee that thou dost reveal thyself to the pure in heart, and dwellest with humble and contrite spirits.

Cleanse our hearts, O thou invisible King, that we

may behold with unveiled face thy glory, and may ourselves be changed into the same image. Cast out all our pollutions and idols, that we may be temples of God, dwelling-places of the Most High; and, being filled with grace and truth, may we have communion with the Father and the Son, and so be made partakers of the divine nature, and comprehend the mystery of thy unfathomable love, that we may be filled with all the fulness of God.—Amen.

Our Father which art in heaven, Hallowed be thy name. Thy kingdom come. Thy will be done on earth, as it is in heaven. Give us day by day our daily bread. And forgive us our debts, as we forgive our debtors. And lead us not into temptation; but deliver us from evil.—Amen.

Praise ye the Lord :
—Praise the Lord, O my soul. *Ps.* cxlvi.

[*Then may be said or sung one or more of these Psalms following.*]

PSALM LVII.

Be merciful unto | me, O | God : || for my | soul... | trusteth in | thee :

Yea, in the shadow of thy wings will I | make my | refuge, || until these ca- | lamities be | over- | past.

I will cry unto | God most | high ; || unto God that per- | formeth | all things | for me.

He shall send from | heaven, and | save me || from the reproach of | him that would | swallow me | up.

God | shall send | forth || his | mercy | and his | truth.

Be thou exalted, O God, a- | bove the | heavens ; || let thy glory | be above | all the | earth.

My heart is fixed, O God, my | heart is | fixed : || I will | sing and | give... | praise.

FIFTH SUNDAY OF THE MONTH.

Awake up, my glory ; awake, | psaltery and | harp : ||
I my- | self will a- | wake... | early.

I will praise thee, O Lord, a- | mong the | people : ||
I will sing unto | thee a- | mong the | nations.

For thy mercy is great | unto the | heavens || and
thy | truth... | unto the | clouds.

Be thou exalted, O God, a- | bove the | heavens : ||
let thy glory | be above | all the | earth.

ISAIAH XII.

O Lord, | I will | praise thee : || though | thou wast |
angry | with me,

Thine anger is | turned a- | way, || and | thou didst |
comfort | me.

Behold, God is | my sal- | vation ; || I will | trust,
and | not be a- | fraid :

For the Lord Jehovah is my | strength and my |
song ; || he also is be- | come... | my sal- | vation.

Therefore with joy shall | ye draw | water || out of
the | wells... | of sal- | vation.

And in that day | shall ye | say, || Praise the Lord, |
call up- | on his | name.

Declare his doings a- | mong the | people, || make |
mention that his | name is ex- | alted.

Sing unto the Lord ; for he hath done | excellent |
things : || this is | known in | all the | earth.

Cry | out and | shout, || thou in- | habi- | tant of | Zion :

For great is the | Holy One of | Israel || in the
midst... | of... | thee.

[*Then may be read the Lesson from the Old Testament : after
which follows*]

The Second Prayer.

I.

We magnify and praise thy great name, O Lord our

heavenly Father, for all the goodness and mercy which thou hast bestowed upon us, and upon our brethren of the human family. Thou didst create us in thine own image; thou hast opened thy hand and supplied all our wants and made our cup to run over; thou hast also, in thy paternal love, chastened us, to make us partakers of thy holiness. But chiefly we give thee thanks, that when, through our disobedience, we had fallen from thee, thou didst ransom us by the sufferings and death of Jesus Christ thy Son; through whom also thou hast given us the blessed hope of everlasting life.

We acknowledge with gratitude thy ever-watchful providence, thy abounding mercy, thy overflowing goodness, thy unwearied patience: But we are miserable sinners.

O God, whom we do daily offend by our manifold iniquities, have mercy upon us, and blot out all our sins. Let it please thee not to cut us down as cumberers of the ground; but spare us, and so quicken us by thy grace, that we may live no longer unto ourselves, but unto him who died for us and rose again, and whom thou hast exalted at thy right hand, that he may be Lord both of the dead and of the living.

As thou hast called us into the marvellous light of thy kingdom, may we not walk in darkness: redeem us from ignorance, error, and unbelief, from unholy desires, evil passions, and unrighteous actions, and from all the power of sin, both in our souls and bodies, that we may know the glorious liberty of the children of God, serving thee in peace, in assured hope, and in perfect love, which casteth out fear.—Amen.

In thee, O Lord, do I put my trust:
—Let me never be put to confusion.
Deliver me in thy righteousness, and cause me to escape:

—Incline thine ear unto me, and save me.
For thou art my hope, O Lord God :
—Thou art my trust from my youth.
By thee have I been holden from the birth :
—My praise shall continually be of thee.
O God, be not far from me :
—O my God, make haste for my help.
My mouth shall shew forth thy righteousness :
—And thy salvation all the day.
My lips shall greatly rejoice when I sing unto thee :
—And my soul, which thou hast redeemed.
It is good for me to draw near unto God :
—I have put my trust in the Lord God, that I may declare all thy works. *Ps.* lxxi., lxxiii.

II.

O God, Redeemer of Israel, who wentest before thy Church in the wilderness in the fiery and cloudy pillar, guiding them to the rest which thou hadst promised, We thank thee that Christ our Passover is sacrificed for us, whereby we are redeemed from the house of bondage, and the dominion of him that had the power of death. By the washing of regeneration and renewing of the Holy Ghost, may we be cleansed from all the pollutions of our servile state; and daily may we eat of the hidden manna, even the word of thy truth, and be made strong for our journey through the wilderness by this bread which cometh down from heaven; till at length we enter thy promised rest, that eternal inheritance which thou hast prepared for all that love thee, whither the Forerunner is for us entered, Jesus Christ our Lord.—Amen.

Sing unto the Lord; bless his name :
—Shew forth his salvation from day to day.
Ps. xcvi.

AFTERNOON SERVICE.   111

[*Here a Psalm may be sung: after which the Lesson from the New Testament is read. Then follows*]

The Third Prayer.

I.

O thou great Master and Lord, who callest us to serve thee that we may be free, and art intrusting thy talents to us for a season, Grant us mercy to be faithful even in that which is least, not wasting or burying thy talent, but improving it to thy glory; that when the Lord shall reckon with us, we may be found good and faithful servants, and may, with all thine elect, enter into the joy of our Lord.—Amen.

II.

O Lord our heavenly Father, who hast taught us that there is one Body, even as there is one Spirit and one Lord, one Faith and one Baptism, one God and Father of us all, We lift up our hearts unto thee on behalf of all that are called by thy Name. Let thy blessing descend upon the whole Church; preserve her in truth and peace, in unity and safety, in all storms and against all temptations; that she, offering to thy glory the never-ceasing sacrifice of prayer and thanksgiving and all holy obedience, may advance the honour of her Lord, and be filled with his Spirit, and partake of his glory.

Endow the ministers of thy word, and the pastors of thy flock, with faith and wisdom, with charity and zeal, that thy saints may be built up in their holy faith, and may abound in good works, to thy glory and praise.—Amen.

III.

God of all grace and consolation, Look down, we humbly entreat thee, upon the sick, the sorrowful, and the dying; upon widows and orphans; upon the despairing and the tempted, and upon all who are in danger or perplexity, distress or tribulation. Hear their cry, O Lord; and for thy mercy's sake deliver and save them;—and us also, for we are men of like passions, and compassed about with infirmity and danger. May we not be high-minded, but fear, that we may stand in the evil day.—Amen.

IV.

O thou immortal King, with whom do live the spirits of them that depart hence in the Lord, and with whom the souls of the faithful, after they are delivered from the burden of the flesh, are in joy and felicity, We give thee thanks for all those who lived in this world in obedience to thy commands, and died in the hope of thy promises, and now sleep in Jesus, waiting for his second and glorious appearing.

Let not us sorrow as others who have no hope. Thou art not the God of the dead but of the living; and thy children, though dead unto us, still live unto thee. We entreat thee, O God, our Father and their Father, so to guide and sanctify us who are still in the body, that we also in due time may be gathered unto the general assembly and church of the first-born, whose names are written in heaven, to live in everlasting joy, and reign with Christ and his saints, in the glory of thy kingdom, world without end.—Amen.

V.

O God, who art the Author of all being and all blessedness, the Fountain of our life and intelligence, and all our good;—for all comes from thee; the creatures are but instruments of thy grace, and messengers of thy mercy;—We render unto thee all praise and glory. Thou art the first and the last, the beginning and the end, the life and perfection of all things; who comprehendest and fillest all, yet canst not thyself be comprehended; who art above all, through all, in all. Thou remainest unshaken, the eternal Rock, while the stream of creation rushes on in endless succession and ceaseless change, the invisible Spectator, the silent Witness of all good and evil: Before the mountains were brought forth, or ever thou hadst formed the earth and the world, from everlasting to everlasting thou art God.

Our days and weeks glide swiftly away, reminding us of the end of our days, and the night which is at hand, when we shall cease from all our earthly cares and labours, and lie down in the dust in silence and darkness.

May we, by thy grace, O Lord, so redeem the time of our visitation, that we shall close our eyes upon this world without sorrow or fear, and sleep in Jesus, our flesh resting in hope of thy promises; that when the day of God shall dawn, we may arise with joy, and put on immortality, being redeemed from all the power of corruption, and made like unto the Son of God; that we, with all thy saints, may live and reign with Him; who died for us and rose again, and liveth and reigneth with thee the Father, in the unity of the Eternal Spirit, world without end.—Amen.

I will praise thee; for thou hast heard me,
—And art become my salvation. *Ps.* cxviii.

[*Then a Psalm or Doxology may be sung.*]

The Benediction.

Now unto Him that is able to keep you from falling, and to present you faultless before the presence of his glory with exceeding joy, To the only wise God, our Saviour, be glory and majesty, dominion and power, both now and ever.—Amen.

Evening Prayer.

O thou that dwellest in unapproachable light, Keep us thy servants, and all that are dear to us, during the darkness and silence of the night, from all evil, whether of the body or the soul; for thou only knowest our dangers, and thou only canst defend and save us. And when the night and darkness of this dying life are passed away, grant that we may awake to behold the light of thine eternal glory in the kingdom of heaven; through Him that loved us, and hath redeemed us from darkness, sin, and death, Jesus Christ our Lord.—Amen.

A Psalm.

O Lord God Almighty, who art, and wast, and art to come; the blessed and only Potentate, dwelling in unapproachable light;

—To thee shall every knee bow, and every tongue confess. O thou that hearest prayer, unto thee shall all flesh come.

We worship thee; we praise thee; we magnify thy great name. Thou only art holy; thou only art the Lord. All the powers and dominions of heaven do continually worship and praise thee; crying one to another and saying, Holy, holy, holy, Lord God of hosts, the whole earth is full of his glory.

—All thy works shall praise thee, O Lord, and thy saints shall bless thee.

Before the mountains were brought forth, or ever thou hadst formed the earth and the world, from everlasting to everlasting thou art God.

—They shall perish, but thou dost endure; they shall wax old as a garment; but thou art the same, and thy years shall not fail.

Whither shall we go from thy Spirit? or flee from thy presence? The darkness hideth not from thee. Thou compassest our path, and art acquainted with all our ways.

—Thou searchest the hearts of the children of men; and all things are naked and open in thy sight.

Thou hast created the world, and all things that are therein, visible and invisible; and thou upholdest them all by the word of thy power: and this day they continue as thou didst ordain; and thine eternal power and Godhead are clearly seen in the things that are made.

—The heavens declare the glory of God, and the firmament sheweth his handiwork. Day unto day uttereth speech, and night unto night teacheth knowledge.

The heavens are thine; the earth also is thine: the world and the fulness thereof, thou hast founded them. Thou hast set all the borders of the earth; thou hast made summer and winter.

—The day is thine; the night also is thine; thou hast prepared the light and the sun.

Clouds and darkness are round about thee; justice and judgment are the habitation of thy throne.

—Just and true are thy ways, O thou King of saints.

Merciful and gracious, slow to anger, and of great kindness; abundant in goodness and truth.

—A father of the fatherless, and a judge of the widows, is God in his holy habitation.

Sing unto the Lord, O ye saints of his, and give thanks at the remembrance of his holiness.

—For his anger endureth but a moment; in his favour is life.

Bless the Lord, all his works, in all places of his dominions:

—Bless the Lord, O my soul.

A Hymn.

He was wounded for our transgressions;
He was bruised for our iniquities;
The chastisement of our peace was upon him;
And by his stripes we are healed.
All we like sheep have gone astray;
And the Lord hath laid upon him the iniquity of us all.

Christ is risen from the dead;
The first-fruits of them that are fallen asleep.
Thou hast ascended on high;
Thou hast led captivity captive;
Thou hast received gifts for men, even for the rebellious;
That the Lord God might dwell among them.

I will not leave you comfortless.
I will send the Comforter, the Holy Spirit,
Who shall teach you all things,
And shall abide with you for ever.
Because I live, ye shall live also.
Death shall be swallowed up in victory.

Reign, O Christ, in the glory of the Father,
Till all things are put under thy feet;
And Death, the last enemy, is destroyed.
Return again unto thy Church, thy spouse;
She is widowed and desolate upon the earth!
She is sorrowful and sigheth, long waiting for thy return.

Let not the enemy say, " Where is the promise of his
  coming ?
All things continue as they were from the beginning
  of the world."

  Arise, thou Morning Star ! O Prince of Life, shine
    upon the nations ;
That the darkness of sin and death may flee away
And the dayspring from on high may visit us.
Come forth from thy secret chambers, thou Prince of
  all the kings of the earth :
O Christ, thou first-born from the dead, appear in thy
  glory :
For now the voice of thy Bride calls thee ;
And the whole creation sigheth to be renewed.

Te Deum Laudamus.

WE praise thee, for | thou art | God : ‖ we acknow- ledge | thee to | be the | Lord.

All the earth doth | worship | thee : ‖ the | Father | ever- | lasting.

To thee all angels | cry a- | loud : ‖ the heavens and | all the | powers there- | in.

To thee | Cherubim and | Seraphim ‖ con- | tinu- al- | ly do | cry,

Holy, | holy, | holy : Lord | God of | Saba- | oth ;

Heaven and | earth are | full | of the | majesty | of thy | glory.

The | glorious | company ‖ of the a- | postles | praise... | thee.

The | noble | army | of | martyrs | praise... | thee.

The holy church through- | out all the | world | doth ac- | know-... | ledge... | thee ;

God over all | blessed for | ever : ‖ the Father of an | infinite | majes- | ty ;

Thine a- | dorable, | true, | and | only be- | gotten | Son ;

Also thy | Spirit of | truth ; " the Holy | Ghost, the | Comfort- | er.

He is the | King of | glory, even | Jesus | thy... | Christ :

The ever- | lasting | Son | of | the e- | ternal | Father.

He came in the | fulness of | time, to take away the | sin... | of the | world.

And when he had overcome the | sharpness of |

death ‖ he opened the kingdom of | heaven to | all be- | lievers.

He sitteth at the | right hand of | God ‖ in the | glory | of the | Father.

We believe that he will | come a- | gain ‖ to judge the | quick... | and the | dead.

Hasten, we | pray thee, O | Lord, ‖ his glorious ap- | pearing | and his | kingdom.

May we be found without | spot and | blameless ‖ be- | fore him | at that | day.

O Lord, | help thy | servants, ‖ whom | thou... | hast re- | deemed.

Make them to be numbered | with thy | saints ‖ in | glory | ever- | lasting.

O Lord, | save thy | people ‖ and | bless thine | heri- | tage.

Go- | ...vern | them ‖ and | lift them | up for | ever.

Day | ...by | day ‖ we | magni- | fy... | thee :

And we will | worship thy | name ‖ ever | world... | without | end.

O Lord, in | thee have we | trusted : ‖ let us | never | be con- | founded.

A General Intercession.

O GOD, Father of our Lord Jesus Christ, of whom the whole family in heaven and earth is named, and who hast taught us, by the mouth of thine Apostle, that there is one Body even as there is one Spirit, one Faith, one Baptism, one God and Father of all, Remember, we beseech thee, thy whole Church militant here upon earth.

We pray thee to send down thy heavenly grace upon all whom thou hast called to serve thee in the ministry of the Word; that by their labours, the whole body of the faithful may be edified and built up in their holy faith, and may be enriched with all heavenly gifts, waiting for the coming of our Lord Jesus Christ.

Merciful God, look down upon thy heritage; unite thy scattered and divided people; heal their divisions; put away all errors and heresies from the midst of them; cleanse thy sanctuary from all defilement of superstition and impiety, that thy servants everywhere may present unto thee an offering, pure and acceptable, through Jesus Christ.—Amen.

Regard with compassion those who are in bitterness because of their transgressions; give unto them true repentance; restore unto them the joy of thy salvation, and uphold them with thy free Spirit.—Amen.

Comfort and succour all who are in trouble, sorrow, need, sickness, or any other adversity:

Especially we commend unto thee those who are departing this life. May thy presence sustain them in that last hour when flesh and heart do fail. Defend them against the assaults of the enemy; and give them such patient hope and confidence that they may joyfully commit their spirits unto thee; and do thou receive them to thy rest.—Amen.

Stir up the hearts of Christian parents to bring up their children in the nurture and admonition of the Lord, that they may be prepared to fulfil their several callings in this life, and to adorn the doctrine of God their Saviour in all things.—Amen.

We pray for all estates of men in Christian lands; for Kings and for all in authority; for Judges and Magistrates: Especially for this land, and for thy servant, our Sovereign Queen Victoria; for the Prince and Princess of Wales, and all the Royal Family.—Amen.

Grant peace to all nations; and in war do thou favour the righteous cause. Save us from factions and tumults, from confusion and discontent: and vouchsafe unto all Christian men to dwell together as brethren in unity and peace.—Amen.

Vouchsafe unto us seasonable weather, that the fruits of the earth may be perfected and gathered in. Preserve us from famine and from pestilence.—Amen.

Send forth the news of thy salvation unto the ends of the earth; and turn the hearts of all Jews, heathens, and unbelievers, that they may become obedient to thy truth.—Amen.

Hasten, we entreat thee, O Lord, the second and glorious appearing of thy Son, our Saviour Jesus Christ; and grant unto us that, daily looking for that blessed hope, we may not sleep as do others, but may watch and be sober, exercising ourselves unto godliness, and working out our own salvation with fear and trembling; that we, with all thy saints, may be presented holy and unblamable, before the presence of thy glory with exceeding joy: through Him that loved us and washed us from our sins in his own blood.

Now to the only wise God, our Saviour, be glory and majesty, dominion and power, both now and ever.—Amen.

The Lord's Supper.

A PRAYER

[*Which may be used on the Sunday preceding the Communion, on the Fast-Day, etc.*]

O God, Father of our Lord Jesus Christ, whom thou hast, of thine infinite mercy, delivered up for us all, and who gave his flesh for the life of the world, We thank thee that thou art calling us to join in that holy Feast which he commanded us to keep in remembrance of him.

That we may not eat and drink judgment to ourselves, do thou teach us to discern the Lord's body, and so to examine and judge ourselves, that when we are judged of thee, we may not be condemned with the world. Give us, O God, a sincere repentance and a true reformation of life; a lively faith; an ardent love to thee, and a fervent charity toward our brethren; without which our gifts and services are odious in thy sight, and we are accounted as dead before thee. Cleanse thou us from the pollutions of the world; may we abhor that which is evil, and cleave unto that which is good; and endow us with the grace of perseverance, that we may endure to the end and be saved.

O God, who art the Saviour of all men, specially of them that believe, look down, we humbly pray thee, on all the household of the faith: animate all thy people with love to thee and to each other: deliver them from the power of the enemy; from the love of the world: from the spirit of bondage and fear: clothe them with the wedding-garment, that they may be clean; and preserve them in soul and body unto eternal life.

Endow the ministers of thy word with the spirit of power, of love, and of a sound mind. May their labours be abundantly blessed to the turning of many unto righteousness, and the disobedient to the wisdom of the just; and to make ready thy Church for the second coming of her Lord.—Amen.

O Lord, show thy mercy unto us :
—And grant us thy salvation.

What shall I render unto the Lord for all his benefits toward me ?
—I will take the cup of salvation, and call upon the name of the Lord.

I will pay my vows unto the Lord in the presence of all his people.
—I will offer to thee the sacrifice of thanksgiving, and will call upon the name of the Lord.

I will pay my vows unto the Lord in the presence of all his people,
—In the courts of the Lord's house, in the midst of thee, O Jerusalem. Praise ye the Lord. *Ps.* cxvi.

The Administration of the Sacrament

OF

THE LORD'S SUPPER.

[*The Preliminary Services being finished, the Minister may begin with reading the Words of Institution, and then he may recite one or more of the following sentences.*]

FOR I have received of the Lord that which also I delivered unto you, that the Lord Jesus, the same night in which he was betrayed, took bread: and, when he had given thanks, he brake it, and said, Take, eat; this is my body, which is broken for you: this do in remembrance of me. After the same manner also he took the cup, when he had supped, saying, This cup is the new covenant in my blood: This do ye, as oft as ye drink it, in remembrance of me. For as often as ye eat this bread, and drink this cup, ye do shew the Lord's death till he come. Wherefore, whosoever shall eat this bread, and drink this cup of the Lord, unworthily, shall be guilty of the body and blood of the Lord. But let a man examine himself, and so let him eat of that bread, and drink of that cup. For he that eateth and drinketh unworthily, eateth and drinketh judgment to himself, not discerning the Lord's body. 1 *Cor.* xi.

Ye are not come unto the mount that might be touched, and that burned with fire, nor unto blackness, and darkness, and tempest, and the sound of a trumpet, and the voice of words ; which voice they that heard entreated that the word should not be spoken to them any more : but ye are come unto mount Sion, and unto the city of the living God, the heavenly Jerusalem, and to an innumerable company of angels, to the general assembly and church of the first-born, which are written in heaven, and to God the Judge of all, and to the spirits of just men made perfect, and to Jesus the mediator of the new covenant, and to the blood of sprinkling, that speaketh better things than that of Abel. *Heb.* xii.

Christ, our passover, is sacrificed for us : therefore let us keep the feast, not with old leaven ; neither with the leaven of malice and wickedness, but with the unleavened bread of sincerity and truth. 1 *Cor.* v.

The cup of blessing which we bless, is it not the communion of the blood of Christ ? The bread which we break, is it not the communion of the body of Christ ? 1 *Cor.* x.

[*Then may be recited*]

THE CREED.

I believe in God the Father Almighty, maker of heaven and earth ; and in Jesus Christ, his only Son, our Lord ; who was conceived by the Holy Ghost ; born of the Virgin Mary ; suffered under Pontius Pilate ; was crucified, dead, and buried : he descended into hell ; the third day he rose again from the dead ; he ascended into heaven ; and sitteth on the right hand of God the Father Almighty ; from thence he shall come to judge the quick and the dead. I believe in the Holy Ghost ; the holy catholick church ; the communion of saints ; the forgiveness of sins ; the resurrection of the body ; and the life everlasting.—Amen.

THE LORD'S SUPPER.

[Then may be said or sung]

PSALM XXVI.

Judge me, O Lord; for I have walked in mine integrity:

—I have trusted also in the Lord; therefore I shall not slide.

Examine me, O Lord, and prove me; try my reins and my heart.

—For thy loving-kindness is before mine eyes; and I have walked in thy truth.

I have not sat with vain persons, neither will I go in with dissemblers.

—I have hated the congregation of evil-doers; and will not sit with the wicked.

I will wash mine hands in innocency; so will I compass thine altar, O Lord:

—That I may publish with the voice of thanksgiving, and tell of all thy wondrous works.

Lord, I have loved the habitation of thy house, and the place where thine honour dwelleth.

—Gather not my soul with sinners, nor my life with bloody men:

In whose hands is mischief, and their right hand is full of bribes.

—But as for me, I will walk in mine integrity: redeem me, and be merciful unto me.

My foot standeth in an even place:

—In the congregations will I bless the Lord.

Prayer before the Communion.

I.

Almighty God, who hast called us to have communion with thee, through the body and blood of thy dear Son, Jesus Christ, that receiving him in faith and love, we may dwell in him and he in us; Grant us thy Holy Spirit, that approaching to thy presence, and beholding thy divine glory, we may abhor ourselves, and repent in dust and ashes.

We have grievously offended thee in thought, word, and deed, resisting thy will, grieving thy Spirit, breaking our vows, and dishonouring thy name.

Yet now, most gracious Father, have mercy upon us. Pardon all our sins, and cleanse us from all our defilements, both of the flesh and of the spirit; that being forgiven of thee, we may also forgive others their trespasses against us, and may walk in love as Christ loved us, and gave himself for us, an offering and a sacrifice well-pleasing unto thee.—Amen.

II.

O God, who, by thy dear Son, hast consecrated for us a new and living way into the holiest of all, Grant unto us, we beseech thee, the assurance of thy mercy, and sanctify us by thy heavenly grace; that we, approaching unto thee with pure heart and undefiled conscience, may offer unto thee a sacrifice in righteousness, and may be accepted in thy sight, through our great High Priest, Jesus Christ.—Amen.

III.

We magnify and praise thy glorious name, O Lord God Almighty:

For thou didst form us in thine own image, giving us rational souls, and making us only a little lower than the angels:

For thou hast opened thy hand, and supplied all our wants, and hast loaded us with benefits, so that our cup runneth over:

For, as a man pitieth his own son, so hast thou pitied us; and as a father chasteneth the son whom he loveth, so hast thou chastened us, to make us partakers of thy holiness:

For all thy benefits known to us, for all unknown, we give thee thanks: but chiefly that when, through our disobedience, we had fallen from thee and forfeited thy favour, thou didst not suffer us to depart from thee for ever, but didst ransom us from death eternal, by the sufferings and death of Jesus Christ thy Son; and hast given to us the blessed hope of everlasting life by his resurrection, his triumphant exaltation at thy right hand, by the gift of the Holy Ghost, and the glorious promise of his second coming in majesty to judge the quick and the dead.

O God our Saviour, thou hast broken our chains that we might be free: thou hast healed our diseased souls that we might not perish of the second death: thou hast enriched us with the treasures of thy salvation: thou hast made us, who were miserable sinners, to be heirs of God, that we might possess all things: thou hast exalted us in hope to be princes in thy kingdom, and to sit with Christ upon his throne; and even now, all things are ours, the world, and life, and death; and our present affliction, which is but for a moment, worketh for us an exceeding, even an eternal weight of glory.

Therefore do we, with one voice and one heart, laud and magnify thy glorious name; and with thy saints on earth and in heaven, we ascribe blessing and honour, and glory and power, unto Him that sitteth upon the throne, and unto the Lamb, for ever and ever.—Amen.

IV.

Almighty God, we, thy servants, calling to mind the most blessed sacrifice of thy Son, rejoicing in that salvation which he hath accomplished for us, do in this manner, eating of this bread and drinking of this cup, according to his command, shew forth the Lord's death till he come again :

Wherefore, we entreat thee to grant thy heavenly benediction, that these creatures of bread and wine may be set apart and consecrated to this holy use and mystery; that we, by faith, may look upon Christ our Lord, set forth under these symbols, and may receive the bread of everlasting life, and the cup of eternal salvation, so that the hunger and thirst of our souls may be satisfied, that the power of sin and death may be destroyed, both in the flesh and in the spirit, and we may be preserved in soul and body unto eternal life.— Amen.

O send out thy light and thy truth : let them lead me ;
—Let them bring me to thy holy hill, even to thy tabernacles.
Then will I go to the altar of God,
—Unto God my exceeding joy.
I will offer to thee the sacrifice of thanksgiving ;
—And will call upon the name of the Lord.
I will pay my vows unto the Lord
—Now in the presence of all his people. *Ps.* xliii. cxvi.

[*The elements being now sanctified by the word and prayer, the Minister, being at the table, is to take the bread in his hand, and say*]

According to the holy institution, command, and example of our blessed Saviour Jesus Christ, I take this bread, and having given thanks, break it, and give it to you.

[*Here the Minister is to break the bread; and, having himself partaken, is to give it to the Communicants, saying*]

Take ye—eat ye : this is the body of Christ which is broken for you : this do in remembrance of him.

THE LORD'S SUPPER.

[*In like manner, the Minister is to take the cup, and say*]

According to the institution, command, and example of our Lord Jesus Christ, I take this cup and give it unto you.

[*Here, having himself partaken, he gives it to the Communicants, saying*]

This cup is the new covenant in the blood of Christ, which is shed for the remission of the sins of many: drink ye all of it.

[*During the action suitable Psalms may be read (as Ps. xcii., ciii., cxvi.), and after all have communicated, the following may be sung*]

> O thou my soul, bless God the Lord;
>   And all that in me is
> Be stirred up his holy name
>   To magnify and bless.
>
> Bless, O my soul, the Lord thy God;
>   And not forgetful be
> Of all his gracious benefits
>   He hath bestow'd on thee.
>
> All thine iniquities who doth
>   Most graciously forgive;
> Who thy diseases all and pains
>   Doth heal, and thee relieve.
>
> Who doth redeem thy life, that thou
>   To death may'st not go down;
> Who thee with loving-kindness doth
>   And tender mercies crown:
>
> The Lord our God is merciful,
>   And he is gracious;
> Long-suffering, and slow to wrath,
>   In mercy plenteous.

Such pity as a father hath
Unto his children dear;
Like pity shews the Lord to such
As worship him in fear.   *Ps.* ciii.

[*Then the Minister exhorts the Communicants to walk worthy of the grace of God in Christ, held forth in this Sacrament: after which may be said the following*]

Post-Communion Prayer.

I.

Almighty and everlasting God, we most heartily thank thee that thou hast now vouchsafed to feed us with the spiritual food of the most precious body and blood of thy Son, our Saviour Jesus Christ; assuring us thereby that we are very members incorporate in the mystical body of thy Son, and heirs, through hope, of thy everlasting kingdom.

And here we offer and present ourselves, our souls and bodies, to be a holy and living sacrifice unto thee, which is our reasonable service; beseeching thee that all we who have partaken of this sacrament may continue in the holy fellowship and communion of thy saints; in faith, charity, patience, and all the fruits of the Spirit; and may constantly to our life's end do all such good works as thou hast prepared for us to walk in; through Christ our Redeemer.—Amen.

The Lord hath chosen Zion;
—He hath desired it for his habitation:
This is my rest for ever;
—Here will I dwell, for I have desired it.
I will abundantly bless her provision:
—I will satisfy her poor with bread:
I will clothe her priests with salvation;
—And her saints shall shout aloud for joy.

II.

Almighty God, Father of our Lord Jesus Christ, who is the head of his body, even the whole family in heaven and earth; we desire now, at thy holy table, to remember before thee all our brethren, members of the same family, and heirs with us of thy incorruptible kingdom.

Look down, O Father, upon thy whole Church militant on earth:

Upon all pastors and teachers, that, being illuminated by thy Spirit, they may rightly divide the word of truth, and may be examples to the flock; that when the Chief Shepherd shall appear, they may receive a crown of glory that fadeth not away:

And upon all thy people, that they may receive, in faith and love, the word of righteousness, and may bring forth much fruit, that thou mayest be glorified:

Upon thy scattered and divided people, that the desolations of thine heritage may be repaired; and all heresies, schisms, and offences being put away, and thy sanctuary being cleansed of all defilement of superstition and impiety, thy children may serve thee in perfect love, in unity of spirit, and joy of the Holy Ghost.

Regard with thy compassion those who are in bitterness because of their transgressions: give unto them true contrition of heart; and strengthen and uphold them with thy free Spirit.

Comfort and succour, we beseech thee, all thy servants who are in trouble, need, sickness, or any other adversity.

And especially we commend unto thee those who are departing this life; beseeching thee to be present to them in that last hour when flesh and heart do fail; and give them such patient hope and confidence, that they may joyfully commit their spirits into thy hands.

To thee, O Lord, we commit them; and we pray thee to have mercy upon them, and to receive them to thy rest.

And, rejoicing in the blessed communion of thy saints, we remember before thee all thy servants who have departed this life, and who, having finished their course with joy, do rest from their labours, and sleep in Jesus, till the day of God shall dawn, and the shadows flee away:

The faithful patriarchs; thy prophets and saints of old; thy holy apostles and evangelists; the blessed martyrs and confessors, even that great cloud of witnesses by which we are compassed about; all those in every age, who served thee in life, and continued faithful unto death:

Our brethren and friends departed in the Lord, our parents, our children, and those who were as our own souls; believing that, though our eyes behold them no more, they have not perished, but are kept by thy mighty power unto eternal salvation; that their spirits are with thee, and their dust is precious in thy sight:

Thanking thee for all thy graces and mercies bestowed upon them, and beseeching thee that we may follow their good examples; that finally we may be made partakers with them, in soul and body, of thine everlasting glory, through Jesus Christ our Redeemer. —Amen.

III.

Hasten, we beseech thee, O Lord, the coming and kingdom of thy Christ; at whose glorious appearing thy saints departed shall be raised, and they that are alive shall be caught up to meet him, and so shall we ever be with the Lord. Under the veil of earthly things we have now communion with him; but with unveiled face we shall then behold him, rejoicing in his glory; and, by him, with the whole Church, holy and unspotted, shall be presented before the presence of thy glory with exceeding joy.

Glory be to God in the highest;
—Peace on earth; good-will to men.

Our Father which art in heaven, Hallowed be thy name. Thy kingdom come. Thy will be done on earth, as it is in heaven. Give us day by day our daily bread. And forgive us our debts, as we forgive our debtors. And lead us not into temptation; but deliver us from evil.—Amen.

[*Then may be sung*]

PAR. LX.

Father of peace, and God of love!
    We own thy power to save,
That power by which our Shepherd rose
    Victorious o'er the grave.

Him from the dead thou brought'st again.
    When, by his sacred blood,
Confirm'd and seal'd for evermore,
    Th' eternal cov'nant stood.

O may thy Spirit seal our souls,
    And mould them to thy will,
That our weak hearts no more may stray,
    But keep thy precepts still:

That to perfection's sacred height
    We nearer still may rise;
And all we think, and all we do,
    Be pleasing in thine eyes.

The Benediction.

Now the God of peace, that brought again from the dead our Lord Jesus, that great Shepherd of the sheep, through the blood of the everlasting covenant,

Make you perfect in every good work to do His will, working in you that which is well-pleasing in His sight, through Jesus Christ; to whom be glory for ever and ever.—Amen.

A Prayer

[*Which may be used in the Afternoon Service after the Communion, and also on the Sunday following*].

Almighty God, whose goodness bestows upon us not only the things needful for this present life, but all things pertaining to godliness and the life eternal, We unite in giving thee humble and hearty thanks for the gift of thy Son Jesus Christ, and for all those benefits of which thou dost make us partakers through him. And we earnestly beseech thee, O Lord, that thy grace may not be in vain to us; but that henceforth we may walk worthy of thee who hast called us into the fellowship of thy Son. Having received Christ Jesus the Lord, may we walk in him, rooted and grounded in the faith, and abounding in the fruits of the Spirit to the glory of thy name. Being children of the light, may we have no fellowship with the unfruitful works of darkness. Teach us to keep our garments unspotted from the world: deliver us from fleshly lusts which war against the soul, and from the snares and subtilty of the devil: and may our light shine before men, that they seeing our good works may glorify thee.

And for this end do thou, of thy great goodness,

endow us with a humble, sober, watchful, and prayerful spirit; that the enemy surprise us not; and that the Lord, when he cometh, may find us waiting for his appearing.

O God of Israel, the Saviour, who didst of old send unto thy servant, Elijah the prophet, that meat, in the strength of which he went forty days and forty nights, till he came to Horeb the Mount of God, Grant unto us, thy servants and family, that, through that spiritual food which thou givest to all thy faithful people, we may go from strength to strength, till every one of us appear in Zion before thee—to hear thy gracious voice, to see thee as thou art, and to be filled with thy fulness.

Have mercy upon thy whole Church, O Lord. Keep thy people by night and day; feed them with the word of thy truth; guide and govern them by thy holy Spirit; may they follow the good Shepherd whithersoever he goeth; and may they at length obtain eternal life, through Him who gave his life for the sheep.—Amen.

The Administration of Baptism.*

[*The Minister may recite the following Sentences.*]

Go and teach all nations, baptizing them in the name of the Father and of the Son and of the Holy Ghost: teaching them to observe all things whatsoever I have commanded you : and, lo, I am with you alway, even unto the end of the world. *Matt.* xxviii.

The promise is unto you and to your children. *Acts* ii.

Even so it is not the will of your Father which is in heaven that one of these little ones should perish.

Take heed that ye despise not one of these little ones ; for I say unto you, that in heaven their angels do always behold the face of my Father which is in heaven. *Matt.* xviii.

Know ye not that so many of us as were baptized into Jesus Christ, were baptized into his death ? Therefore we were buried with him by our baptism into his death ; that like as Christ was raised up from the dead by the glory of the Father, even so we also should walk in newness of life. *Rom.* vi.

[*The Father (or Sponsor) having presented the child, the Minister asketh of him this question*]

Do you here present this child to be baptized, desiring that [he] may be engrafted in the mystical body of Jesus Christ.

Ans.—Yea, we desire the same.

* Partly taken from the Book of Common Order.

THE ADMINISTRATION OF BAPTISM.

[*The Minister proceeds.*]

Let us therefore understand, dearly beloved, that Almighty God hath not only received us into the fellowship of his church, and made us his children by adoption, but hath also promised the same unto our children. Which promise as he confirmed to his people under the Old Testament by the sacrament of Circumcision, so hath he renewed the same to us by the sacrament of Baptism: hereby signifying to us that our children also are to be reckoned among the number of God's children; and therefore ought they not to be defrauded of those holy signs and badges by which his children are distinguished from pagans and infidels.

Hear ye the words of the holy Gospel—

"And they brought young children to him, that he should touch them: and his disciples rebuked those that brought them. But when Jesus saw it, he was much displeased, and said unto them, Suffer the little children to come unto me, and forbid them not: for of such is the kingdom of God. Verily I say unto you, Whosoever shall not receive the kingdom of God as a little child, he shall not enter therein. And he took them up in his arms, put his hands upon them, and blessed them."—*Mark* x. 13-16.

Not that we think this outward action of such necessity that the lack of it would be hurtful to their salvation, if they should be prevented by death; or that any such virtue or power is included in the water or the outward action, as that all who partake of it are therefore born again of the Spirit, (which apparently many who have been baptized are not;) but we, having respect to that obedience which Christians owe to the voice and ordinance of Jesus Christ, who commanded to baptize all without exception, do judge them only unworthy, who contemptuously refuse such means of grace as his wisdom hath appointed.

This Baptism with water doth signify and set forth unto us the virtue of Christ's blood and righteousness, for cleansing our souls from the guilt and deadly poison of sin; that being born again of the Spirit, we may walk in newness of life, of which grace Baptism is the sign and seal.

Moreover, ye that be fathers and mothers may take from hence most singular comfort in seeing your children thus received into the bosom of Christ's Church: and by this also ye are daily admonished that ye bring up in piety and virtue, these children of God's favour and mercy, over whom his fatherly providence watcheth continually.

Wherein if ye be negligent, ye shall not only do injury to your children, hiding from them the good pleasure of Almighty God their Father, but ye shall bring judgment upon yourselves, in suffering his children, bought with the blood of his dear Son, so traitorously for lack of knowledge to turn back from him.

Finally,—that we may be assured that you the Father [or Sponsor] consent to the performance of these things,—declare here, before the face of God's congregation, the sum of that Faith wherein you believe and will instruct this child.

[*Then the Father or Sponsor shall, after the Minister, rehearse the Apostles' Creed.*]

I believe in God the Father Almighty, maker of heaven and earth; and in Jesus Christ, his only Son, our Lord; who was conceived by the Holy Ghost; born of the Virgin Mary; suffered under Pontius Pilate; was crucified, dead, and buried: he descended into hell; the third day he rose again from the dead; he ascended into heaven; and sitteth on the right hand

THE ADMINISTRATION OF BAPTISM. 141

of God the Father Almighty; from thence he shall come to judge the quick and the dead. I believe in the Holy Ghost; the holy catholick church; the communion of saints; the forgiveness of sins; the resurrection of the body; and the life everlasting.—Amen.

[*Then follows this Prayer.*]

Almighty and everlasting God, who of thine infinite mercy and goodness hast promised unto us that thou wilt be not only our God, but also the God and Father of our children, We beseech thee, that as thou hast vouchsafed to call us to be partakers of this thy great mercy, in the fellowship of faith, so it may please thee to sanctify with thy Spirit, and to receive into the number of thy children, this infant whom we are about to baptize according to thy word; to the end that *he*, coming to mature age, may confess thee the only true God, and Jesus Christ whom thou hast sent; and may serve thee and be profitable unto thy Church, all the days of *his* life; that, after this life ended, *he* may be brought as a lively member of thy Son's body, unto the full fruition of thy joys in the heavens, where our Saviour Christ is exalted and reigneth with thee the Father, in the unity of the Spirit, world without end; in whose name we pray, as he has taught us, saying—

Our Father which art in heaven, Hallowed be thy name. Thy kingdom come. Thy will be done on earth, as it is in heaven. Give us this day our daily bread. And forgive us our debts, as we forgive our debtors. And lead us not into temptation; but deliver us from evil.—Amen.

[*When they have prayed in this sort, the Minister asketh the child's name: which known, he saith: " N., I baptize thee in the name of the Father and of the Son and of the Holy Ghost." And as he speaketh these words, he taketh water in his hand,*

and sprinkleth it upon the child's face: which done he giveth thanks, as follows]

I.

Most holy and merciful Father, who dost not only bestow upon us the common benefits of thy providence, but also dost enrich and beautify us with the blessings of grace and salvation, We, as it is meet and our bounden duty, do lift up our eyes and hearts unto thee; thanking thee for thy great mercy and grace, in that thou hast been pleased not only to number us among thy saints, but also dost call our children unto thee, marking them with this sacrament, in token of thy favour, and as a badge and seal of thy love.

Wherefore, notwithstanding our great unworthiness, we entreat thee, most holy and loving Father, through thy dear Son, to confirm thy grace toward us more and more; and take into thy favour and protection this infant, whom, with common supplications, we present unto thee. Defend, guide, and sanctify *him*, both in soul and body; that *he* may never so fall away from thy faith and love as to lose the force of baptism, but may acknowledge thee continually as *his* merciful Father, in faith and obedience, through thy Holy Spirit working in *his* heart; by whose divine power *he* may increase in wisdom and in all goodness from day to day, may prevail against the devil, the world, and the flesh; till in the end, having obtained a final victory, and being perfect in all thy will, *he* may be exalted to the liberty of thy sons and the glory of thy kingdom, at the appearing of our Lord and Saviour Jesus Christ.—Amen.

II.

Most gracious God, who settest the solitary in families, and hast promised unto thy handmaidens that they shall be saved in childbearing, if they continue in faith and holiness, We thank thee for thy great goodness to thy handmaid the mother of this child, and with her to thy servant the father, [and the other members of their family.] Grant them thy blessing : may they live together as heirs of the grace of life, in sobriety, charity, and peace : and prosper them in all good things.

And as they have now dedicated their child to thee in baptism, may they bring *him* up in the way that *he* should go, diligently instructing *him* in the doctrine which is according to godliness, and both by precept and example, guiding *his* steps in the ways of righteousness and peace.

Graciously receive these our prayers, we beseech thee, O Lord, through thy well-beloved Son, our Saviour Jesus Christ.—Amen.

The Benediction.

The grace of the Lord Jesus Christ, and the love of God, and the fellowship of the Holy Ghost, be with you all.—Amen.

The Marriage Service.*

[*The Minister may begin with reciting one or more of these Sentences.*]

Marriage is honourable among all men. *Heb.* xiii.

He that made them at the beginning, made them male and female, and said, For this cause a man shall leave his father and his mother, and shall cleave unto his wife; and they two shall be one flesh. *Matt.* xix.

Whoso findeth a wife, findeth a good thing, and obtaineth favour of the Lord. *Prov.* xviii.

Be not unequally yoked together with unbelievers. 2 *Cor.* vi.

Let us pray.

INTRODUCTORY PRAYER.

Almighty God, our heavenly Father, who hast created us, and dost from day to day load us with thy benefits; and who hast sent thy well-beloved Son into the world, that we might not perish but might have everlasting life, We thankfully acknowledge thy great goodness and mercy. We confess and lament our great unworthiness, and our manifold sins against thy divine majesty: and we beseech thee to forgive all our trespasses, and to accept us and bless us with thy favour and love; through Jesus Christ our Lord.—Amen.

O God, who didst in the beginning create man out of the earth, and who, because it was not good for the man that he should be alone, didst form the woman to

---
* Partly taken from the Book of Common Order.

THE MARRIAGE SERVICE. 145

be an help meet for him; and didst bring her unto the man that they two might be one flesh; and didst bless them and say, that for this cause a man should leave his father and his mother, and should cleave unto his wife; and who hast, by thine apostle, declared that marriage is honourable in all, We pray that thy blessing may rest upon these thy servants, who are now to be joined together according to thy holy institution and ordinance; that acknowledging thee, and seeking to please thee, in this and in all things, they may enjoy thy favour which is life, and thy loving-kindness which is better than life. And this we beg in the name of Jesus Christ our Lord.—Amen.

[*Then the Minister speaketh to the parties that are to be married, in this wise*]

I charge you both, as ye shall answer at the day of judgment, that if either of you do know any impediment why ye may not be lawfully joined together in matrimony, that ye confess it: for be ye well assured that so many as be coupled together otherwise than as God's Word doth allow, are not joined together by God; neither is their matrimony lawful.

[*If no impediment be by them declared, then the Minister saith to the whole congregation*]

If there be any of you who know that either of these parties be contracted to any other, or knoweth any other lawful impediment to their union, let them now make declaration thereof.

[*If no cause be alleged, the Minister proceedeth, saying—to the Man*]

Forasmuch as no man speaketh against this thing,— Do you, M., protest here before God and his holy congregation, that you have taken, and are now contented to have N., here present, for your lawful wife; promising to keep her, and love her, and to entreat her in all things, according to the duty of a faithful husband, forsaking all other; and to live in a holy conversation with her, keeping faith and truth in all points, according as the Word of God and his holy gospel doth command?

[*The Man shall answer*]

Even so I take her, before God and in the presence of this his congregation.—So help me God.

[*The Minister also saith to the Woman*]

Do you, N., protest here, before the face of God, and in the presence of this his congregation, that you have taken, and are contented to have M., here present, for your lawful husband; promising to him love, honour, and obedience in all things lawful and honest; and that, forsaking all other, you will live in a holy conversation with him, keeping faith and truth in all points, even as God's Word doth require?

[*The Woman shall answer*]

Even so I take him, before God and in the presence of this his congregation.—So help me God.

[*The Minister may here say to the Man*]

In pledge whereof, put you the marriage ring upon the ring finger of the woman's left hand, and join hands.

[*Which being done, the Minister addeth*]

I declare you married persons; and what God hath joined together, let no man put asunder.

THE MARRIAGE SERVICE. 147

[*Adding this*]

Benediction.

The Lord bless you and keep you. The Lord make his face to shine upon you, and be gracious to you. The Lord lift up the light of his countenance upon you, and give you peace. *Numb.* vi.

[*The Minister proceedeth*]

Dearly beloved, seeing ye are now knit together in this holy estate of marriage, that ye may understand how God, our heavenly Father, would have this holy contract kept and observed in which ye have now been joined together, hearken to the words of the Apostle St. Paul:—

Wives, submit yourselves unto your own husbands, as unto the Lord. For the husband is the head of the wife, even as Christ is the head of the Church: and he is the Saviour of the body. Therefore, as the Church is subject unto Christ, so let the wives be to their own husbands in everything.

Husbands, love your wives, even as Christ also loved the Church, and gave himself for her; that he might sanctify and cleanse her with the washing of water by the word, that he might present her to himself, a pure Church, not having spot or wrinkle, or any such thing; but that she should be holy and without blemish. So ought men to love their wives as their own bodies. He that loveth his wife loveth himself. For no man ever yet hated his own flesh; but nourisheth and cherisheth it, even as the Lord the Church: for ye are members of his body, of his flesh, and of his bones.

For this cause shall a man leave his father and mother, and shall be joined unto his wife, and they two shall be one flesh.

This is a great mystery: but I speak concerning Christ and the Church.

Nevertheless, let every one of you in particular so love his wife even as himself; and the wife see that she reverence her husband. *Eph.* v.

Hear also the words of the Apostle Peter :—

Likewise, ye wives, be in subjection to your own husbands; that, if any obey not the word, they also may without the word be won by the conversation of the wives; while they behold your chaste conversation coupled with fear. Whose adorning, let it not be that outward adorning of plaiting the hair, and of wearing of gold, or of putting on of apparel; but let it be the hidden man of the heart, in that which is not corruptible, even the ornament of a meek and quiet spirit, which is in the sight of God of great price.

Likewise, ye husbands, dwell with them according to knowledge, giving honour unto the wife, as unto the weaker vessel, and as being heirs together of the grace of life; that your prayers be not hindered. 1 *Pet.* iii.

If ye assuredly believe these words, and study to observe the same, then may ye be certain that God hath even so knit you together in this holy estate of wedlock. Wherefore apply yourselves to live together in godliness, in Christian peace, and good example, ever holding fast the bond of charity without any breach, keeping faith and truth to each other, even as God's Word doth appoint.

Ye are not your own: for ye are bought with a price; therefore glorify God in your body, and in your spirit, which are God's. 1 *Cor.* vi.

But this I say, brethren, the time is short: it remaineth that both they that have wives be as though they had none; and they that weep, as though they wept not; and they that rejoice, as though they rejoiced not; and they that buy as though they possessed not; and they that use this world, as not abusing it; for the fashion of this world passeth away.   1 *Cor.* vii.

[*Then may follow these Prayers.*]

O God, the author and giver of all good things, who hast consecrated this estate of marriage, and made it holy, by thine own institution and blessing, and by the mystery whereby it sets forth the union of all faithful souls with Jesus Christ, our great Husband and Head, Let thy blessing, we humbly entreat thee, descend and rest upon these thy servants, who have now been joined together. Grant unto them health, prosperity, and peace. May they dwell together in unity and love all the days of their life. And, above all things, O Lord, we pray thee to enrich their souls with thy heavenly grace, that they may obey and serve thee all their days, walking in the steps of Jesus Christ thy Son, and adorning his doctrine; that, finally, when the joys and sorrows, and all the good and evil of this transitory world are ended, they may inherit thy promises, and be made partakers of eternal joy in the kingdom of heaven; where they neither marry nor are given in marriage, but are as the angels of God.—Amen.

O thou Almighty King, who dost invite us all, in thy Gospel, to the great marriage supper of thy Son, So incline our hearts by thy good Spirit, that we may yield obedience to thy gracious call and come to the wedding; and may we, each one, be so clothed in the garments of righteousness and true holiness, that we may be accepted of thee, and may sit down with Abraham, and Isaac, and Jacob, and all thy saints, to enjoy for ever that banquet of unutterable felicity, which thou hast prepared for them that love thee.—Amen.

O Lord, whose only Son, Jesus Christ, did first display his divine power by turning water into wine at that marriage in Cana, which he beautified with his presence, Turn, O Lord, we pray thee, the water into wine, to us thy servants; that all our temporal mercies, being sanctified to us, may become spiritual blessings, and means of life and salvation; through Jesus Christ our Redeemer.—Amen.

Our Father which art in heaven, Hallowed be thy name. Thy kingdom come. Thy will be done on earth, as it is in heaven. Give us this day our daily bread. And forgive us our debts, as we forgive our debtors. And lead us not into temptation; but deliver us from evil.—Amen.

[*Then may be said or sung :—*]

Blessed is every one that feareth the Lord;
—That walketh in his ways.
For thou shalt eat the labour of thine hands:
—Happy shalt thou be, and it shall be well with thee.
Thy wife shall be as a fruitful vine by the sides of thy house;
—Thy children like olive plants round about thy table.
Behold, that thus shall the man be blessed
—That feareth the Lord.
The Lord shall bless thee out of Zion:
—And thou shalt see the good of Jerusalem all the days of thy life.
Yea, thou shalt see thy children's children,
—And peace upon Israel. *Ps.* cxxviii.

The Benediction.

The grace of the Lord Jesus Christ, and the love of God, and the communion of the Holy Ghost, be with you all.—Amen.

Service at the Burial of the Dead.

[*The Minister may recite the following Introductory Sentences.*]

Man that is born of a woman is of few days, and full of trouble. He cometh forth as a flower, and is cut down : he fleeth also as a shadow, and continueth not.

Man dieth and wasteth away : yea, man giveth up the ghost, and where is he ? *Job* xiv.

I am the resurrection and the life, saith the Lord : he that believeth in me, though he were dead, yet shall he live : and whosoever liveth and believeth in me shall never die. *John* xi.

[*Then may be said or sung this Psalm.*]

Lord, thou hast been our dwelling-place in all generations.

Before the mountains were brought forth, or ever thou hadst formed the earth and the world, even from everlasting to everlasting thou art God.

Thou turnest man to destruction; and sayest, Return, ye children of men.

For a thousand years in thy sight are but as yesterday when it is past, and as a watch in the night.

Thou carriest them away as with a flood ; they are as a sleep : in the morning they are like grass which groweth up.

In the morning it flourisheth and groweth up ; in the evening it is cut down and withereth.

The days of our years are threescore years and ten ;

and if by reason of strength they be fourscore years, yet is their strength labour and sorrow ; for it is soon cut off, and we fly away.

So teach us to number our days, that we may apply our hearts unto wisdom. *Ps.* xc.

[*Or this.*]

Lord, make me to know mine end, and the measure of my days, what it is ; that I may know how frail I am.

Behold, thou hast made my days as an handbreadth, and mine age is as nothing before thee : verily every man at his best state is altogether vanity.

Surely every man walketh in a vain show ; surely they are disquieted in vain : he heapeth up riches, and knoweth not who shall gather them.

And now, Lord, what wait I for ? my hope is in thee.

Deliver me from all my transgressions ; make me not the reproach of the foolish.

I was dumb, I opened not my mouth; because thou didst it.

When thou with rebukes dost correct man for iniquity, thou makest his beauty to consume away like a moth : surely every man is vanity.

Hear my prayer, O Lord, and give ear unto my cry ; hold not thy peace at my tears ; for I am a stranger with thee, and a sojourner, as all my fathers were.

Ps. xxxix.

[*After which may follow this Lesson.*]

Now is Christ risen from the dead, and become the first-fruits of them that slept. For since by man came death, by man came also the resurrection of the dead. For as in Adam all die, even so in Christ shall all be made alive. But every man in his own order : Christ the first-fruits ; afterwards they that are Christ's at his coming. Then cometh the end, when he shall have delivered up the kingdom to God, even the Father ;

when he shall have put down all rule, and all authority and power. For he must reign till he hath put all enemies under his feet. The last enemy that shall be destroyed is death. For he hath put all things under his feet.

But some man will say, How are the dead raised up? and with what body do they come?—It is sown in corruption; it is raised in incorruption: it is sown in dishonour; it is raised in glory: it is sown in weakness; it is raised in power: it is sown a natural body; it is raised a spiritual body. There is a natural body, and there is a spiritual body. And so it is written, The first man Adam was made a living soul; the last Adam was made a quickening spirit. Howbeit that was not first which is spiritual, but that which is natural; and afterward that which is spiritual. The first man is of the earth, earthy; the second man is the Lord from heaven.

As is the earthy, such are they also that are earthy; and as is the heavenly, such are they also that are heavenly. And as we have borne the image of the earthy, we shall also bear the image of the heavenly. Now this I say, brethren, that flesh and blood cannot inherit the kingdom of God; neither doth corruption inherit incorruption. Behold, I shew you a mystery; We shall not all sleep, but we shall all be changed, in a moment, in the twinkling of an eye, at the last trump, (for the trumpet shall sound, and the dead shall be raised incorruptible, and we shall be changed.) For this corruptible must put on incorruption, and this mortal must put on immortality. So when this corruptible shall have put on incorruption, and this mortal shall have put on immortality, then shall be brought to pass the saying that is written, Death is swallowed up in victory. O death, where is thy sting? O grave, where is thy victory? The sting of death is sin; and the strength of sin is the law. But thanks be to God, which giveth us the victory, through our Lord Jesus Christ. Therefore, my beloved brethren, be ye steadfast, unmoveable, always abounding in the work of the Lord, forasmuch as ye know that your labour is not in vain in the Lord. 1 *Cor.* xv.

[*Or this.*]

But I would not have you to be ignorant, brethren, concerning them which are asleep, that ye sorrow not, even as others which have no hope. For if we believe that Jesus died and rose again, even so them also which sleep in Jesus will God bring with him. For this we say unto you, by the word of the Lord, that we which are alive and remain unto the coming of the Lord, shall not prevent them which are asleep. For the Lord himself shall descend from heaven with a shout, with the voice of the archangel, and with the trump of God : and the dead in Christ shall rise first. Then we which are alive and remain shall be caught up together with them in the clouds, to meet the Lord in the air : and so shall we ever be with the Lord. Wherefore comfort one another with these words. 1 *Thess.* iv.

[*Then may follow these Prayers.*]

Let us pray.

I.

We humble ourselves, O Lord God, before the face of thy Divine Majesty, acknowledging that we are guilty in thy sight ; for we have sinned and done wickedly, both we and our fathers : and the wages of sin is death.

But we thank and praise thee, that of thy unspeakable compassion and grace, thou hast sent thy wellbeloved Son into the world, to redeem and deliver us, that we, who by our sins lay in death, might be made

SERVICE AT THE BURIAL OF THE DEAD.

heirs, according to the hope of everlasting life; that as sin hath reigned unto death, so might grace reign through righteousness unto eternal life, by Jesus Christ our Lord.—Amen.

II.

Almighty and everlasting God, who sendest forth thy Spirit and we are created, and who takest away our breath, and we die and return to our dust, We bow in reverence before thy inscrutable judgments; remembering that thou, who orderest all things according to thine own will in heaven and earth, art also our merciful and loving Father, who dost not willingly afflict or grieve the children of men, but dost correct us, that we may be partakers of thy holiness. We would therefore be subject unto thee, saying, The Lord gave, and the Lord hath taken away; blessed be the name of the Lord.—Amen.

III.

And now we follow to the house appointed for all living, the dust of our dear *brother*, whom thou hast been pleased to call out of this sinful and dying world:

We commit *his* body to the grave; dust to dust, ashes to ashes, earth to earth, till that great day of thy judgment, when earth and sea shall give up their dead:

Not sorrowing as others who have no hope; but believing, that as Jesus died and rose again, so them that sleep in Jesus thou wilt bring with him; that being cleansed from sin, and redeemed from the bondage of death, they may reign in immortal life, with Christ our Lord, who shall change our vile body, that it may be fashioned like unto his glorious body, according to that working whereby he is able to subdue all things unto himself.—Amen.

I heard a voice from heaven, saying unto me, Write,

Blessed are the dead that die in the Lord from henceforth : yea, saith the Spirit, that they may rest from their labours, and their works do follow them. *Rev.* xiv.

IV.

Lord, increase our faith.

Merciful God, Father of our Lord Jesus Christ, we give thee humble and hearty thanks for all thy servants who are fallen asleep in the Lord, and have received the end of their faith, even the salvation of their souls.

For all thy goodness and mercy vouchsafed to them in their earthly pilgrimage, we give thee praise and glory.

It is of thy grace that they fought the good fight and kept the faith, and have obtained the unfading crown, being conquerors, yea, more than conquerors, through him that loved us.

We magnify thy name, O God, our Father and their Father, that their trials and temptations being ended, sickness and death being past, with all the dangers and miseries of this present life, they have entered into the joy of their Lord, and are in perfect peace and felicity in thy presence for ever : their spirits being with thee, and their bodies resting in the grave until the resurrection of the just.

May we, animated by their good examples, run the race that is set before us ; not being weary in welldoing, or fainting when we are rebuked of thee; that when this transitory world is passed away, we may again be joined with our dear friends, departed in the Lord, in a perfect union and communion for ever, in thy kingdom of glory, where there shall be no more sickness or sighing, pain, sorrow, or death, for the former things shall have passed away.—Amen.

V.

Grant us true repentance, and remission of all our sins: cleanse us from all our iniquities: deliver us from the dominion of sin, that we may be delivered from the fear and the power of death. And not knowing at what hour the Lord shall come, may we be sober and watch unto prayer, daily meditating on mortality and immortality, and giving all diligence to make our calling and election sure; that when Christ, who is our life, shall appear the second time in glory, we may appear with him, and receive that sentence, Come, ye blessed of my Father, inherit the kingdom prepared for you from the foundation of the world.

These things we ask, not in our own name, or trusting in our own worthiness, but for thy mercy's sake, through our Lord and Saviour Jesus Christ, who died for our sins, and rose again for our justification, and who taught us thus to pray,—

Our Father which art in heaven, Hallowed be thy name. Thy kingdom come. Thy will be done on earth, as it is in heaven. Give us this day our daily bread. And forgive us our debts, as we forgive our debtors. And lead us not into temptation; but deliver us from evil.—Amen.

Benediction.

The grace of the Lord Jesus Christ, and the love of God, and the communion of the Holy Ghost, be with you all.—Amen.

[*Or, instead of the foregoing, the following shorter form* may be used.*]

I.

O merciful God, Father of our Lord Jesus Christ,

---

* Slightly altered from the Dutch Reformed Liturgy.

who hath said, Blessed are they that mourn, for they shall be comforted: Under the shadow of thy judgments we come to thee, and acknowledge thee to be Lord alone. Thou hast entered this house with thy chastenings : O be thou nigh in thy tender compassion to these afflicted ones. Bless thy sorrowing servants with thy consolations, which are neither few nor small. Convert them wholly to thyself, and fill their bleeding hearts with thy love. Make the night of their grief to be light by thy grace. Deliver us thy servants, we pray thee, from the bondage of our sins, that we may be free from fear of death, and be ready at thy coming. Yea, Lord, do thou sanctify us by thy Holy Spirit, that whether we live, we may live unto the Lord, or whether we die, we may die unto the Lord; so that whether we live or die, we may be the Lord's.—Amen.

II.

Almighty and everlasting God, we thine unworthy servants beseech thee, through Christ thy Son, to have mercy upon us. From the borders of the grave we cry unto thee, Have mercy upon us. It hath pleased thee to call out of this world the soul of our departed *brother*, whose body we now follow to *his* burial. We humbly entreat thee that we may with true penitence of heart receive the warning of thy providence, and consider that by reason of our guilt it is appointed unto us to die, and that in a moment when we think not we may appear before thee. Yea, Lord, by reason of our sins we lie in the midst of death. Spare us, O Lord; O most pitiful and long-suffering Lord God, spare us a little longer, that we may turn unto thee with true repentance and with lively faith in thy Son Jesus Christ, that when he shall appear we may have confidence, and not be ashamed at his coming. O merciful God,

Father of our Lord Jesus Christ, suffer none of us to live without God in the world, and to die without hope; but constrain us mightily by thy love: that we, being renewed by thy grace, and accepted through Christ's intercession, may walk before thee in newness of life, and praise thee for ever among the assembly of thy saints, where there shall be no more death; and sorrow and sighing shall flee away: which things we implore in the name of Him who has taught us to say, —Our Father, etc.—Amen.

The Benediction.

The grace of the Lord Jesus Christ, and the love of God, and the communion of the Holy Ghost, be with you all.—Amen.

Psalms.

(1)   Psalm III.   *Saxony.*

1 O Lord, how are my foes increas'd?
   Against me many rise.
2 Many say of my soul, For him
   In God no succour lies.
3 Yet thou my shield and glory art,
   Th' uplifter of mine head.
4 I cry'd, and, from his holy hill,
   The Lord me answer made.
5 I laid me down and slept, I wak'd,
   For God sustained me.
6 I will not fear though thousands ten
   Set round against me be.

8 Salvation doth appertain
   Unto the Lord alone:
Thy blessing, Lord, for evermore
   Thy people is upon.

(2)   Psalm IV.   *St. Paul's.*

1 Give ear unto me when I call,
   God of my righteousness:
Have mercy, hear my pray'r; thou hast
   Enlarged me in distress.

6 O who will shew us any good?
   Is that which many say;
But of thy countenance the light,
   Lord, lift on us alway.

7 Upon my heart, bestow'd by thee,
  More gladness I have found
Than they, ev'n then, when corn and wine
  Did most with them abound.

8 I will both lay me down in peace,
  And quiet sleep will take;
Because thou only me to dwell
  In safety, Lord, dost make.

(3)   PSALM V.   *St. Nicholas.*

1 GIVE ear unto my words, O Lord,
  My meditation weigh.
2 Hear my loud cry, my King, my God;
  For I to thee will pray.

3 Lord, thou shalt early hear my voice:
  I early will direct
My pray'r to thee; and, looking up,
  An answer will expect.

4 For thou art not a God that doth
  In wickedness delight;
 Neither shall evil dwell with thee,
5 Nor fools stand in thy sight.

7 But I into thy house will come
  In thine abundant grace;
And I will worship in thy fear
  Toward thy holy place.

(4)   PSALM V.   *St. David's.*

8 BECAUSE of those mine enemies,
  Lord, in thy righteousness
Do thou me lead; do thou thy way
  Make straight before my face.

11 But let all joy that trust in thee,
    And still make shouting noise ;
For them thou sav'st : let all that love
    Thy name in thee rejoice.

12 For, Lord, unto the righteous man
    Thou wilt thy blessing yield :
With favour thou wilt compass him
    About, as with a shield.

(5)   PSALM VI.   *Soldau.*

1 LORD, in thy wrath rebuke me not ;
  Nor in thy hot rage chasten me.
2 Lord, pity me, for I am weak :
  Heal me, for my bones vexed be.

3 My soul is also vexed sore ;
  But, Lord, how long stay wilt thou make ?
4 Return, O Lord, my soul set free ;
  O save me, for thy mercies' sake.

5 Because those that deceased are
  Of thee shall no remembrance have ;
  And who is he that will to thee
  Give praises lying in the grave ?

9 God hath my supplication heard,
  My pray'r received graciously.
10 Shamed and sore vex'd be all my foes,
   Shamed and back turned suddenly.

(6)   PSALM VIII.   *Tallis's Chant.*

1 How excellent in all the earth,
    Lord, our Lord, is thy name !
Who hast thy glory far advanced
    Above the starry frame.

3 When I look up unto the heav'ns,
    Which thine own fingers framed,
  Unto the moon, and to the stars,
    Which were by thee ordain'd ;

4 Then say I, What is man, that he
    Remember'd is by thee ?
  Or what the son of man, that thou
    So kind to him shouldst be ?

5 For thou a little lower hast
    Him than the angels made ;
  With glory and with dignity
    Thou crowned hast his head.

6 Of thy hands' works thou mad'st him lord,
    All under 's feet didst lay ;
7 All sheep and oxen, yea, and beasts
    That in the field do stray ;

8 Fowls of the air, fish of the sea,
    All that pass through the same.
9 How excellent in all the earth,
    Lord, our Lord, is thy name !

(7)   Psalm IX.   *Manchester.*

1 Lord, thee I'll praise with all my heart,
    Thy wonders all proclaim.
2 In thee, most High, I'll greatly joy,
    And sing unto thy name.

7 God shall endure for aye ; he doth
    For judgment set his throne ;
8 In righteousness to judge the world,
    Justice to give each one.

9 God also will a refuge be
    For those that are oppress'd ;

    A refuge will he be in times
      Of trouble to distress'd.

10 And they that know thy name, in thee
      Their confidence will place :
    For thou hast not forsaken them
      That truly seek thy face.

(8)   Psalm IX.   *Jackson's.*

11 O SING ye praises to the Lord
      That dwells in Sion hill ;
    And all the nations among
      His deeds record ye still.

16 The Lord is by the judgment known
      Which he himself hath wrought :
    The sinners' hands do make the snares
      Wherewith themselves are caught.

17 They who are wicked into hell
      Each one shall turned be ;
    And all the nations that forget
      To seek the Lord most high.

18 For they that needy are shall not
      Forgotten be alway ; '
    The expectation of the poor
      Shall not be lost for aye.

(9)   Psalm X.   *Glasgow.*

12 O LORD, do thou arise ; O God,
      Lift up thine hand on high :
    Put not the meek afflicted ones
      Out of thy memory.

16 The Lord is king through ages all,
      Ev'n to eternity ;

The heathen people from his land
Are perish'd utterly.

17 O Lord, of those that humble are
Thou the desire didst hear;
Thou wilt prepare their heart, and thou
To hear wilt bend thine ear.

18 To judge the fatherless, and those
That are oppressed sore;
That man, that is but sprung of earth,
May them oppress no more.

(10)   PSALM XI.   *St. Magnus.*

1 I IN the Lord do put my trust;
How is it then that ye
Say to my soul, Flee, as a bird,
Unto your mountain high?

2 For, lo, the wicked bend their bow,
Their shafts on string they fit,
That those who upright are in heart
They privily may hit.

3 If the foundations be destroy'd,
What hath the righteous done?

4 God in his holy temple is,
In heaven in his throne:

His eyes do see, his eyelids try
5   Men's sons. The just he proves:
But his soul hates the wicked man,
And him that vi'lence loves.

6 Snares, fire and brimstone, furious storms,
On sinners he shall rain:
This, as the portion of their cup,
Doth unto them pertain.

7 Because the Lord most righteous doth
  In righteousness delight;
  And with a pleasant countenance
  Beholdeth the upright.

(11)   Psalm XII.   *Newington.*

1 Help, Lord, because the godly man
  Doth daily fade away;
  And from among the sons of men
  The faithful do decay.

3 God shall cut off all flatt'ring lips,
  Tongues that speak proudly thus,
4 We'll with our tongue prevail, our lips
  Are ours: who's lord o'er us?

5 For poor oppress'd, and for the sighs
  Of needy, rise will I,
  Saith God, and him in safety set
  From such as him defy.

6 The words of God are words most pure;
  They be like silver try'd
  In earthen furnace, seven times
  That hath been purify'd.

(12)   Psalm XIII.   *French.*

1 How long wilt thou forget me, Lord?
  Shall it for ever be?
  O how long shall it be that thou
  Wilt hide thy face from me?

3 O Lord my God, consider well,
  And answer to me make:
  Mine eyes enlighten, lest the sleep
  Of death me overtake.

5 But I have all my confidence
 Thy mercy set upon ;
 My heart within me shall rejoice
 In thy salvation.

6 I will unto the Lord my God
 Sing praises cheerfully,
 Because he hath his bounty shewn
 To me abundantly.

(13)   Psalm XV.   *London New.*

1 WITHIN thy tabernacle, Lord,
 Who shall abide with thee ?
 And in thy high and holy hill
 Who shall a dweller be ?

2 The man that walketh uprightly,
 And worketh righteousness,
 And as he thinketh in his heart,
 So doth he truth express.

3 Who doth not slander with his tongue,
 Nor to his friend doth hurt ;
 Nor yet against his neighbour doth
 Take up an ill report.

4 In whose eyes vile men are despised ;
 But those that God do fear
 He honoureth ; and changeth not,
 Though to his hurt he swear.

5 His coin puts not to usury,
 Nor take reward will he
 Against the guiltless. Who doth thus
 Shall never moved be.

(14)   Psalm XVI.   *St. Paul's.*

5 God is of mine inheritance
    And cup the portion;
The lot that fallen is to me
    Thou dost maintain alone.

6 Unto me happily the lines
    In pleasant places fell;
Yea, the inheritance I got
    In beauty doth excel.

7 I bless the Lord, because he doth
    By counsel me conduct;
And in the seasons of the night
    My reins do me instruct.

(15)   Psalm XVI.   *Bedford.*

8 Before me still the Lord I set:
    Sith it is so that he
Doth ever stand at my right hand,
    I shall not moved be.

9 Because of this my heart is glad,
    And joy shall be exprest
Ev'n by my glory; and my flesh
    In confidence shall rest.

10 Because my soul in grave to dwell
    Shall not be left by thee;
Nor wilt thou give thine Holy One
    Corruption to see.

11 Thou wilt me shew the path of life:
    Of joys there is full store
Before thy face; at thy right hand
    Are pleasures evermore.

(16)   PSALM XVII.   *St. Stephen's.*

5 HOLD up my goings, Lord, me guide
In those thy paths divine,
So that my footsteps may not slide
Out of those ways of thine.

6 I called have on thee, O God,
Because thou wilt me hear:
That thou may'st hearken to my speech,
To me incline thine ear.

7 Thy wondrous loving-kindness shew,
Thou that, by thy right hand,
Sav'st them that trust in thee from those
That up against them stand.

15 But as for me, I thine own face
In righteousness will see;
And with thy likeness, when I wake,
I satisfy'd shall be.

(17)   PSALM XVIII.   *St. Matthew's.*

1 THEE will I love, O Lord, my strength.
2   My fortress is the Lord,
My rock, and he that doth to me
Deliverance afford.

3 Upon the Lord, who worthy is
Of praises, will I cry;
And then shall I preserved be
Safe from mine enemy.

4 Floods of ill men affrighted me,
Death's pangs about me went;
5 Hell's sorrows me environed;
Death's snares did me prevent.

6 In my distress I call'd on God,
    Cry to my God did I;
  He from his temple heard my voice,
    To his ears came my cry.

(18)   PSALM XIX.   *St. Gregory.*

1 THE heav'ns God's glory do declare,
    The skies his hand-works preach :
2 Day utters speech to day, and night
    To night doth knowledge teach.

3 There is no speech nor tongue to which
    Their voice doth not extend :
4 Their line is gone through all the earth,
    Their words to the world's end.

7 God's law is perfect, and converts
    The soul in sin that lies :
  God's testimony is most sure,
    And makes the simple wise.

10 They more than gold, yea, much fine gold,
    To be desired are :
  Than honey, honey from the comb
    That droppeth, sweeter far.

(19)   PSALM XIX.   *St. Andrew's.*

8 THE statutes of the Lord are right,
    And do rejoice the heart :
  The Lord's command is pure, and doth
    Light to the eyes impart.

12 Who can his errors understand?
    O cleanse thou me within
13 From secret faults. Thy servant keep
    From all presumptuous sin :

And do not suffer them to have
Dominion over me :
Then, righteous and innocent,
I from much sin shall be.

14 The words which from my mouth proceed,
The thoughts sent from my heart,
Accept, O Lord, for thou my strength
And my Redeemer art.

(20)   PSALM XX.   *Bedford.*

1 JEHOVAH hear thee in the day
When trouble he doth send;
And let the name of Jacob's God
Thee from all ill defend.

2 O let him help send from above,
Out of his sanctuary :
From Sion, his own holy hill,
Let him give strength to thee.

3 Let him remember all thy gifts,
Accept thy sacrifice :

4 Grant thee thine heart's wish, and fulfil
Thy thoughts and counsel wise.

5 In thy salvation we will joy;
In our God's name we will
Display our banners : and the Lord
Thy prayers all fulfil.

7 In chariots some put confidence,
Some horses trust upon :
But we remember will the name
Of our Lord God alone.

(21)   PSALM XXII.   *St. Mary's.*

1 MY God, my God, why hast thou me
Forsaken? why so far

Art thou from helping me, and from
   My words that roaring are ?

2 All day, my God, to thee I cry,
    Yet am not heard by thee ;
   And in the season of the night
    I cannot silent be.

3 But thou art holy, thou that dost
    Inhabit Israel's praise.
4 Our fathers hoped in thee, they hoped,
    And thou didst them release.

5 When unto thee they sent their cry,
    To them deliv'rance came :
  Because they put their trust in thee,
    They were not put to shame.

(22)   Psalm XXII.   *Eastgate.*

23 Praise ye the Lord, who do him fear ;
    Him glorify all ye
   The seed of Jacob ; fear him all
    That Israel's children be.

24 For he despised not nor abhorr'd
    Th' afflicted's misery ;
   Nor from him hid his face, but heard
    When he to him did cry.

25 Within the congregation great
    My praise shall be of thee ;
   My vows before them that him fear
    Shall be perform'd by me.

26 The meek shall eat, and shall be fill'd ;
    They also praise shall give
   Unto the Lord that do him seek :
    Your heart shall ever live.

(23)   PSALM XXII.   *Sheffield.*

27 ALL ends of th' earth remember shall,
    And turn the Lord unto ;
    All kindreds of the nations
    To him shall homage do :

28 Because the kingdom to the Lord
    Doth appertain as his ;
    Likewise among the nations
    The Governor he is.

30 A seed shall service do to him ;
    Unto the Lord it shall
    Be for a generation
    Reckon'd in ages all.

31 They shall come, and they shall declare
    His truth and rightcousness
    Unto a people yet unborn,
    And that he hath done this.

(24)   PSALM XXIII.   *St. Ann's New.*

1 THE Lord 's my shepherd, I 'll not want.
2   He makes me down to lie
    In pastures green : he leadeth me
    The quiet waters by.

3 My soul he doth restore again ;
    And me to walk doth make
    Within the paths of righteousness,
    Ev'n for his own name's sake.

4 Yea, though I walk in death's dark vale,
    Yet will I fear none ill :
    For thou art with me ; and thy rod
    And staff me comfort still.

5 My table thou hast furnished
  In presence of my foes;
My head thou dost with oil anoint,
  And my cup overflows.

6 Goodness and mercy all my life
  Shall surely follow me:
And in God's house for evermore
  My dwelling-place shall be.

(25)   Psalm XXIV.   *St. Gregory.*

1 The earth belongs unto the Lord,
  And all that it contains;
The world that is inhabited,
  And all that there remains.

2 For the foundations thereof
  He on the seas did lay,
And he hath it established
  Upon the floods to stay.

3 Who is the man that shall ascend
  Into the hill of God?
Or who within his holy place
  Shall have a firm abode?

4 Whose hands are clean, whose heart is pure,
  And unto vanity
Who hath not lifted up his soul,
  Nor sworn deceitfully.

5 He from th' Eternal shall receive
  The blessing him upon,
And righteousness ev'n from the God
  Of his salvation.

(26)   Psalm XXIV.   *St. George's Edinburgh.*

7 Ye gates, lift up your heads on high;
  Ye doors that last for aye,

Be lifted up, that so the King
　Of glory enter may.

8　But who of glory is the King?
　　The mighty Lord is this;
　Ev'n that same Lord, that great in might
　　And strong in battle is.

9　Ye gates, lift up your heads; ye doors,
　　Doors that do last for aye,
　Be lifted up, that so the King
　　Of glory enter may.

10　But who is he that is the King
　　Of glory? who is this?
　The Lord of hosts, and none but he,
　　The King of glory is.

(27)　　　　　Psalm XXV.　　　Chant No. 5.

1　To thee I lift my soul:
2　　O Lord, I trust in thee:
　My God, let me not be ashamed,
　　Nor foes triumph o'er me.

4　Shew me thy ways, O Lord;
　　Thy paths, O teach thou me:
5　And do thou lead me in thy truth,
　　Therein my teacher be:

　For thou art God that dost
　　To me salvation send,
　And I upon thee all the day
　　Expecting do attend.

7　My sins and faults of youth
　　Do thou, O Lord, forget:
　After thy mercy think on me,
　　And for thy goodness great.

8 God good and upright is:
   The way he'll sinners show.
9 The meek in judgment he will guide,
   And make his path to know.
10 The whole paths of the Lord
   Are truth and mercy sure,
   To those that do his cov'nant keep,
   And testimonies pure.

(28)   PSALM XXV.   *Aynhoe.*

11 Now, for thine own name's sake,
   O Lord, I thee entreat
   To pardon mine iniquity;
   For it is very great.
12 What man is he that fears
   The Lord, and doth him serve?
   Him shall he teach the way that he
   Shall choose, and still observe.
14 With those that fear him is
   The secret of the Lord;
   The knowledge of his covenant
   He will to them afford.
15 Mine eyes upon the Lord
   Continually are set;
   For he it is that shall bring forth
   My feet out of the net.

(29)   PSALM XXV.   *St. Bride's.*

16 TURN unto me thy face,
   And to me mercy show;
   Because that I am desolate,
   And am brought very low.
17 My heart's griefs are increas'd:
   Me from distress relieve.

18 See mine affliction and my pain,
    And all my sins forgive.
20 O do thou keep my soul,
    Do thou deliver me :
    And let me never be ashamed,
    Because I trust in thee.
21 Let uprightness and truth
    Keep me, who thee attend.
22 Redemption, Lord, to Israel
    From all his troubles send.

(30)   Psalm XXVI.   *Huddersfield.*

1 Judge me, O Lord, for I have walk'd
    In mine integrity :
    I trusted also in the Lord ;
    Slide therefore shall not I.

2 Examine me, and do me prove;
    Try heart and reins, O God :
3 For thy love is before mine eyes,
    Thy truth's paths I have trode.

6 Mine hands in innocence, O Lord,
    I'll wash and purify ;
    So to thine holy altar go,
    And compass it will I :

7 That I, with voice of thanksgiving,
    May publish, and declare,
    And tell of all thy mighty works,
    That great and wondrous are.

(31)   Psalm XXVI.   *St. Thomas's.*

8 The habitation of thy house,
    Lord, I have loved well ;

Yea, in that place I do delight
  Where doth thine honour dwell.

11 But as for me, I will walk on
   In mine integrity :
 Do thou redeem me, and, O Lord,
   Be merciful to me.

12 My foot upon an even place
   Doth stand with stedfastness :
 Within the congregations
   Th' Eternal I will bless.

(32) Psalm XXVII. *Jackson's.*

1 The Lord 's my light and saving health,
   Who shall make me dismay'd ?
 My life's strength is the Lord, of whom
   Then shall I be afraid ?

3 Against me though an host encamp,
   My heart yet fearless is :
 Though war against me rise, I will
   Be confident in this.

4 One thing I of the Lord desired,
   And will seek to obtain,
 That all days of my life I may
   Within God's house remain ;

 That I the beauty of the Lord
   Behold may and admire,
 And that I in his holy place
   May rev'rently inquire.

5 For he in his pavilion shall
   Me hide in evil days ;
 In secret of his tent me hide,
   And on a rock me raise.

(33)   PSALM XXVII.   *St. Nicholas.*

7 O LORD, give ear unto my voice,
   When I do cry to thee;
Upon me also mercy have,
   And do thou answer me.

8 When thou didst say, Seek ye my face,
   Then unto thee reply
Thus did my heart, Above all things
   Thy face, Lord, seek will I.

9 Far from me hide not thou thy face;
   Put not away from thee
Thy servant in thy wrath: thou hast
   An helper been to me.

O God of my salvation,
   Leave me not, nor forsake:
10 Though me my parents both should leave,
   The Lord will me up take.

(34)   PSALM XXVII.   *St. Magnus.*

6 AND now, ev'n at this present time,
   Mine head shall lifted be
Above all those that are my foes,
   And round encompass me:

Therefore unto his tabernacle
   I'll sacrifices bring
Of joyfulness; I'll sing, yea, I
   To God will praises sing.

11 O Lord, instruct me in thy way,
   To me a leader be
In a plain path, because of those
   That hatred bear to me.

13 I fainted had, unless that I
   Believed had to see

The Lord's own goodness in the land
   Of them that living be.
14 Wait on the Lord, and be thou strong,
   And he shall strength afford
Unto thine heart; yea, do thou wait,
   I say, upon the Lord.

(35)   Psalm XXVIII.   *St. David's.*

1 To thee I'll cry, O Lord, my rock;
   Hold not thy peace to me;
Lest like those that to pit descend
   I by thy silence be.

2 The voice hear of my humble pray'rs,
   When unto thee I cry;
When to thine holy oracle
   I lift mine hands on high.

5 God shall not build, but them destroy,
   Who would not understand
The Lord's own works, nor did regard
   The doing of his hand.

6 For ever blessed be the Lord,
   For graciously he heard
The voice of my petitions,
   And prayers did regard.

(36)   Psalm XXVIII.   *Manchester.*

7 The Lord's my strength and shield; my heart
   Upon him did rely;
And I am helped: hence my heart
   Doth joy exceedingly,
And with my song I will him praise.
8   Their strength is God alone:
He also is the saving strength
   Of his anointed one.

9 O thine own people do thou save,
  Bless thine inheritance ;
  Them also do thou feed, and them
  For evermore advance.

(37)   PSALM XXIX.   *French.*

1 GIVE ye unto the Lord, ye sons
  That of the mighty be,
  All strength and glory to the Lord
  With cheerfulness give ye.
3 The Lord's voice on the waters is ;
  The God of majesty
  Doth thunder, and on multitudes
  Of waters sitteth he.
4 A pow'rful voice it is that comes
  Out from the Lord most high ;
  The voice of that great Lord is full
  Of glorious majesty.
10 The Lord sits on the floods ; the Lord
   Sits King, and ever shall.
11 The Lord will give his people strength,
   And with peace bless them all.

(38)   PSALM XXX.   *Stroudwater.*

1 LORD, I will thee extol, for thou
  Hast lifted me on high,
  And over me thou to rejoice
  Mad'st not mine enemy.
2 O thou who art the Lord my God,
  I in distress to thee
  With loud cries lifted up my voice,
  And thou hast healed me.
3 O Lord, my soul thou hast brought up,
  And rescued from the grave ;

           That I to pit should not go down,
              Alive thou didst me save.
       4 O ye that are his holy ones,
              Sing praise unto the Lord ;
           And give unto him thanks, when ye
              His holiness record.

(39)   Psalm XXXI.   St. James's.
       1 In thee, O Lord, I put my trust,
              Shamed let me never be ;
           According to thy righteousness
              Do thou deliver me.
       2 Bow down thine ear to me, with speed
              Send me deliverance :
           To save me, my strong rock be thou,
              And my house of defence.
       3 Because thou art my rock, and thee
              I for my fortress take ;
           Therefore do thou me lead and guide,
              Ev'n for thine own name's sake.
       5 Into thine hands I do commit
              My sp'rit : for thou art he,
           O thou, JEHOVAH, God of truth,
              That hast redeemed me.

(40)   Psalm XXXI.   St. Ann's New.
       7 I'll in thy mercy gladly joy :
              For thou my miseries
           Consider'd hast ; thou hast my soul
              Known in adversities ;
       8 And thou hast not enclosed me
              Within the en'my's hand ;
           And by thee have my feet been made
              In a large room to stand.

19 How great's the goodness thou for them
   That fear thee keep'st in store,
   And wrought'st for them that trust in thee
   The sons of men before!
23 O love the Lord, all ye his saints;
   Because the Lord doth guard
   The faithful, and he plenteously
   Proud doers doth reward.
24 Be of good courage, and he strength
   Unto your heart shall send,
   All ye whose hope and confidence
   Do on the Lord depend.

(41) PSALM XXXII. *Bedford.*

1 O BLESSED is the man to whom
   Is freely pardoned
   All the transgression he hath done,
   Whose sin is covered.
2 Bless'd is the man to whom the Lord
   Imputeth not his sin,
   And in whose sp'rit there is no guile,
   Nor fraud is found therein.
5 I will confess unto the Lord
   My trespasses, said I;
   And of my sin thou freely didst
   Forgive th' iniquity.
6 For this shall ev'ry godly one
   His prayer make to thee;
   In such a time he shall thee seek,
   As found thou mayest be.
   Surely, when floods of waters great
   Do swell up to the brim,
   They shall not overwhelm his soul,
   Nor once come near to him.

(42)   Psalm XXXII.   *Warwick.*

7 Thou art my hiding-place, thou shalt
   From trouble keep me free:
  Thou with songs of deliverance
   About shalt compass me.

8 I will instruct thee, and thee teach
   The way that thou shalt go;
  And, with mine eye upon thee set,
   I will direction show.

10 Unto the man that wicked is
   His sorrows shall abound;
  But him that trusteth in the Lord
   Mercy shall compass round.

11 Ye righteous, in the Lord be glad,
   In him do ye rejoice:
  All ye that upright are in heart,
   For joy lift up your voice.

(43)   Psalm XXXIII.   *Irish.*

1 Ye righteous, in the Lord rejoice;
   It comely is and right,
  That upright men, with thankful voice,
   Should praise the Lord of might.

2 Praise God with harp, and unto him
   Sing with the psaltery;
  Upon a ten-string'd instrument
   Make ye sweet melody.

3 A new song to him sing, and play
   With loud noise skilfully;
4 For right is God's word, all his works
   Are done in verity.

5 To judgment and to righteousness
   A love he beareth still ;
   The loving-kindness of the Lord
   The earth throughout doth fill.

(44)   Psalm XXXIII.   *St. Lawrence.*

6 The heavens by the word of God
   Did their beginning take ;
   And by the breathing of his mouth
   He all their hosts did make.

7 The waters of the seas he brings
   Together as an heap ;
   And in storehouses, as it were,
   He layeth up the deep.

8 Let earth, and all that live therein,
   With rev'rence fear the Lord ;
   Let all the world's inhabitants
   Dread him with one accord.

9 For he did speak the word, and done
   It was without delay ;
   Established it firmly stood,
   Whatever he did say.

(45)   Psalm XXXIII.   *Farrant.*

12 That nation blessed is, whose God
    Jehovah is, and those
    A blessed people are, whom for
    His heritage he chose.

13 The Lord from heav'n sees and beholds
    All sons of men full well :
14 He views all from his dwelling-place
    That in the earth do dwell.

18 Behold, on those that do him fear
    The Lord doth set his eye ;
    Ev'n those who on his mercy do
    With confidence rely.

21 Sith in his holy name we trust,
    Our heart shall joyful be.
22 Lord, let thy mercy be on us,
    As we do hope in thee.

(46)   Psalm XXXIV.   *St. Ann's.*

1 God will I bless all times ; his praise
    My mouth shall still express.
2 My soul shall boast in God : the meek
    Shall hear with joyfulness.

3 Extol the Lord with me, let us
    Exalt his name together.
4 I sought the Lord, he heard, and did
    Me from all fears deliver.

7 The angel of the Lord encamps,
    And round encompasseth
  All those about that do him fear,
    And them delivereth.

8 O taste and see that God is good :
    Who trusts in him is bless'd.
9 Fear God his saints : none that him fear
    Shall be with want oppress'd.

(47)   Psalm XXXIV.   *St. Matthew's.*

18 The Lord is ever nigh to them
    That be of broken sp'rit ;
  To them he safety doth afford
    That are in heart contrite.

19 The troubles that afflict the just
    In number many be ;
    But yet at length out of them all
    The Lord doth set him free.

20 He carefully his bones doth keep,
    Whatever can befall ;
    That not so much as one of them
    Can broken be at all.

21 Ill shall the wicked slay ; laid waste
    Shall be who hate the just.
22 The Lord redeems his servants' souls ;
    None perish that him trust.

(48)   Psalm XXXVI.   *London New.*

5 THY mercy, Lord, is in the heav'ns :
    Thy truth doth reach the clouds :
6 Thy justice is like mountains great :
    Thy judgments deep as floods :

    Lord, thou preservest man and beast.
7   How precious is thy grace !
    Therefore in shadow of thy wings
    Men's sons their trust shall place.

8 They with the fatness of thy house
    Shall be well satisfy'd :
    From rivers of thy pleasures thou
    Wilt drink to them provide.

9 Because of life the fountain pure
    Remains alone with thee ;
    And in that purest light of thine
    We clearly light shall see.

(49)   Psalm XXXIX.   *Martyrdom.*

4 Mine end, and measure of my days,
   O Lord, unto me show
What is the same ; that I thereby
   My frailty well may know.

5 Lo, thou my days an handbreadth mad'st ;
   Mine age is in thine eye
As nothing : sure each man at best
   Is wholly vanity.

6 Sure each man walks in a vain show ;
   They vex themselves in vain :
He heaps up wealth, and doth not know
   To whom it shall pertain.

7 And now, O Lord, what wait I for ?
   My hope is fix'd on thee.
8 Free me from all my trespasses,
   The fool's scorn make not me.

(50)   Psalm XXXIX.   *French.*

9 Dumb was I, op'ning not my mouth,
   Because this work was thine.
10 Thy stroke take from me ; by the blow
   Of thine hand I do pine.

11 When with rebukes thou dost correct
   Man for iniquity,
Thou wast'st his beauty like a moth :
   Sure each man's vanity.

12 Attend my cry, Lord, at my tears
   And pray'rs not silent be :
I sojourn as my fathers all,
   And stranger am with thee.

13 O spare thou me, that I my strength
   Recover may again,
   Before from hence I do depart,
   And here no more remain.

(51)   PSALM XL.   *Manchester*, or *St. Ann's New.*

1 I WAITED for the Lord my God,
   And patiently did bear;
   At length to me he did incline
   My voice and cry to hear.

2 He took me from a fearful pit,
   And from the miry clay,
   And on a rock he set my feet,
   Establishing my way.

3 He put a new song in my mouth,
   Our God to magnify:
   Many shall see it, and shall fear,
   And on the Lord rely.

4 O blessed is the man whose trust
   Upon the Lord relies;
   Respecting not the proud, nor such
   As turn aside to lies.

(52)   PSALM XL.   *St. Ann's.*

5 O LORD my God, full many are
   The wonders thou hast done;
   Thy gracious thoughts to us-ward far
   Above all thoughts are gone:

   In order none can reckon them
   To thee: if them declare,
   And speak of them I would, they more
   That can be number'd are.

16 In thee let all be glad, and joy,
    Who seeking thee abide;
    Who thy salvation love, say still,
    The Lord be magnify'd.

17 I 'm poor and needy, yet the Lord
    Of me a care doth take :
    Thou art my help and saviour,
    My God, no tarrying make.

(53)   Psalm XL.   *Farrant.*

6 No sacrifice nor offering
    Didst thou at all desire ;
    Mine ears thou bor'd'st : sin-off'ring thou
    And burnt didst not require :

7 Then to the Lord these were my words,
    I come, behold and see ;
    Within the volume of the book
    It written is of me,

8 To do thy will I take delight,
    O thou my God that art ;
    Yea, that most holy law of thine
    I have within my heart.

11 Thy tender mercies, Lord, from me
    O do thou not restrain :
    Thy loving-kindness, and thy truth,
    Let them me still maintain.

(54)   Psalm XLI.   *St. David's.*

1 Blessed is he that wisely doth
    The poor man's case consider ;
    For when the time of trouble is,
    The Lord will him deliver.

2 God will him keep, yea, save alive;
   On earth he bless'd shall live;
   And to his enemies' desire
   Thou wilt him not up give.

3 God will give strength when he on bed
   Of languishing doth mourn;
   And in his sickness sore, O Lord,
   Thou all his bed wilt turn.

4 I said, O Lord, do thou extend
   Thy mercy unto me;
   O do thou heal my soul; for why?
   I have offended thee.

(55)   Psalm XLII.   *Jenkensdale.*

1 Like as the hart for water-brooks
   In thirst doth pant and bray;
   So pants my longing soul, O God,
   That come to thee I may.

2 My soul for God, the living God,
   Doth thirst: when shall I near
   Unto thy countenance approach,
   And in God's sight appear?

3 My tears have unto me been meat,
   Both in the night and day,
   While unto me continually,
   Where is thy God? they say.

4 My soul is poured out in me,
   When this I think upon;
   Because that with the multitude
   I heretofore had gone;

   With them into God's house I went
   With voice of joy and praise;

    Yea, with the multitude that kept
       The solemn holy days.

5 O why art thou cast down, my soul?
    Why in me so dismay'd?
  Trust God, for I shall praise him yet,
    His count'nance is mine aid.

(56)   Psalm XLII.   *Durham,*
                                             or *St. Paul's.*

6 My God, my soul's cast down in me;
    Thee therefore mind I will
  From Jordan's land, the Hermonites,
    And ev'n from Mizar hill.

7 At the noise of thy water-spouts
    Deep unto deep doth call;
  Thy breaking waves pass over me,
    Yea, and thy billows all.

8 His loving-kindness yet the Lord
    Command will in the day,
  His song's with me by night; to God,
    By whom I live, I'll pray.

9 And I will say to God my rock,
    Why me forgett'st thou so?
  Why, for my foes' oppression,
    Thus mourning do I go?

(57)   Psalm XLIII.   *Invocation.*

3 O send thy light forth and thy truth;
    Let them be guides to me,
  And bring me to thine holy hill,
    Ev'n where thy dwellings be.

4 Then will I to God's altar go,
    To God my chiefest joy:

>   Yea, God, my God, thy name to praise
>   My harp I will employ.
>
> 5 Why art thou then cast down, my soul?
>   What should discourage thee?
>   And why with vexing thoughts art thou
>   Disquieted in me?
>
>   Still trust in God; for him to praise
>   Good cause I yet shall have:
>   He of my count'nance is the health,
>   My God that doth me save.

(58)   PSALM XLV.   *Prague.*

> 1 My heart inditing is
>   Good matter in a song:
>   I speak the things that I have made
>   Which to the King belong:
>
>   My tongue shall be as quick,
>   His honour to indite,
>   As is the pen of any scribe
>   That useth fast to write.
>
> 2 Thou 'rt fairest of all men;
>   Grace in thy lips doth flow:
>   And therefore blessings evermore
>   On thee doth God bestow.
>
> 3 Thy sword gird on thy thigh,
>   Thou that art most of might:
>   Appear in dreadful majesty,
>   And in thy glory bright.
>
> 4 For meekness, truth, and right,
>   Ride prosp'rously in state;
>   And thy right hand shall teach to thee
>   Things terrible and great.

(59)   Psalm XLV.   *St. Michael's.*

5 Thy shafts shall pierce their hearts
    That foes are to the King;
 Whereby into subjection
    The people thou shalt bring.

6 Thy royal seat, O Lord,
    For ever shall remain:
 The sceptre of thy kingdom doth
    All righteousness maintain.

7 Thou lov'st right, and hat'st ill;
    For God, thy God, most high,
 Above thy fellows hath with th' oil
    Of joy anointed thee.

17 I will shew forth thy name
    To generations all:
 Therefore the people evermore
    To thee give praises shall.

(60)   Psalm XLVI.   *Stroudwater.*

1 God is our refuge and our strength,
    In straits a present aid;
2 Therefore, although the earth remove,
    We will not be afraid:

 Though hills amidst the seas be cast;
3   Though waters roaring make,
 And troubled be; yea, though the hills
    By swelling seas do shake.

4 A river is, whose streams do glad
    The city of our God;
 The holy place, wherein the Lord
    Most high hath his abode.

5 God in the midst of her doth dwell;
　Nothing shall her remove :
　The Lord to her an helper will,
　And that right early, prove.

(61) PSALM XLVI. *St. Gregory.*

8 COME, and behold what wondrous works
　Have by the Lord been wrought;
　Come, see what desolations
　He on the earth hath brought.

9 Unto the ends of all the earth
　Wars into peace he turns :
　The bow he breaks, the spear he cuts,
　In fire the chariot burns.

10 Be still, and know that I am God;
　Among the heathen I
　Will be exalted; I on earth
　Will be exalted high.

11 Our God, who is the Lord of hosts,
　Is still upon our side;
　The God of Jacob our refuge
　For ever will abide.

(62) PSALM XLVII. *Newington.*

1 ALL people, clap your hands; to God
　With voice of triumph shout :
2 For dreadful is the Lord most high,
　Great King the earth throughout.

4 The lot of our inheritance
　Choose out for us shall he,
　Of Jacob, whom he loved well,
　Ev'n the excellency.

5 God is with shouts gone up, the Lord
   With trumpets sounding high.
6 Sing praise to God, sing praise, sing praise,
   Praise to our King sing ye.

7 For God is King of all the earth;
   With knowledge praise express.
8 God rules the nations: God sits on
   His throne of holiness.

(63)   Psalm XLVIII.   *Bedford.*

10 O Lord, according to thy name,
      Through all the earth's thy praise;
   And thy right hand, O Lord, is full
      Of righteousness always.

11 Because thy judgments are made known,
      Let Sion mount rejoice;
   Of Judah let the daughters all
      Send forth a cheerful voice.

12 Walk about Sion, and go round:
      The high towers thereof tell:
13 Consider ye her palaces,
      And mark her bulwarks well;

   That ye may tell posterity.
14   For this God doth abide
   Our God for evermore: he will
      Ev'n unto death us guide.

(64)   Psalm L.   *Aynhoe.*

1 The mighty God, the Lord,
      Hath spoken, and did call
   The earth, from rising of the sun,
      To where he hath his fall.

2 From out of Sion hill,
    Which of excellency
  And beauty the perfection is,
    God shined gloriously.

3 Our God shall surely come;
    Keep silence shall not he:
  Before him fire shall waste; great storms
    Shall round about him be.

4 Unto the heavens clear
    He from above shall call,
  And to the earth likewise, that he
    May judge his people all.

5 Together let my saints
    Unto me gather'd be,
  Those that by sacrifice have made
    A covenant with me.

6 And then the heavens shall
    His righteousness declare:
  Because the Lord himself is he
    By whom men judged are.

(65)   PSALM LI.   *Dundee.*

1 AFTER thy loving-kindness, Lord,
    Have mercy upon me:
  For thy compassions great, blot out
    All mine iniquity.

2 Me cleanse from sin, and throughly wash
    From mine iniquity:
3 For my transgressions I confess;
    My sin I ever see.

7 Do thou with hyssop sprinkle me,
    I shall be cleansed so;
  Yea, wash thou me, and then I shall
    Be whiter than the snow.

8 Of gladness and of joyfulness
   Make me to hear the voice;
   That so these very bones which thou
   Hast broken may rejoice.

(66)　　　　　Psalm LI.　　　　*Solomon.*

9 All mine iniquities blot out;
   Thy face hide from my sin.
10 Create a clean heart, Lord; renew
   A right sp'rit me within.
11 Cast me not from thy sight, nor take
   Thy Holy Sp'rit away.
12 Restore me thy salvation's joy;
   With thy free Sp'rit me stay.
13 Then will I teach thy ways unto
   Those that transgressors be;
   And those that sinners are shall then
   Be turned unto thee.

(67)　　　　　Psalm LI.　　　　*Manchester.*

15 My closed lips, O Lord, by thee
   Let them be opened;
   Then shall thy praises by my mouth
   Abroad be published.
16 For thou desir'st not sacrifice,
   Else would I give it thee;
   Nor wilt thou with burnt-offering
   At all delighted be.
17 A broken spirit is to God
   A pleasing sacrifice:
   A broken and a contrite heart,
   Lord, thou wilt not despise.

(68)   PSALM LV.   *Harrington.*

6 O THAT I, like a dove, had wings,
   Said I, then would I flee
   Far hence, that I might find a place
   Where I in rest might be.

7 Lo, then far off I wander would,
   And in the desert stay;
8 From windy storm and tempest I
   Would haste to 'scape away.

16 I'll call on God: God will me save.
17   I'll pray, and make a noise
   At ev'ning, morning, and at noon;
   And he shall hear my voice.

22 Cast thou thy burden on the Lord,
   And he shall thee sustain;
   Yea, he shall cause the righteous man
   Unmoved to remain.

(69)   PSALM LVII.   *Martyrdom.*

1 BE merciful to me, O God;
   Thy mercy unto me
   Do thou extend; because my soul
   Doth put her trust in thee:

Yea, in the shadow of thy wings
   My refuge I will place,
   Until these sad calamities
   Do wholly overpass.

2 My cry I will cause to ascend
   Unto the Lord most high;
   To God, who doth all things for me
   Perform most perfectly.

3 From heav'n he shall send down, and me
    From his reproach defend
  That would devour me : God his truth
    And mercy forth shall send.

(70)   Psalm LVII.   St Ann's New.

5 Be thou exalted very high
    Above the heav'ns, O God ;
  Let thou thy glory be advanced
    O'er all the earth abroad.

7 My heart is fix'd, my heart is fix'd,
    O God ; I'll sing and praise.
8 My glory wake; wake psalt'ry, harp ;
    Myself I'll early raise.

9 I'll praise thee 'mong the people, Lord ;
    'Mong nations sing will I :
10 For great to heav'n thy mercy is,
    Thy truth is to the sky.

11 O Lord, exalted be thy name
    Above the heav'ns to stand :
  Do thou thy glory far advance
    Above both sea and land.

(71)   Psalm LXI.   *St. Paul's*, or *Durham*.

1 O God, give ear unto my cry ;
    Unto my pray'r attend.
2 From th' utmost corner of the land
    My cry to thee I'll send.

  What time my heart is overwhelm'd,
    And in perplexity,
  Do thou me lead unto the Rock
    That higher is than I.

3 For thou hast for my refuge been
  A shelter by thy power;
  And for defence against my foes
  Thou hast been a strong tower.

4 Within thy tabernacle I
  For ever will abide;
  And under covert of thy wings
  With confidence me hide.

5 For thou the vows that I did make,
  O Lord my God, didst hear:
  Thou hast giv'n me the heritage
  Of those thy name that fear.

(72)   PSALM LXII.   *St. Stephen's.*

5 MY soul, wait thou with patience
  Upon thy God alone;
  On him dependeth all my hope
  And expectation.

6 He only my salvation is,
  And my strong rock is he:
  He only is my sure defence;
  I shall not moved be.

7 In God my glory placed is,
  And my salvation sure:
  In God the rock is of my strength,
  My refuge most secure.

8 Ye people, place your confidence
  In him continually:
  Before him pour ye out your heart:
  God is our refuge high.

(73)   PSALM LXIII.   *London New.*

1 LORD, thee my God, I'll early seek:
  My soul doth thirst for thee;

My flesh longs in a dry parch'd land,
　　Wherein no waters be.
3 Since better is thy love than life,
　　My lips thee praise shall give.
4 I in thy name will lift my hands,
　　And bless thee while I live.

6 When I do thee upon my bed
　　Remember with delight,
　And when on thee I meditate
　　In watches of the night.
7 In shadow of thy wings I'll joy;
　　For thou mine help has been.
8 My soul thee follows hard; and me
　　Thy right hand doth sustain.

(74)   Psalm LXV.   *St. Magnus,* or *St Thomas's.*

1 Praise waits for thee in Sion, Lord:
　　To thee vows paid shall be.
2 O thou that hearer art of pray'r,
　　All flesh shall come to thee.

3 Iniquities, I must confess,
　　Prevail against me do:
　But as for our transgressions,
　　Them purge away shalt thou.
4 Bless'd is the man whom thou dost choose,
　　And mak'st approach to thee,
　That he within thy courts, O Lord,
　　May still a dweller be:

　We surely shall be satisfy'd
　　With thy abundant grace,
　And with the goodness of thy house,
　　Ev'n of thy holy place.

(75)   PSALM LXV.   *Old 68th.*

5 O GOD of our salvation,
    Thou, in thy righteousness,
By fearful works unto our pray'rs
    Thine answer dost express;

Therefore the ends of all the earth,
    And those afar that be
Upon the sea, their confidence,
    O Lord, will place in thee:

6 Who, being girt with power, sets fast
    By his great strength the hills:
7 Who noise of seas, noise of their waves,
    And people's tumult, stills.

8 Those in the utmost parts that dwell
    Are at thy signs afraid:
Th' outgoings of the morn and ev'n
    By thee are joyful made.

(76)   PSALM LXV.   *Glasgow.*

9 THE earth thou visit'st, wat'ring it;
    Thou mak'st it rich to grow
With God's full flood; thou corn prepar'st,
    When thou provid'st it so.

10 Her rigs thou wat'rest plenteously:
    Her furrows settelest:
With showers thou dost her mollify:
    Her spring by thee is blest.

11 So thou the year most lib'rally
    Dost with thy goodness crown:
And all thy paths abundantly
    On us drop fatness down.

13 With flocks the pastures clothed be,
    The vales with corn are clad;
And now they shout and sing to thee,
    For thou hast made them glad.

(77)   Psalm LXVI.   *Tiverton, or Sheffield.*

1 All lands to God, in joyful sounds,
    Aloft your voices raise.
2 Sing forth the honour of his name,
    And glorious make his praise.
3 Say unto God, How terrible
    In all thy works art thou!
Through thy great power thy foes to thee
    Shall be constrain'd to bow.
4 All on the earth shall worship thee:
    They shall thy praise proclaim
In songs: they shall sing cheerfully
    Unto thy holy name.
5 Come, and the works that God hath wrought
    With admiration see:
In's working to the sons of men
    Most terrible is he.

(78)   Psalm LXVI.   *Lancaster.*

8 Ye people, bless our God; aloud
    The voice speak of his praise:
9 Our soul in life who safe preserves,
    Our foot from sliding stays.
16 All that fear God, come, hear, I'll tell
    What he did for my soul.
17 I with my tongue unto him cry'd,
    My tongue did him extol.

18 If in my heart I sin regard,
  The Lord me will not hear :
19 But surely God me heard, and to
  My prayer's voice gave ear.
20 O let the Lord, our gracious God,
  For ever blessed be,
  Who turned not my pray'r from him,
  Nor yet his grace from me.

(79) Psalm LXVII. *Selma.*

1 Lord, bless and pity us,
  Shine on us with thy face ;
2 That th' earth thy way, and nations all
  May know thy saving grace.
3 Let people praise thee, Lord ;
  Let people all thee praise.
4 O let the nations be glad,
  In songs their voices raise :
  Thou 'lt justly people judge,
   On earth rule nations all.
5 Let people praise thee, Lord ; let them
  Praise thee, both great and small.
6 The earth her fruit shall yield ;
  Our God shall blessing send.
7 God shall us bless ; men shall him fear
  Unto earth's utmost end.

(80) Psalm LXVIII. *Old 23d.*

1 Let God arise, and scattered
  Let all his en'mies be ;
  And let all those that do him hate
  Before his presence flee.

3 But let the righteous be glad :
   Let them before God's sight
 Be very joyful; yea, let them
   Rejoice with all their might.

4 To God sing, to his name sing praise :
   Extol him with your voice,
 That rides on heav'n, by his name JAH :
   Before his face rejoice.

5 Because the Lord a father is
   Unto the fatherless;
 God is the widow's judge, within
   His place of holiness.

(81)   PSALM LXVIII.   *Old* 68*th.*

7 O GOD, what time thou didst go forth
   Before thy people's face;
 And when through the great wilderness
   Thy glorious marching was;

8 Then at God's presence shook the earth,
   Then drops from heaven fell;
 This Sinai shook before the Lord,
   The God of Israel.

9 O God, thou to thine heritage
   Didst send a plenteous rain,
 Whereby thou, when it weary was,
   Didst it refresh again.

10 Thy congregation then did make
   Their habitation there :
 Of thine own goodness for the poor,
   O God, thou didst prepare.

(82)   PSALM LXVIII.   *Sheffield.*

16 WHY do ye leap, ye mountains high?
   This is the hill where God

Desires to dwell; yea, God in it
      For aye will make abode.
17 God's chariots twenty thousand are,
      Thousands of angels strong;
   In's holy place God is, as in
      Mount Sinai, them among.
18 Thou hast, O Lord, most glorious,
      Ascended up on high;
   And in triumph victorious led
      Captive captivity:
   Thou hast received gifts for men,
      For such as did rebel;
   Yea, ev'n for them, that God the Lord
      In midst of them might dwell.

(83)   PSALM LXVIII.   *Warwick.*

19 BLESS'D be the Lord, who is to us
      Of our salvation God;
   Who daily with his benefits
      Us plenteously doth load.
32 O all ye kingdoms of the earth,
      Sing praises to this King;
   For he is Lord that ruleth all,
      Unto him praises sing:
33 To him that rides on heav'ns of heav'ns,
      Which he of old did found;
   Lo, he sends out his voice, a voice
      In might that doth abound.
34 Strength unto God do ye ascribe;
      For his excellency
   Is over Israel, his strength
      Is in the clouds most high.

(84)   Psalm LXIX.   *Farrant.*

1 Save me, O God, because the floods
    Do so environ me,
  That ev'n unto my very soul
    Come in the waters be.

14 Deliver me out of the mire,
    From sinking do me keep :
  Free me from those that do me hate,
    And from the waters deep.

15 Let not the flood on me prevail,
    Whose water overflows ;
  Nor deep me swallow, nor the pit
    Her mouth upon me close.

16 Hear me, O Lord, because thy love
    And kindness are most good :
  Turn unto me, according to
    Thy mercies' multitude.

(85)   Psalm LXIX.   *Jackson.*

30 The name of God I with a song
    Most cheerfully will praise ;
  And I, in giving thanks to him,
    His name shall highly raise.

31 This to the Lord a sacrifice
    More gracious shall prove
  Than bullock, ox, or any beast
    That hath both horn and hoof.

32 When this the humble men shall see,
    It joy to them shall give :
  O all ye that do seek the Lord,
    Your hearts shall ever live.

33 For God the poor hears, and will not
   His prisoners contemn.
34 Let heav'n, and earth, and seas, him praise,
   And all that move in them.

(86)   Psalm LXX.   *Arran.*

1 Lord, haste me to deliver ;
   With speed, Lord, succour me.
2 Let them that for my soul do seek
   Shamed and confounded be :

Turn'd back be they, and shamed,
   That in my hurt delight.
3 Turn'd back be they, Ha, ha ! that say,
   Their shaming to requite.

4 In thee let all be glad
   And joy that seek for thee :
Let them who thy salvation love
   Say still, God praised be.

5 I poor and needy am ;
   Come, Lord, and make no stay :
My help thou and deliv'rer art ;
   O Lord, make no delay.

(87)   Psalm LXXI.   *Old 8th.*

1 O Lord, my hope and confidence
   Are placed in thee alone ;
Then let thy servant never be
   Put to confusion.

2 And let me, in thy righteousness,
   From thee deliv'rance have :
Cause me escape, incline thine ear
   Unto me, and me save.

3 Be thou my dwelling-rock, to which
    I ever may resort :
  Thou gav'st commandment me to save,
    For thou 'rt my rock and fort.

4 Free me, my God, from wicked hands,
    Hands cruel and unjust :
5 For thou, O Lord God, art my hope,
    And from my youth my trust.

(88)   Psalm LXXI.   *Bedford.*

14 But I with expectation
      Will hope continually ;
    And yet with praises more and more
      I will thee magnify.

15 Thy justice and salvation
      My mouth abroad shall show,
    Ev'n all the day ; for I thereof
      The numbers do not know.

16 And I will constantly go on
      In strength of God the Lord ;
    And thine own righteousness, ev'n thine
      Alone, I will record.

17 For even from my youth, O God,
      By thee I have been taught ;
    And hitherto I have declared
      The wonders thou hast wrought.

(89)   Psalm LXXI.   *St. Thomas's* or *St. Magnus.*

18 And now, Lord, leave me not, when I
      Old and grey-headed grow :
    Till to this age thy strength, and power
      To all to come, I show.

19 And thy most perfect righteousness,
　　O Lord, is very high,
　Who hast so great things done : O God,
　　Who is like unto thee?
22 Thee, ev'n thy truth, I'll also praise,
　　My God, with psaltery:
　Thou Holy One of Israel,
　　With harp I'll sing to thee.
23 My lips shall much rejoice in thee,
　　When I thy praises sound:
　My soul, which thou redeemed hast,
　　In joy shall much abound.

(90)　　　　Psalm LXXII.　　　*French.*
1 O Lord, thy judgments give the King,
　　His son thy righteousness.
2 With right he shall thy people judge,
　　Thy poor with uprightness.
4 The people's poor ones he shall judge,
　　The needy's children save;
　And those shall he in pieces break
　　Who them oppressed have.
5 They shall thee fear, while sun and moon
　　Do last, through ages all.
6 Like rain on mown grass he shall drop,
　　Or showers on earth that fall.
7 The just shall flourish in his days,
　　And prosper in his reign:
　He shall, while doth the moon endure,
　　Abundant peace maintain.

(91)　　　　Psalm LXXII.　　　*St. Gregory.*
16 Of corn an handful in the earth
　　On tops of mountains high,

With prosp'rous fruit shall shake, like trees
    On Lebanon that be.
The city shall be flourishing,
    Her citizens abound
In number shall, like to the grass
    That grows upon the ground.

17 His name for ever shall endure;
    Last like the sun it shall:
Men shall be bless'd in him; and bless'd
    All nations shall him call.

18 Now blessed be the Lord our God,
    The God of Israel;
For he alone doth wondrous works,
    In glory that excel.

19 And blessed be his glorious name
    To all eternity:
The whole earth let his glory fill.
    Amen, so let it be.

(92)   Psalm LXXIII.   *Solomon.*

24 Thou, with thy counsel, while I live,
    Wilt me conduct and guide;
And to thy glory afterward
    Receive me to abide.

25 Whom have I in the heavens high
    But thee, O Lord, alone?
And in the earth whom I desire
    Besides thee there is none.

26 My flesh and heart do faint and fail,
    But God doth fail me never:
For of my heart God is the strength
    And portion for ever.

28 But surely it is good for me
   That I draw near to God :
   In God I trust, that all thy works
   I may declare abroad.

(93)   Psalm LXXIV.   *Durham.*

12 For certainly God is my King,
   Ev'n from the times of old,
   Working in midst of all the earth
   Salvation manifold.

13 The sea, by thy great power, to part
   Asunder thou didst make :
   Thou didst the dragons' heads, O Lord,
   Within the waters break.

16 Thine only is the day, O Lord,
   Thine also is the night ;
   And thou alone prepared hast
   The sun and shining light.

17 By thee the borders of the earth
   Were settled ev'rywhere :
   The summer and the winter both
   By thee created were.

(94)   Psalm LXXVI.   *St. Paul's.*

7 Thou, Lord, ev'n thou art he that should
   Be fear'd ; and who is he
   That may stand up before thy sight,
   If once thou angry be ?

8 From heav'n thou judgment mad'st be heard ;
   The earth was still with fear,
9 When God to judgment rose, to save
   All meek on earth that were.

10 Surely the very wrath of man
    Unto thy praise redounds :
  Thou to the remnant of his wrath
    Wilt set restraining bounds.

(95)   PSALM LXXVII.   *Dunfermline.*

13 O GOD, thy way most holy is
    Within thy sanctuary :
  And what God is so great in power
    As is our God most high ?
14 Thou art the God that wonders dost
    By thy right hand most strong :
  Thy mighty power thou hast declared
    The nations among.
15 To thine own people with thine arm
    Thou didst redemption bring ;
  To Jacob's sons, and to the tribes
    Of Joseph that do spring.
18 Thy thunder's voice alongst the heav'n
    A mighty noise did make :
  By lightnings lighten'd was the world :
    Th' earth tremble did and shake.
19 Thy way is in the sea, and in
    The waters great thy path ;
  Yet are thy footsteps hid, O Lord ;
    None knowledge thereof hath.

(96)   PSALM LXXIX.   *Burford.*

8 AGAINST us mind not former sins :
    Thy tender mercies show :
  Let them prevent us speedily ;
    For we 're brought very low.

9 For thy name's glory help us, Lord,
   Who hast our Saviour been :
Deliver us; for thy name's sake,
   O purge away our sin.
11 O let the pris'ner's sighs ascend
   Before thy sight on high ;
Preserve those in thy mighty power
   That are design'd to die.
13 So we thy folk, and pasture-sheep,
   Shall give thee thanks always ;
And unto generations all
   We will shew forth thy praise.

(97)   PSALM LXXX.   *York.*

1 HEAR, Isr'el's Shepherd ! like a flock
   Thou that dost Joseph guide :
Shine forth, O thou that dost between
   The cherubim abide.
2 In Ephraim's, and Benjamin's,
   And in Manasseh's sight,
O come for our salvation ;
   Stir up thy strength and might.
3 Turn us again, O Lord our God,
   And upon us vouchsafe
To make thy countenance to shine ;
   And so we shall be safe.
4 O Lord of hosts, almighty God,
   How long shall kindled be
Thy wrath against the prayer made
   By thine own folk to thee ?

(98)   PSALM LXXX.   *Old 68th.*

7 TURN us again, O God of hosts,
   And upon us vouchsafe

To make thy countenance to shine ;
   And so we shall be safe.

17 O let thy hand be still upon
   The Man of thy right hand,
   The Son of man, whom for thyself
   Thou madest strong to stand.

18 So henceforth we will not go back,
   Nor turn from thee at all :
   O do thou quicken us, and we
   Upon thy name will call.

19 Turn us again, Lord God of hosts,
   And upon us vouchsafe
   To make thy countenance to shine ;
   And so we shall be safe.

(99)   Psalm LXXXIV.   *Lewes.*

1 How lovely is thy dwelling-place,
   O Lord of hosts, to me !
   The tabernacles of thy grace
   How pleasant, Lord, they be !

2 My thirsty soul longs veh'mently,
   Yea faints, thy courts to see :
   My very heart and flesh cry out,
   O living God, for thee.

4 Bless'd are they in thy house that dwell :
   They ever give thee praise.
5 Bless'd is the man whose strength thou art,
   In whose heart are thy ways.

7 So they from strength unwearied go
   Still forward unto strength,
   Until in Sion they appear
   Before the Lord at length.

(100)   PSALM LXXXIV.   *St. James's.*

8 LORD God of hosts, my prayer hear;
    O Jacob's God, give ear.
9 See God our shield; look on the face
    Of thine anointed dear.

10 For in thy courts one day excels
    A thousand: rather in
    My God's house will I keep a door,
    Than dwell in tents of sin.

11 For God the Lord's a sun and shield:
    He'll grace and glory give;
    And will withhold no good from them
    That uprightly do live.

12 O thou that art the Lord of hosts,
    That man is truly blest,
    Who by assured confidence
    On thee alone doth rest.

(101)   PSALM LXXXV.   *St. Thomas's.*

6 THAT in thee may thy people joy,
    Wilt thou not us revive?
7 Shew us thy mercy, Lord; to us
    Do thy salvation give.

8 I'll hear what God the Lord will speak:
    To his folk he'll speak peace,
    And to his saints; but let them not
    Return to foolishness.

9 To them that fear him, surely near
    Is his salvation;
    That glory in our land may have
    Her habitation.

10 Truth met with mercy : righteousness
     And peace kiss'd mutually :
11 Truth springs from earth ; and righteousness
     Looks down from heaven high.

(102)   Psalm LXXXVI.   *St. Mary's.*

1 O Lord, do thou bow down thine ear,
    And hear me graciously ;
  Because I sore afflicted am,
    And am in poverty.

3 Sith unto thee I daily cry,
    Be merciful to me.
4 Rejoice thy servant's soul ; for, Lord,
    I lift my soul to thee.

5 For thou art gracious, O Lord,
    And ready to forgive ;
  And rich in mercy, all that call
    Upon thee to relieve.

6 Hear, Lord, my pray'r : unto the voice
    Of my request attend.
7 In troublous times I'll call on thee ;
    For thou wilt answer send.

(103)   Psalm LXXXVI.   *St. Ann's.*

8 Lord, there is none among the gods
    That may with thee compare ;
  And like the works which thou hast done,
    Not any work is there.

9 All nations whom thou mad'st shall come
    And worship rev'rently
  Before thy face ; and they, O Lord,
    Thy name shall glorify.

10 Because thou art exceeding great,
    And works by thee are done
    Which are to be admired ; and thou
    Art God thyself alone.
11 Teach me thy way, and in thy truth,
    O Lord, then walk will I :
    Unite my heart, that I thy name
    May fear continually.

(104)   PSALM LXXXVI.   *London New.*

12 O LORD my God, with all my heart
    To thee I will give praise ;
    And I the glory will ascribe
    Unto thy name always :
13 Because thy mercy toward me
    In greatness doth excel ;
    And thou deliver'd hast my soul
    Out from the lowest hell.
15 For thou art full of pity, Lord ;
    A God most gracious,
    Long-suffering, and in thy truth
    And mercy plenteous.
16 O turn to me thy countenance,
    And mercy on me have :
    Thy servant strengthen, and the son
    Of thine own handmaid save.

(105)   PSALM LXXXVII.   *St. Lawrence.*

1 UPON the hills of holiness
    He his foundation sets.
2 God, more than Jacob's dwellings all,
    Delights in Sion's gates.
3 Things glorious are said of thee,
    Thou city of the Lord.

4 Rahab and Babel I, to those
    That know me, will record :
  Behold, ev'n Tyrus, and with it
    The land of Palestine,
  And likewise Ethiopia ;
    This man was born therein.

5 And it of Sion shall be said,
    This man and that man there
  Was born ; and he that is most High
    Himself shall stablish her.

6 When God the people writes, he'll count
    That this man was born there.
7 There be that sing and play ; and all
    My well-springs in thee are.

(106)   Psalm LXXXIX.   *St. David's.*

5 The praises of thy wonders, Lord,
    The heavens shall express ;
  And in the congregation
    Of saints thy faithfulness.

6 For who in heaven with the Lord
    May once himself compare ?
  Who is like God among the sons
    Of those that mighty are ?

7 Great fear in meeting of the saints
    Is due unto the Lord ;
  And he of all about him should
    With rev'rence be adored.

8 O thou that art the Lord of hosts,
    What Lord in mightiness
  Is like to thee, who compass'd round
    Art with thy faithfulness ?

(107)   PSALM LXXXIX.   *Manchester.*

11 THE heav'ns are thine; thou for thine own
   The earth dost also take :
   The world, and fulness of the same,
   Thy power did found and make.

12 The north and south from thee alone
   Their first beginning had :
   Both Tabor mount and Hermon hill
   Shall in thy name be glad.

13 Thou hast an arm that's full of power :
   Thy hand is great in might;
   And thy right hand exceedingly
   Exalted is in height.

14 Justice and judgment of thy throne
   Are made the dwelling-place :
   Mercy, accompany'd with truth,
   Shall go before thy face.

(108)   PSALM LXXXIX.   *St. Gregory.*

15 O GREATLY bless'd the people are
   The joyful sound that know :
   In brightness of thy face, O Lord,
   They ever on shall go.

16 They in thy name shall all the day
   Rejoice exceedingly;
   And in thy righteousness shall they
   Exalted be on high.

17 Because the glory of their strength
   Doth only stand in thee;
   And in thy favour shall our horn
   And power exalted be.

18 For God is our defence ; and he
    To us doth safety bring :
   The Holy One of Israel
    Is our almighty King.

(109)   Psalm XC.   *Jenkensdale.*

1 Lord, thou hast been our dwelling-place
    In generations all.
2 Before thou ever hadst brought forth
    The mountains great or small ;

   Ere ever thou hadst form'd the earth,
    And all the world abroad ;
   Even thou from everlasting art
    To everlasting God.

3 Thou dost unto destruction
    Man that is mortal turn ;
   And unto them thou say'st, Again,
    Ye sons of men, return.

4 Because a thousand years appear
    No more before thy sight
   Than yesterday, when it is past,
    Or than a watch by night.

(110)   Psalm XC.   *St. Neot's.*

5 As with an overflowing flood
    Thou carry'st them away :
   They like a sleep are, like the grass
    That grows at morn are they.

6 At morn it flourishes and grows :
    Cut down at ev'n doth fade.
7 For by thine anger we're consumed :
    Thy wrath makes us afraid.

8 Our sins thou and iniquities
   Dost in thy presence place,
And sett'st our secret faults before
   The brightness of thy face.
9 For in thine anger all our days
   Do pass on to an end;
And as a tale that hath been told,
   So we our years do spend.

(111)   Psalm XC.   *Huddersfield.*
11 Who knows the power of thy wrath!
   According to thy fear
12 So is thy wrath: Lord, teach thou us
   Our end in mind to bear;
And so to count our days, that we
   Our hearts may still apply
To learn thy wisdom and thy truth,
   That we may live thereby.
13 Turn yet again to us, O Lord,
   How long thus shall it be?
Let it repent thee now for those
   That servants are to thee.
14 O with thy tender mercies, Lord,
   Us early satisfy;
So we rejoice shall all our days,
   And still be glad in thee.

(112)   Psalm XC.   *St. Paul's.*
15 According as the days have been,
   Wherein we grief have had,
And years wherein we ill have seen,
   So do thou make us glad.
16 O let thy work and power appear
   Thy servants' face before;

And shew unto their children dear
   Thy glory evermore :
17 And let the beauty of the Lord
   Our God be us upon :
   Our handy-works establish thou,
   Establish them each one.

(113)   Psalm XCI.   *Old 8th.*

1 He that doth in the secret place
   Of the most High reside,
   Under the shade of him that is
   Th' Almighty shall abide.

2 I of the Lord my God will say,
   He is my refuge still :
   He is my fortress, and my God ;
   And in him trust I will.

3 Assuredly he shall thee save,
   And give deliverance
   From subtle fowler's snare, and from
   The noisome pestilence.

4 His feathers shall thee hide ; thy trust
   Under his wings shall be :
   His faithfulness shall be a shield
   And buckler unto thee.

(114)   Psalm XCII.   *Harrington.*

1 To render thanks unto the Lord
   It is a comely thing,
   And to thy name, O thou most High,
   Due praise aloud to sing.

2 Thy loving-kindness to shew forth
   When shines the morning light ;

And to declare thy faithfulness
With pleasure ev'ry night,

3 On a ten-stringed instrument,
Upon the psaltery,
And on the harp with solemn sound,
And grave sweet melody.

4 For thou, Lord, by thy mighty works
Hast made my heart right glad;
And I will triumph in the works
Which by thine hands were made.

(115) PSALM XCII. *Jackson's.*

9 FOR, lo, thine enemies, O Lord,
Thine en'mies perish shall:
The workers of iniquity
Shall be dispersed all.

12 But like the palm-tree flourishing
Shall be the righteous one:
He shall like to the cedar grow
That is in Lebanon.

13 Those that within the house of God
Are planted by his grace,
They shall grow up, and flourish all
In our God's holy place.

14 And in old age, when others fade,
They fruit still forth shall bring:
They shall be fat, and full of sap,
And aye be flourishing.

(116) PSALM XCIII. *Bromfield.*

1 THE Lord doth reign, and clothed is he
With majesty most bright:

His works do show him clothed to be,
  And girt about with might.
The world is also stablished,
  That it cannot depart.
2 Thy throne is fix'd of old, and thou
  From everlasting art.

3 The floods, O Lord, have lifted up,
  They lifted up their voice :
The floods have lifted up their waves,
  And made a mighty noise.

4 But yet the Lord, that is on high,
  Is more of might by far,
Than noise of many waters is,
  Or great sea-billows are.

5 Thy testimonies ev'ry one
  In faithfulness excel ;
And holiness for ever, Lord,
  Thine house becometh well.

(117)   PSALM XCIV.   *Farrant.*

11 Man's thoughts to be but vanity
  The Lord doth well discern.
12 Bless'd is the man thou chast'nest, Lord,
  And mak'st thy law to learn :
13 That thou may'st give him rest from days
  Of sad adversity,
Until the pit be digg'd for those
  That work iniquity.
14 For sure the Lord will not cast off
  Those that his people be ;
Neither his own inheritance
  Quit and forsake will he :

15 But judgment unto righteousness
　　Shall yet return again;
　　And all shall follow after it
　　That are right-hearted men.

(118)　　　　Psalm XCV.　　　Tiverton.

1 O COME, let us sing to the Lord:
　　Come, let us ev'ry one
　　A joyful noise make to the Rock
　　Of our salvation.

2 Let us before his presence come
　　With praise and thankful voice:
　　Let us sing psalms to him with grace,
　　And make a joyful noise.

3 For God, a great God, and great King,
　　Above all gods he is.
4 Depths of the earth are in his hand:
　　The strength of hills is his.

5 To him the spacious sea belongs,
　　For he the same did make:
　　The dry land also from his hands
　　Its form at first did take.

6 O come, and let us worship him:
　　Let us bow down withal,
　　And on our knees before the Lord
　　Our Maker let us fall.

(119)　　　　Psalm XCVI.　　　*St. Ann's New.*

1 O SING a new song to the Lord:
　　Sing all the earth to God.
2 To God sing, bless his name, shew still
　　His saving health abroad.

3 Among the heathen nations
   His glory do declare;
  And unto all the people shew
   His works that wondrous are.

4 For great's the Lord, and greatly he
   Is to be magnify'd;
  Yea, worthy to be fear'd is he
   Above all gods beside.

5 For all the gods are idols dumb,
   Which blinded nations fear;
  But our God is the Lord, by whom
   The heav'ns created were.

(120)   Psalm XCVI.   *St. Andrew's.*

6 GREAT honour is before his face,
   And majesty divine:
  Strength is within his holy place,
   And there doth beauty shine.

7 Do ye ascribe unto the Lord,
   Of people ev'ry tribe,
  Glory do ye unto the Lord,
   And mighty power ascribe.

8 Give ye the glory to the Lord
   That to his name is due:
  Come ye into his courts, and bring
   An offering with you.

9 In beauty of his holiness,
   O do the Lord adore:
  Likewise let all the earth throughout
   Tremble his face before.

(121)   Psalm XCVI.   *St. Thomas's.*

10 AMONG the heathen say, God reigns:
    The world shall stedfastly

Be fix'd from moving : he shall judge
    The people righteously.
11 Let heav'ns be glad before the Lord,
    And let the earth rejoice :
  Let seas, and all that is therein,
    Cry out, and make a noise.
12 Let fields rejoice, and ev'rything
    That springeth of the earth :
  Then woods and ev'ry tree shall sing
    With gladness and with mirth
13 Before the Lord ; because he comes,
    To judge the earth comes he :
  He 'll judge the world with righteousness,
    The people faithfully.

(122)   Psalm XCVII.   *Bedford.*

1 God reigneth, let the earth be glad,
    And isles rejoice each one.
2 Dark clouds him compass ; and in right
    With judgment dwells his throne.
6 The heav'ns declare his righteousness,
    All men his glory see.
7 All who serve graven images,
    Confounded let them be.

  Who do of idols boast themselves,
    Let shame upon them fall :
  Ye that are called gods, see that
    Ye do him worship all.
9 For thou, O Lord, art high above
    All things on earth that are :
  Above all other gods thou art
    Exalted very far.

(123)   Psalm XCVII.   *St. Lawrence.*

8 Sion did hear, and joyful was,
    Glad Judah's daughters were :
  They much rejoiced, O Lord, because
    Thy judgments did appear.

10 Hate ill, all ye that love the Lord :
    His saints' souls keepeth he;
  And from the hands of wicked men
    He sets them safe and free.

11 For all those that be righteous
    Sown is a joyful light;
  And gladness sown is for all those
    That are in heart upright.

12 Ye righteous, in the Lord rejoice :
    Express your thankfulness,
  When ye into your memory
    Do call his holiness.

(124)   Psalm XCVIII.   *Warwick.*

1 O sing a new song to the Lord,
    For wonders he hath done :
  His right hand and his holy arm
    Him victory hath won.

2 The Lord God his salvation
    Hath caused to be known :
  His justice in the heathen's sight
    He openly hath shown.

3 He mindful of his grace and truth
    To Isr'el's house hath been ;
  And the salvation of our God
    All ends of th' earth have seen.

(125)   Psalm XCVIII.   *Old* 137*th.*

4 LET all the earth unto the Lord
   Send forth a joyful noise :
   Lift up your voice aloud to him,
   Sing praises, and rejoice.

5 With harp, with harp, and voice of psalms,
   Unto JEHOVAH sing :
6 With trumpets, cornets, gladly sound
   Before the Lord the King.

7 Let seas and all their fulness roar ;
   The world, and dwellers there.
8 Let floods clap hands ; and let the hills
   Together joy declare

9 Before the Lord ; because he comes,
   To judge the earth comes he ;
   He'll judge the world with righteousness,
   His folk with equity.

(126)   Psalm XCIX.   *St. David's.*

1 TH' eternal Lord doth reign as king ;
   Let all the people quake :
   He sits between the cherubim ;
   Let th' earth be moved and shake.

2 The Lord in Sion great and high
   Above all people is :
3 Thy great and dreadful name (for it
   Is holy) let them bless.

4 The king's strength also judgment loves :
   Thou settlest equity :
   Just judgment thou dost execute
   In Jacob righteously.

5 The Lord our God exalt on high,
    And rev'rently do ye
  Before his footstool worship him :
    The Holy One is he.

(127)   PSALM XCIX.   *Durham.*

6 Moses and Aaron 'mong his priests ;
    Samuel, with them that call
  Upon his name : these call'd on God,
    And he them answer'd all.

7 Within the pillar of the cloud
    He unto them did speak :
  The testimonies he them taught,
    And laws, they did not break.

8 Thou answer'dst them, O Lord our God :
    Thou wast a God that gave
  Pardon to them, though on their deeds
    Thou wouldest vengeance have.

9 Do ye exalt the Lord our God,
    And at his holy hill
  Do ye him worship : for the Lord
    Our God is holy still.

(128)   PSALM C.   *Old 100th.*

1 ALL people that on earth do dwell,
  Sing to the Lord with cheerful voice.
2 Him serve with mirth, his praise forth tell :
  Come ye before him and rejoice.

3 Know that the Lord is God indeed :
  Without our aid he did us make :
  We are his flock ; he doth us feed,
  And for his sheep he doth us take.

4 O enter then his gates with praise :
Approach with joy his courts unto :
Praise, laud, and bless his name always ;
For it is seemly so to do.

5 For why ? the Lord our God is good ;
His mercy is for ever sure ;
His truth at all times firmly stood,
And shall from age to age endure.

(129)   Psalm CII.   *Soldau.*

1 LORD, hear my pray'r, and let my cry
Have speedy access unto thee.
2 In day of my calamity
O hide not thou thy face from me :

Hear when I call to thee : that day
An answer speedily return.
3 My days like smoke consume away,
And as an hearth my bones do burn.

11 My days are like a shade alway,
Which doth declining swiftly pass
And I am withered away,
Much like unto the fading grass.

12 But thou, O Lord, shalt still endure,
From change and all mutation free :
And to all generations sure
Shall thy remembrance ever be.

(130)   Psalm CII.   *Melcombe,* or *Doversdale.*

13 THOU shalt arise, and mercy yet
Thou to mount Sion shalt extend :
Her time for favour which was set,
Behold, is now come to an end.

14 Thy saints take pleasure in her stones;
    Her very dust to them is dear.
15 All heathen lands and kingly thrones
    On earth thy glorious name shall fear.
16 God in his glory shall appear,
    When Sion he builds and repairs.
17 He shall regard and lend his ear
    Unto the needy's humble pray'rs:
    Th' afflicted's pray'r he will not scorn.
18 All times this shall be on record:
    And generations yet unborn
    Shall praise and magnify the Lord.

(131)   Psalm CII.   *Norwich,* or *St. Pancras.*

19 He from his holy place look'd down,
    The earth he view'd from heav'n on high,
20 To hear the pris'ner's mourning groan,
    And free them that are doom'd to die;
21 That Sion, and Jerus'lem too,
    His name and praise may well record,
22 When people and the kingdoms do
    Assemble all to praise the Lord.

(132)   Psalm CII.   *Hamburgh.*

23 My strength he weaken'd in the way;
    My days of life he shortened.
24 My God, O take me not away
    In mid-time of my days, I said.
    Thy years throughout all ages last.
25 Of old thou hast established
    The earth's foundation firm and fast:
    Thy mighty hands the heav'ns have made.
26 They perish shall as garments do,
    But thou shalt evermore endure:

As vestures, thou shalt change them so ;
And they shall all be changed sure :
27 But from all changes thou art free ;
Thy endless years do last for aye.
28 Thy servants, and their seed who be,
Establish'd shall before thee stay.

(133)   PSALM CIII.   *Lord Mornington's Chant.*

1 O THOU my soul, bless God the Lord ;
And all that in me is
Be stirred up his holy name
To magnify and bless.

2 Bless, O my soul, the Lord thy God,
And not forgetful be
Of all his gracious benefits
He hath bestow'd on thee.

3 All thine iniquities who doth
Most graciously forgive :
Who thy diseases all and pains
Doth heal, and thee relieve :

4 Who doth redeem thy life, that thou
To death may'st not go down :
Who thee with loving-kindness doth
And tender mercies crown :

5 Who with abundance of good things
Doth satisfy thy mouth ;
So that, ev'n as the eagle's age
Renewed is thy youth.

6 God righteous judgment executes
For all oppressed ones.
7 His ways to Moses, he his acts
Made known to Isr'el's sons.

(134)   Psalm CIII.   *French.*

  8 The Lord our God is merciful,
      And he is gracious,
    Long-suffering, and slow to wrath,
      In mercy plenteous.

  9 He will not chide continually,
      Nor keep his anger still.
10 With us he dealt not as we sinn'd,
      Nor did requite our ill.

11 For as the heaven in its height
      The earth surmounteth far;
    So great to those that do him fear
      His tender mercies are.

12 As far as east is distant from
      The west, so far hath he
    From us removed, in his love,
      All our iniquity.

(135)   Psalm CIII.   *St. Paul's.*

13 Such pity as a father hath
      Unto his children dear;
    Like pity shews the Lord to such
      As worship him in fear.

14 For he remembers we are dust,
      And he our frame well knows.
15 Frail man, his days are like the grass,
      As flower in field he grows.

16 For over it the wind doth pass,
      And it away is gone;
    And of the place where once it was
      It shall no more be known.

17 But unto them that do him fear
   God's mercy never ends;
   And to their children's children still
   His righteousness extends:
18 To such as keep his covenant,
   And mindful are alway
   Of his most just commandements,
   That they may them obey.

(136)　　　Psalm CIII.　　　*Sheffield.*
19 The Lord prepared hath his throne
   In heavens firm to stand;
   And ev'ry thing that being hath
   His kingdom doth command.
20 O ye his angels, that excel
   In strength, bless ye the Lord;
   Ye who obey what he commands,
   And hearken to his word.
21 O bless and magnify the Lord,
   Ye glorious hosts of his;
   Ye ministers, that do fulfil
   Whate'er his pleasure is.
22 O bless the Lord, all ye his works,
   Wherewith the world is stored
   In his dominions ev'ry where.
   My soul, bless thou the Lord.

(137)　　　Psalm CIV.　　　*St. Gregory.*
31 The glory of the mighty Lord
   Continue shall for ever:
   The Lord Jehovah shall rejoice
   In all his works together.
33 I will sing to the Lord most high,
   So long as I shall live;

And while I being have I shall
    To my God praises give.
34 Of him my meditation shall
    Sweet thoughts to me afford ;
  And as for me, I will rejoice
    In God, my only Lord.
35 From earth, let sinners be consumed ;
    Let ill men no more be.
  O thou my soul, bless thou the Lord.
    Praise to the Lord give ye.

(138)   PSALM CV.   *Glasgow.*
1 GIVE thanks to God, call on his name :
    To men his deeds make known.
2 Sing ye to him, sing psalms : proclaim
    His wondrous works each one.
3 See that ye in his holy name
    To glory do accord ;
  And let the heart of ev'ry one
    Rejoice that seeks the Lord.
4 The Lord Almighty, and his strength,
    With stedfast hearts seek ye :
  His blessed and his gracious face
    Seek ye continually.
7 Because he, and he only, is
    The mighty Lord our God ;
  And his most righteous judgments are
    In all the earth abroad.

(139)   PSALM CVI.   *St. Magnus.*
1 GIVE praise and thanks unto the Lord,
    For bountiful is he :
  His tender mercy doth endure
    Unto eternity.

2 God's mighty works who can express?
   Or shew forth all his praise?
3 Blessed are they that judgment keep,
   And justly do always.

4 Remember me, Lord, with that love
   Which thou to thine dost bear;
   With thy salvation, O my God,
   To visit me draw near:
5 That I thy chosen's good may see,
   And in their joy rejoice;
   And may with thine inheritance
   Triumph with cheerful voice.

(140)   PSALM CVII.   *Harrington.*
1 PRAISE God, for he is good : for still
   His mercies lasting be.
2 Let God's redeem'd say so, whom he
   From th' en'my's hand did free;
3 And gather'd them out of the lands,
   From north, south, east, and west.
4 They stray'd in desert's pathless way,
   No city found to rest.
5 For thirst and hunger in them faints
6   Their soul. When straits them press,
   They cry unto the Lord, and he
   Them frees from their distress.

7 Them also in a way to walk
   That right is he did guide,
   That they might to a city go,
   Wherein they might abide.

(141)   PSALM CVII.   *Tiverton.*
8 O THAT men to the Lord would give
   Praise for his goodness then,

And for his works of wonder done
   Unto the sons of men!

9 For he the soul that longing is
   Doth fully satisfy:
  With goodness he the hungry soul
   Doth fill abundantly.

21 O that men to the Lord would give
    Praise for his goodness then,
   And for his works of wonder done
    Unto the sons of men!

22 And let them sacrifice to him
    Off'rings of thankfulness;
   And let them shew abroad his works
    In songs of joyfulness.

(142)   Psalm CVII.   *London New.*

40 He upon princes pours contempt,
    And causeth them to stray,
   And wander in a wilderness,
    Wherein there is no way.

41 Yet setteth he the poor on high
    From all his miseries,
   And he, much like unto a flock,
    Doth make him families.

42 They that are righteous shall rejoice,
    When they the same shall see;
   And, as ashamed, stop her mouth,
    Shall all iniquity.

43 Whoso is wise, and will these things
    Observe, and them record,
   Ev'n they shall understand the love
    And kindness of the Lord.

(143)   Psalm CVIII.   *Old* 23*d*.

1 My heart is fix'd, Lord ; I will sing,
   And with my glory praise.
2 Awake up psaltery and harp ;
   Myself I 'll early raise.

3 I 'll praise thee 'mong the people, Lord ;
   'Mong nations sing will I :
4 For above heav'n thy mercy's great,
   Thy truth doth reach the sky.

5 Be thou above the heavens, Lord,
   Exalted gloriously ;
   Thy glory all the earth above
   Be lifted up on high ;

6 That those who thy beloved are
   Delivered may be :
   O do thou save with thy right hand,
   And answer give to me.

(144)   Psalm CX.   *Old* 68*th*.

1 The Lord did say unto my Lord,
   Sit thou at my right hand,
   Until I make thy foes a stool,
   Whereon thy feet may stand.

2 The Lord shall out of Sion send
   The rod of thy great power :
   In midst of all thine enemies
   Be thou the governor.

3 A willing people in thy day
   Of power shall come to thee :
   In holy beauties from morn's womb,
   Thy youth like dew shall be.

4 The Lord himself hath made an oath,
       And will repent him never;
    Of th' order of Melchisedec
       Thou art a priest for ever.

(145)   Psalm CXI.   *Newington.*
  1 Praise ye the Lord : with my whole heart
       I will God's praise declare,
    Where the assemblies of the just
       And congregations are.
  2 The whole works of the Lord our God
       Are great above all measure ;
    Sought out they are of ev'ry one
       That doth therein take pleasure.
  3 His work most honourable is,
       Most glorious and pure ;
    And his untainted righteousness
       For ever doth endure.
  4 His works most wonderful he hath
       Made to be thought upon :
    The Lord is gracious, and he is
       Full of compassion.

(146)   Psalm CXI.   *York.*
  5 He giveth meat unto all those
       That truly do him fear ;
    And evermore his covenant
       He in his mind will bear.
  7 His handy-works are truth and right :
       All his commands are sure :
  8 And, done in truth and uprightness,
       They evermore endure.
  9 He sent redemption to his folk :
       His covenant for aye

He did command : holy his name
And rev'rend is alway.
10 Wisdom's beginning is God's fear :
Good understanding they
Have all, that his commands fulfil :
His praise endures for aye.

(147) PSALM CXII. *St. Andrews.*

1 PRAISE ye the Lord. The man is bless'd
That fears the Lord aright,
He who in his commandements
Doth greatly take delight.

4 Unto the upright light doth rise,
Though he in darkness be :
Compassionate, and merciful,
And righteous is he.

6 Surely there is not any thing
That ever shall him move :
The righteous man's memorial
Shall everlasting prove.

9 He hath dispersed, giv'n to the poor :
His righteousness shall be
To ages all : with honour shall
His horn be raised high.

(148) PSALM CXIII. *St. Thomas's.*

1 PRAISE God : ye servants of the Lord,
O praise, the Lord's name praise.
2 Yea, blessed be the name of God
From this time forth always.

3 From rising sun to where it sets,
God's name is to be praised.
4 Above all nations God is high :
'Bove heav'ns his glory raised.

5 Unto the Lord our God that dwells
   On high, who can compare?
6 Himself that humbleth things to see
   In heaven and earth that are.

7 He from the dust doth raise the poor,
   That very low doth lie;
   And from the dunghill lifts the man
   Oppress'd with poverty.

9 The barren woman house to keep
   He maketh, and to be
   Of sons a mother full of joy.
   Praise to the Lord give ye.

(149)   Psalm CXV.   *Dunfermline.*

1 Not unto us, Lord, not to us,
   But do thou glory take
   Unto thy name, ev'n for thy truth,
   And for thy mercy's sake.

2 O wherefore should the heathen say,
   Where is their God now gone?
3 But our God in the heavens is:
   What pleased him he hath done.

4 Their idols silver are and gold,
   Work of men's hands they be.
5 Mouths have they, but they do not speak;
   And eyes, but do not see.

8 Like them their makers are, and all
   On them their trust that build.
9 O Isr'el, trust thou in the Lord:
   He is their help and shield.

10 O Aaron's house, trust in the Lord:
    Their help and shield is he.
11 Ye that fear God, trust in the Lord:
    Their help and shield he'll be.

(150)   Psalm CXV.   *St. Matthew's.*

12 The Lord of us hath mindful been,
    And he will bless us still:
    He will the house of Isr'el bless,
    Bless Aaron's house he will.
13 Both small and great, that fear the Lord,
    He will them surely bless.
14 The Lord will you, you and your seed,
    Aye more and more increase.
15 O blessed are ye of the Lord,
    Who made the earth and heav'n.
16 The heav'n, ev'n heav'ns, are God's, but he
    Earth to men's sons hath giv'n.
17 The dead, nor who to silence go,
    God's praise do not record.
18 But henceforth we for ever will
    Bless God.   Praise ye the Lord.

(151)   Psalm CXVI.   *Handel's Chant.*

1 I LOVE the Lord, because my voice
    And prayers he did hear.
2 I, while I live, will call on him,
    Who bow'd to me his ear.
3 Of death the cords and sorrows did
    About me compass round:
    The pains of hell took hold on me:
    I grief and trouble found.
4 Upon the name of God the Lord
    Then did I call, and say,
    Deliver thou my soul, O Lord,
    I do thee humbly pray.
5 God merciful and righteous is;
    Yea, gracious is our Lord.

6 God saves the meek : I was brought low,
   He did me help afford.
7 O thou my soul, do thou return
   Unto thy quiet rest;
For, largely, lo, the Lord to thee
   His bounty hath exprest.
8 For my distressed soul from death
   Deliver'd was by thee :
Thou didst my mourning eyes from tears,
   My feet from falling, free.

(152)   Psalm CXVI.   *Jenkensdale.*

13 I'll of salvation take the cup,
   On God's name will I call.
14 I'll pay my vows now to the Lord
   Before his people all.
15 Dear in God's sight is his saints' death.
16   Thy servant, Lord, am I ;
Thy servant sure, thine handmaid's son :
   My bands thou didst untie.
17 Thank-off'rings I to thee will give,
   And on God's name will call.
18 I'll pay my vows now to the Lord
   Before his people all ;
19 Within the courts of God's own house,
   Within the midst of thee,
   O city of Jerusalem.
   Praise to the Lord give ye.

(153)   Psalm CXVII.   *Peterborough.*

1 O give ye praise unto the Lord,
   All nations that be ;
Likewise, ye people all, accord
   His name to magnify.

2 For great to us-ward ever are
His loving-kindnesses :
His truth endures for evermore.
The Lord O do ye bless.

(154)   Psalm CXVIII.   *Tiverton.*

1 O PRAISE the Lord, for he is good;
His mercy lasteth ever.
2 Let those of Israel now say,
His mercy faileth never.

3 Now let the house of Aaron say,
His mercy lasteth ever.
4 Let those that fear the Lord now say,
His mercy faileth never.

5 I in distress call'd on the Lord ;
The Lord did answer me :
He in a large place did me set,
From trouble made me free.

6 The mighty Lord is on my side,
I will not be afraid :
For any thing that man can do
I shall not be dismay'd.

(155)   Psalm CXVIII.   *St. Gregory.*

15 IN dwellings of the righteous
Is heard the melody
Of joy and health : the Lord's right hand
Doth ever valiantly.

16 The right hand of the mighty Lord
Exalted is on high :
The right hand of the mighty Lord
Doth ever valiantly.

17 I shall not die, but live, and shall
    The works of God discover.
18 The Lord hath me chastised sore,
    But not to death giv'n over.
19 O set ye open unto me
    The gates of righteousness :
    Then will I enter into them,
    And I the Lord will bless.

(156)   Psalm CXVIII.   *St. Andrew's.*
24 This is the day God made, in it
    We 'll joy triumphantly.
25 Save now, I pray thee, Lord : I pray,
    Send now prosperity.
26 Blessed is he in God's great name
    That cometh us to save :
    We, from the house which to the Lord
    Pertains, you blessed have.
27 God is the Lord, who unto us
    Hath made light to arise :
    Bind ye unto the altar's horns
    With cords the sacrifice.
28 Thou art my God, I 'll thee exalt :
    My God, I will thee praise.
29 Give thanks to God, for he is good :
    His mercy lasts always.

(157)   Psalm CXIX.   *St. Stephen's.*
1 Blessed are they that undefiled,
    And straight are in the way ;
    Who in the Lord's most holy law
    Do walk, and do not stray.
2 Blessed are they who to observe
    His statutes are inclined ;

And who do seek the living God
    With their whole heart and mind.
3 Such in his ways do walk, and they
    Do no iniquity.
4 Thou hast commanded us to keep
    Thy precepts carefully.
5 O that thy statutes to observe
    Thou wouldst my ways direct!
6 Then shall I not be shamed, when I
    Thy precepts all respect.

(158)   PSALM CXIX.   *St. Paul's.*
11 THY word I in my heart have hid,
    That I offend not thee.
12 O Lord, thou ever blessed art:
    Thy statutes teach thou me.
13 The judgments of thy mouth each one
    My lips declared have.
14 More joy thy testimonies' way
    Than riches all me gave.
15 I will thy holy precepts make
    My meditation;
    And carefully I'll have respect
    Unto thy ways each one.
16 Upon thy statutes my delight
    Shall constantly be set:
    And, by thy grace, I never will
    Thy holy word forget.

(159)   PSALM CXIX.   *Farrant.*
17 WITH me thy servant, in thy grace,
    Deal bountifully, Lord;
    That by thy favour I may live,
    And duly keep thy word.

18 Open mine eyes, that of thy law
   The wonders I may see.
 I am a stranger on this earth :
   Hide not thy laws from me.
20 My soul within me breaks, and doth
   Much fainting still endure,
 Through longing that it hath all times
   Unto thy judgments pure.
24 My comfort, and my heart's delight,
   Thy testimonies be ;
 And they, in all my doubts and fears,
   Are counsellors to me.

(160)   PSALM CXIX.   *London New.*
25 My soul to dust cleaves : quicken me,
   According to thy word.
26 My ways I shew'd, and me thou heard'st :
   Teach me thy statutes, Lord.
27 The way of thy commandements
   Make me aright to know ;
 So all thy works that wondrous are
   I shall to others show.
30 I chosen have the perfect way
   Of truth and verity :
 Thy judgments that most righteous are
   Before me laid have I.

(161)   PSALM CXIX.   *Sheffield.*
33 TEACH me, O Lord, the perfect way
   Of thy precepts divine ;
 And to observe it to the end
   I shall my heart incline.
34 Give understanding unto me,
   So keep thy law shall I ;

Yea, ev'n with my whole heart I shall
Observe it carefully.
35 In thy law's path make me to go;
For I delight therein.
36 My heart unto thy testimonies,
And not to greed, incline.
37 Turn thou away my sight and eyes
From viewing vanity;
And in thy good and holy way
Be pleased to quicken me.

(162) Psalm CXIX. *Durham.*

57 Thou my sure portion art alone,
Which I did choose, O Lord:
I have resolved, and said, that I
Would keep thy holy word.
58 With my whole heart I did entreat
Thy face and favour free:
According to thy gracious word
Be merciful to me.
59 I thought upon my former ways,
And did my life well try;
And to thy testimonies pure
My feet then turned I.
60 I did not stay, nor linger long,
As those that slothful are;
But hastily thy laws to keep
Myself I did prepare.

(163) Psalm CXIX. *Old 8th.*

65 Well hast thou with thy servant dealt,
As thou didst promise give.
66 Good judgment me, and knowledge teach;
For I thy word believe.

67 Ere I afflicted was I stray'd;
    But now I keep thy word.
    Both good thou art, and good thou dost:
    Teach me thy statutes, Lord.

71 It hath been very good for me
    That I afflicted was;
    That I might well instructed be,
    And learn thy holy laws.

75 That very right thy judgments are,
    I know, and do confess;
    And that thou hast afflicted me
    In truth and faithfulness.

(164)   PSALM CXIX.   *St. Ann's.*

89 THY word for ever is, O Lord,
    In heaven settled fast:
90 Unto all generations,
    Thy faithfulness doth last.

    The earth thou hast established,
    And it abides by thee.
91 This day they stand as thou ordain'dst;
    For all thy servants be.

92 Unless in thy most perfect law
    My soul delights had found,
    I should have perished, when as
    My troubles did abound.

93 Thy precepts I will ne'er forget:
    They quick'ning to me brought.
94 Lord, I am thine; O save thou me:
    Thy precepts I have sought.

(165)   PSALM CXIX.   *Solomon.*

97 O how love I thy law! it is
    My study all the day:

98 It makes me wiser than my foes;
    For it doth with me stay.
99 Than all my teachers now I have
    More understanding far;
    Because my meditation
    Thy testimonies are.

101 My feet from each ill way I stay'd,
    That I may keep thy word.
102 I from thy judgments have not swerved;
    For thou hast taught me, Lord.

103 How sweet unto my taste, O Lord,
    Are all thy words of truth!
    Yea, I do find them sweeter far
    Than honey to my mouth.

(166)   Psalm CXIX.   *Old* 68*th.*

129 Thy statutes, Lord, are wonderful:
    My soul them keeps with care.
130 The entrance of thy words gives light;
    Makes wise who simple are.

131 My mouth I have wide opened,
    And panted earnestly,
    While after thy commandements
    I long'd exceedingly.

132 Look on me, Lord, and merciful
    Do thou unto me prove,
    As thou art wont to do to those
    Thy name who truly love.

133 O let my footsteps in thy word
    Aright still order'd be:
    Let no iniquity obtain
    Dominion over me.

(167)   PSALM CXIX.   *Manchester.*

164 SEV'N times a day it is my care
    To give due praise to thee;
Because of all thy judgments, Lord,
    Which righteous ever be.

165 Great peace have they who love thy law:
    Offence they shall have none.
166 I hoped for thy salvation, Lord,
    And thy commands have done.

167 My soul thy testimonies pure
    Observèd carefully:
On them my heart is set, and them
    I love exceedingly.

(168)   PSALM CXIX.   *Farrant.*

169 O LET my earnest pray'r and cry
    Come near before thee, Lord:
Give understanding unto me,
    According to thy word.

170 Let my request before thee come:
    After thy word me free.
171 My lips shall utter praise, when thou
    Hast taught thy laws to me.

172 My tongue of thy most blessed word
    Shall speak, and it confess;
Because all thy commandements
    Are perfect righteousness.

(169)   PSALM CXIX.   *Huddersfield.*

173 LET thy strong hand make help to me:
    Thy precepts are my choice.
174 I long'd for thy salvation, Lord;
    And in thy law rejoice.

175 O let my soul live, and it shall
Give praises unto thee;
And let thy judgments gracious
Be helpful unto me.

176 I, like a lost sheep, went astray;
Thy servant seek, and find :
For thy commands I suffer'd not
To slip out of my mind.

(170)   Psalm CXXI.   *French.*

1 I to the hills will lift mine eyes,
From whence doth come mine aid:
2 My safety cometh from the Lord,
Who heav'n and earth hath made.

3 Thy foot he'll not let slide, nor will
He slumber that thee keeps.
4 Behold, he that keeps Israel,
He slumbers not, nor sleeps.

5 The Lord thee keeps: the Lord thy shade
On thy right hand doth stay.
6 The moon by night thee shall not smite,
Nor yet the sun by day.

7 The Lord shall keep thy soul : he shall
Preserve thee from all ill.
8 Henceforth thy going out and in
God keep for ever will.

(171)   Psalm CXXII.   *St. Stephen's.*

1 I joy'd when to the house of God,
Go up, they said to me.
2 Jerusalem, within thy gates
Our feet shall standing be.

6 Pray that Jerusalem may have
    Peace and felicity:
  Let them that love thee and thy peace
    Have still prosperity.

7 Therefore I wish that peace may still
    Within thy walls remain;
  And ever may thy palaces
    Prosperity retain.

8 Now, for my friends' and brethren's sakes,
    Peace be in thee, I'll say.
9 And for the house of God our Lord,
    I'll seek thy good alway.

(172)   Psalm CXXIV.   *Old* 124*th.*

1 Now Israel
    May say, and that truly,
  If that the Lord
    Had not our cause maintain'd;
2 If that the Lord
    Had not our right sustain'd,
  When cruel men
    Against us furiously
  Rose up in wrath,
    To make of us their prey;

3 Then certainly
    They had devour'd us all,
  And swallow'd quick,
    For aught that we could deem:
  Such was their rage,
    As we might well esteem.
4 And as fierce floods
    Before them all things drown,
  So had they brought
    Our soul to death quite down.

5 The raging streams,
　　With their proud swelling waves,
　Had then our soul
　　O'erwhelmed in the deep.
6 But bless'd be God,
　　Who doth us safely keep,
　And hath not giv'n
　　Us for a living prey
　Unto their teeth,
　　And bloody cruelty.
7 Ev'n as a bird
　　Out of the fowler's snare
　Escapes away,
　　So is our soul set free :
　Broke are their nets,
　　And thus escaped we.
8 Therefore our help
　　Is in the Lord's great name,
　Who heav'n and earth
　　By his great power did frame.

(173)　　　　　　Psalm CXXV.　　　*St. Gregory.*

1 They in the Lord that firmly trust
　　Shall be like Sion hill,
　Which at no time can be removed,
　　But standeth ever still.

2 As round about Jerusalem
　　The mountains stand alway,
　The Lord his folk doth compass so,
　　From henceforth and for aye.

3 For ill men's rod upon the lot
　　Of just men shall not lie ;
　Lest righteous men stretch forth their hands
　　Unto iniquity.

4 Do thou to all those that be good
 Thy goodness, Lord, impart;
 And do thou good to those that are
 Upright within their heart.

(174)   Psalm CXXVI.   *Comfort.*

1 When Sion's bondage God turn'd back,
 As men that dream'd were we.
2 Then fill'd with laughter was our mouth,
 Our tongue with melody :
 They 'mong the heathen said, The Lord
 Great things for them hath wrought.
3 The Lord hath done great things for us,
 Whence joy to us is brought.
4 As streams of water in the south,
 Our bondage, Lord, recall.
5 Who sow in tears, a reaping time
 Of joy enjoy they shall.
6 That man who, bearing precious seed,
 In going forth doth mourn,
 He doubtless, bringing back his sheaves,
 Rejoicing shall return.

(175)   Psalm CXXVIII.   *Sheffield.*

1 Bless'd is each one that fears the Lord,
 And walketh in his ways.
2 For of thy labour thou shalt eat,
 And happy be always.
3 Thy wife shall as a fruitful vine
 By thy house' sides be found :
 Thy children like to olive-plants
 About thy table round.
4 Behold, the man that fears the Lord,
 Thus blessed shall he be.

5 The Lord shall out of Sion give
    His blessing unto thee :
  Thou shalt Jerus'lem's good behold
    Whilst thou on earth dost dwell.
6 Thou shalt thy children's children see,
    And peace on Israel.

(176)   PSALM CXXX.   *St. Mary's.*
1 LORD, from the depths to thee I cry'd.
2   My voice, Lord, do thou hear :
  Unto my supplication's voice
    Give an attentive ear.
3 Lord, who shall stand, if thou, O Lord,
    Shouldst mark iniquity ?
4 But yet with thee forgiveness is,
    That fear'd thou mayest be.
5 I wait for God, my soul doth wait,
    My hope is in his word.
6 More than they that for morning watch,
    My soul waits for the Lord :
  I say, more than they that do watch,
    The morning light to see.
7 Let Israel hope in the Lord,
    For with him mercies be ;
  And plenteous redemption
    Is ever found with him.
8 And from all his iniquities
    He Isr'el shall redeem.

(177)   PSALM CXXXI.   *Huddersfield.*
1 My heart not haughty is, O Lord,
    Mine eyes not lofty be ;
  Nor do I deal in matters great,
    Or things too high for me.

PSALMS. 261

   2 I surely have myself behaved
      With quiet sp'rit and mild,
     As child of mother wéan'd : my soul
      Is like a weaned child.
   3 Upon the Lord let all the hope
      Of Israel rely,
     Ev'n from the time that present is
      Unto eternity.

(178)   PSALM CXXXII.   *Lancaster.*
   7 WE'LL go into his tabernacles,
      And at his footstool bow.
   8 Arise, O Lord, into thy rest,
      Th' ark of thy strength, and thou.
   9 O let thy priests be clothed, Lord,
      With truth and righteousness;
     And let all those that are thy saints
      Shout loud for joyfulness.
 13 For God of Sion hath made choice;
      There he desires to dwell.
 14 This is my rest, here still I'll stay;
      For I do like it well.
 15 Her food I'll greatly bless; her poor
      With bread will satisfy.
 16 Her priests I'll clothe with health: her saints
      Shall shout forth joyfully.

(179)   PSALM CXXXIII.   *Irish.*
   1 BEHOLD, how good a thing it is,
      And how becoming well,
     Together such as brethren are
      In unity to dwell!
   2 Like precious ointment on the head,
      That down the beard did flow,

Ev'n Aaron's beard, and to the skirts
Did of his garments go.
3 As Hermon's dew, the dew that doth
On Sion' hills descend :
For there the blessing God commands,
Life that shall never end.

(180)   Psalm CXXXIV.   *St. Magnus.*

1 BEHOLD, bless ye the Lord, all ye
That his attendants are,
Ev'n you that in God's temple be,
And praise him nightly there.

2 Your hands within God's holy place
Lift up, and praise his name.
3 From Sion' hill the Lord thee bless,
That heaven and earth did frame.

(181)   Psalm CXXXVI.   *Berlin,* or *Handel's Chant.*

1 GIVE thanks to God, for good is he :
For mercy hath he ever.
2 Thanks to the God of gods give ye :
For his grace faileth never.
3 Thanks give the Lord of lords unto :
For mercy hath he ever.
4 Who only wonders great can do :
For his grace faileth never.
5 Who by his wisdom made heav'ns high :
For mercy hath he ever.
6 Who stretch'd the earth above the sea :
For his grace faileth never.
7 To him that made the great lights shine
For mercy hath he ever.

8 The sun to rule till day decline :
    For his grace faileth never.
23 In our low state who on us thought :
    For he hath mercy ever.
24 And from our foes our freedom wrought :
    For his grace faileth never.
25 Who doth all flesh with food relieve :
    For he hath mercy ever.
26 Thanks to the God of heaven give :
    For his grace faileth never.

(182)   Psalm CXXXVI.   *Old* 136*th*.

1 Praise God, for he is kind :
    His mercy lasts for aye.
2 Give thanks with heart and mind
    To God of gods alway :
        For certainly
          His mercies dure
            Most firm and sure
        Eternally.
3 The Lord of lords praise ye,
    Whose mercies still endure.
4 Great wonders only he
    Doth work by his great power :
        For certainly, *&c.*

7 Great lights he made to be ;
    For his grace lasteth aye :
8 Such as the sun we see,
    To rule the lightsome day :
        For certainly, *&c.*

9 Also the moon so clear,
    Which shineth in our sight ;

  The stars that do appear,
  To guide the darksome night :
   For certainly, &c.

25 Who to all flesh gives food ;
  For his grace faileth never.
26 Give thanks to God most good,
  The God of heav'n, for ever :
   For certainly, &c.

(183)   Psalm CXXXVIII.   *Newington.*

1 THEE will I praise with all my heart :
  I will sing praise to thee
2 Before the gods ; and worship will
  Toward thy sanctuary.

 I 'll praise thy name, ev'n for thy truth,
  And kindness of thy love ;
 For thou thy word hast magnify'd
  All thy great name above.

3 Thou didst me answer in the day
  When I to thee did cry ;
 And thou my fainting soul with strength
  Didst strengthen inwardly.

4 All kings upon the earth that are
  Shall give thee praise, O Lord ;
 When as they from thy mouth shall hear
  Thy true and faithful word.

(184)   Psalm CXXXVIII.   *Manchester.*

6 THOUGH God be high, yet he respects
  All those that lowly be ;
 Whereas the proud and lofty ones
  Afar off knoweth he.

7 Though I in midst of trouble walk,
   I life from thee shall have :
 'Gainst my foes' wrath thou 'lt stretch thine
   Thy right hand shall me save.   [hand :

8 Surely that which concerneth me
   The Lord will perfect make :
 Lord, still thy mercy lasts; do not
   Thine own hands' works forsake.

(185)   Psalm CXXXIX.   *Old* 68*th.*

1 O Lord, thou hast me search'd and known.
2   Thou know'st my sitting down,
   And rising up; yea, all my thoughts
     Afar to thee are known.

3 My footsteps, and my lying down,
   Thou compassest always ;
 Thou also most entirely art
   Acquaint with all my ways.

4 For in my tongue, before I speak,
   Not any word can be,
 But altogether, lo, O Lord,
   It is well known to thee.

5 Behind, before, thou hast beset,
   And laid on me thine hand.
6 Such knowledge is too strange for me,
   Too high to understand.

(186)   Psalm CXXXIX.   *Old* 8*th.*

7 From thy Sp'rit whither shall I go ?
   Or from thy presence fly ?
8 Ascend I heav'n, lo, thou art there ;
   There, if in hell I lie.

9 Take I the morning wings, and dwell
     In utmost parts of sea;
10 Ev'n there, Lord, shall thy hand me lead,
     Thy right hand hold shall me.
11 If I do say that darkness shall
     Me cover from thy sight;
   Then surely shall the very night
     About me be as light.
12 Yea, darkness hideth not from thee,
     But night doth shine as day:
   To thee the darkness and the light
     Are both alike alway.

(187)   Psalm CXXXIX.   *St. David's.*

14 THEE will I praise; for fearfully
     And strangely made I am:
   Thy works are marv'llous, and right well
     My soul doth know the same.
17 How precious also are thy thoughts,
     O gracious God, to me!
   And in their sum how passing great
     And numberless they be!
18 If I should count them, than the sand
     They more in number be:
   What time soever I awake,
     I ever am with thee.

(188)   Psalm CXLI.   *Huddersfield.*

 1 O LORD, I unto thee do cry;
     Do thou make haste to me,
   And give an ear unto my voice,
     When I cry unto thee.

2 As incense let my prayer be
   Directed in thine eyes;
  And the uplifting of my hands
   As th' ev'ning sacrifice.
3 Set, Lord, a watch before my mouth:
   Keep of my lips the door.
4 My heart incline thou not unto
   The ill I should abhor,
  To practise wicked works with men
   That work iniquity;
  And with their delicates my taste
   Let me not satisfy.

(189)   Psalm CXLIII.   *St. Mary's.*

1 Lord, hear my pray'r, attend my suits;
   And in thy faithfulness
  Give thou an answer unto me,
   And in thy righteousness.
2 Thy servant also bring thou not
   In judgment to be try'd:
  Because no living man can be
   In thy sight justify'd.
10 Because thou art my God, to do
   Thy will do me instruct:
  Thy Sp'rit is good; me to the land
   Of uprightness conduct.
11 Revive and quicken me, O Lord,
   Ev'n for thine own name's sake;
  And do thou, for thy righteousness,
   My soul from trouble take.

(190)   Psalm CXLIII.   *St. Neot's.*

5 I call to mind the days of old:
   To meditate I use

On all thy works ; upon the deeds
I of thy hands do muse.

6 My hands to thee I stretch : my soul
Thirsts, as dry land, for thee.
7 Haste, Lord, to hear ; my spirit fails :
Hide not thy face from me ;

Lest like to them I do become
That go down to the dust.
8 At morn let me thy kindness hear ;
For in thee do I trust.

Teach me the way that I should walk :
I lift my soul to thee.
9 Lord, free me from my foes : I flee
To thee to cover me.

(191) PSALM CXLIII. *St. Columba.*

1 OH, hear my prayer, Lord,
And unto my desire
To bow thine ear accord,
I humbly thee require ;
And, in thy faithfulness,
Unto me answer make,
And, in thy righteousness,
Upon me pity take.

2 In judgment enter not
With me thy servant poor ;
For why, this well I wot,
No sinner can endure
The sight of thee, O God :
If thou his deeds shalt try,
He dare make none abode
Himself to justify.

7 Lord, let my pray'r prevail,
  To answer it make speed;
  For, lo, my sp'rit doth fail:
  Hide not thy face in need;
  Lest I be like to those
  That do in darkness sit,
  Or him that downward goes
  Into the dreadful pit.

8 Because I trust in thee,
  O Lord, cause me to hear
  Thy loving-kindness free,
  When morning doth appear:
  Cause me to know the way
  Wherein my path should be;
  For why, my soul on high
  I do lift up to thee.

(192) PSALM CXLV. *Green's 145th.*

1 O LORD, thou art my God and King;
  Thee will I magnify and praise:
  I will thee bless, and gladly sing
  Unto thy holy name always.

2 Each day I rise I will thee bless,
  And praise thy name time without end.
3 Much to be praised, and great God is;
  His greatness none can comprehend.

4 Race shall thy works praise unto race,
  The mighty acts shew done by thee.
5 I will speak of the glorious grace,
  And honour of thy majesty:

  Thy wondrous works I will record.
6 By men the might shall be extoll'd
  Of all thy dreadful acts, O Lord:
  And I thy greatness will unfold.

(193)   PSALM CXLV.   *Winchester,* or *Wareham.*

7 THEY utter shall abundantly
The mem'ry of thy goodness great;
And shall sing praises cheerfully,
Whilst they thy righteousness relate.

8 The Lord our God is gracious;
Compassionate is he also:
In mercy he is plenteous,
But unto wrath and anger slow.

9 Good unto all men is the Lord:
O'er all his works his mercy is.
10 Thy works all praise to thee afford:
Thy saints, O Lord, thy name shall bless.

(194)   PSALM CXLV.   *St. Pancras,* or *Warrington.*

13 THY kingdom hath none end at all,
It doth through ages all remain.
14 The Lord upholdeth all that fall,
The cast-down raiseth up again.

15 The eyes of all things, Lord, attend,
And on thee wait that here do live;
And thou, in season due, doth send
Sufficient food them to relieve.

16 Yea, thou thine hand dost open wide,
And ev'ry thing dost satisfy
That lives, and doth on earth abide,
Of thy great liberality.

(195)   PSALM CXLV.   *Mount Sinai.*

17 THE Lord is just in his ways all,
And holy in his works each one.

18 He's near to all that on him call,
   Who call in truth on him alone.

19 God will the just desire fulfil
   Of such as do him fear and dread :
   Their cry regard, and hear he will,
   And save them in the time of need.

20 The Lord preserves all, more and less,
   That bear to him a loving heart :
   But workers all of wickedness
   Destroy will he, and clean subvert.

21 Therefore my mouth and lips I'll frame
   To speak the praises of the Lord :
   To magnify his holy name
   For ever let all flesh accord.

(196)   PSALM CXLVI.   *Saxony*, or *New St Ann's*.

1 PRAISE God. The Lord praise, O my soul.
2   I'll praise God while I live :
   While I have being to my God
     In songs I'll praises give.

3 Trust not in princes, nor man's son,
     In whom there is no stay :
4 His breath departs, to's earth he turns :
     That day his thoughts decay.

5 O happy is that man and blest,
     Whom Jacob's God doth aid ;
   Whose hope upon the Lord doth rest,
     And on his God is stay'd :

6 Who made the earth and heavens high,
     Who made the swelling deep,
   And all that is within the same :
     Who truth doth ever keep.

(197)   PSALM CXLVI.   *St. David's.*

7 GOD righteous judgment executes
　For those oppress'd that be :
　He to the hungry giveth food :
　　God sets the pris'ners free.

8 The Lord doth give the blind their sight;
　The bowed down doth raise :
　The Lord doth dearly love all those
　　That walk in upright ways.

9 The stranger's shield, the widow's stay,
　The orphan's help, is he :
　But yet by him the wicked's way
　　Turn'd upside down shall be.

10 The Lord shall reign for evermore :
　Thy God, O Sion, he
　Reigns to all generations.
　　Praise to the Lord give ye.

(198)   PSALM CXLVII.   *Old* 68*th.*

1 PRAISE ye the Lord ; for it is good
　Praise to our God to sing :
　For it is pleasant, and to praise
　　It is a comely thing.

2 God doth build up Jerusalem ;
　And he it is alone
　That the dispersed of Israel
　　Doth gather into one.

3 Those that are broken in their heart,
　And grieved in their minds,
　He healeth, and their painful wounds
　　He tenderly up-binds.

4 He counts the number of the stars;
  He names them ev'ry one.
5 Great is our Lord, and of great power;
  His wisdom search can none.

(199)　　　　Psalm CXLVII.　　　　*Lancaster.*

6 The Lord lifts up the meek; and casts
  The wicked to the ground.
7 Sing to the Lord, and give him thanks;
  On harp his praises sound;
8 Who covereth the heav'n with clouds,
  Who for the earth below
  Prepareth rain, who maketh grass
  Upon the mountains grow.
9 He gives the beast his food, he feeds
  The ravens young that cry.
10 His pleasure not in horses' strength,
  Nor in man's legs, doth lie.
11 But in all those that do him fear
  The Lord doth pleasure take;
  In those that to his mercy do
  By hope themselves betake.

(200)　　　　Psalm CXLVII.　　　　*Farrant.*

12 The Lord praise, O Jerusalem;
  Sion, thy God confess:
13 For thy gates' bars he maketh strong;
  Thy sons in thee doth bless.
14 He in thy borders maketh peace;
  With fine wheat filleth thee.
15 He sends forth his command on earth;
  His word runs speedily.
16 Hoar-frost, like ashes, scatt'reth he;
  Like wool he snow doth give:

17 Like morsels casteth forth his ice ;
    Who in its cold can live ?
18 He sendeth forth-his mighty word,
    And melteth them again ;
    His wind he makes to blow, and then
    The waters flow amain.
19 The doctrine of his holy word
    To Jacob he doth shew ;
    His statutes and his judgments he
    Gives Israel to know.
20 To any nation never he
    Such favour did afford ;
    For they his judgments have not known.
    O do ye praise the Lord.

(201)   PSALM CXLVIII.   *Old* 148*th*, or *Benedicite*.

1 THE Lord of heav'n confess,
    On high his glory raise.
2 Him let all angels bless,
    Him all his armies praise.
3   Him glorify
        Sun, moon, and stars ;
4   Ye higher spheres,
    And cloudy sky.
5 From God your beings are,
    Him therefore famous make ;
    You all created were,
    When he the word but spake.
6   And from that place,
        Where fix'd you be
    By his decree,
        You cannot pass.
7 Praise God from earth below,
    Ye dragons, and ye deeps :

8 Fire, hail, clouds, wind, and snow,
　　Whom in command he keeps.
9　　　Praise ye his name,
　　　　Hills great and small,
　　　　Trees low and tall ;
10　　　Beasts wild and tame ;

13 O let God's name be praised
　　Above both earth and sky ;
14 For he his saints hath raised.
　　And set their horn on high :
　　　Ev'n those that be
　　　　Of Isr'el's race,
　　　　Near to his grace.
　　　The Lord praise ye.

(202)　　　　Psalm CXLIX.　　　　*Irish.*

1 Praise ye the Lord : unto him sing
　　A new song, and his praise
　In the assembly of his saints
　　In sweet psalms do ye raise.

2 Let Isr'el in his Maker joy,
　　And to him praises sing :
　Let all that Sion's children are
　　Be joyful in their King.

3 O let them unto his great name
　　Give praises in the dance ;
　Let them with timbrel and with harp
　　In songs his praise advance.

4 For God doth pleasure take in those
　　That his own people be ;
　And he with his salvation
　　The meek will beautify.

(203)   PSALM CL.   *Newington.*

1 PRAISE ye the Lord. God's praise within
His sanctuary raise ;
And to him in the firmament
Of his power give ye praise.

2 Because of all his mighty acts,
With praise him magnify :
O praise him, as he doth excel
In glorious majesty.

3 Praise him with trumpet's sound ; his praise
With psaltery advance :
4 With timbrel, harp, string'd instruments,
And organs, in the dance.

5 Praise him on cymbals loud : him praise
On cymbals sounding high.
6 Let each thing breathing praise the Lord.
Praise to the Lord give ye.

Paraphrases.

(204)   II.   *Harrington.*

1 O God of Bethel! by whose hand
    Thy people still are fed;
Who through this weary pilgrimage
    Hast all our fathers led:

2 Our vows, our prayers, we now present
    Before thy throne of grace:
God of our fathers! be the God
    Of their succeeding race.

3 Through each perplexing path of life
    Our wand'ring footsteps guide;
Give us each day our daily bread,
    And raiment fit provide.

4 O spread thy cov'ring wings around,
    Till all our wand'rings cease,
And at our Father's loved abode
    Our souls arrive in peace.

5 Such blessings from thy gracious hand
    Our humble prayers implore;
And thou shalt be our chosen God,
    And portion evermore.

(205)   III.   *Durham.*

1 Naked as from the earth we came,
    And enter'd life at first;
Naked we to the earth return,
    And mix with kindred dust.

2 Whate'er we fondly call our own
    Belongs to heav'n's great Lord;

The blessings lent us for a day
Are soon to be restored.

3 'Tis God that lifts our comforts high,
Or sinks them in the grave :
He gives ; and when he takes away,
He takes but what he gave.

4 Then, ever blessed be his name!
His goodness swell'd our store ;
His justice but resumes its own ;
'Tis ours still to adore.

(206) IV. *Bangor.*

1 How still and peaceful is the grave!
Where, life's vain tumults past,
Th' appointed house, by Heav'n's decree,
Receives us all at last.

2 The wicked there from troubling cease,
Their passions rage no more ;
And there the weary pilgrim rests
From all the toils he bore.

3 There rest the pris'ners, now released
From slav'ry's sad abode :
No more they hear th' oppressor's voice,
Or dread the tyrant's rod.

4 There servants, masters, small and great,
Partake the same repose ;
And there, in peace, the ashes mix
Of those who once were foes.

5 All, levell'd by the hand of Death,
Lie sleeping in the tomb ;
Till God in judgment calls them forth,
To meet their final doom.

PARAPHRASES. 279

(207)   V.   *St. Mary's.*

1 Though trouble springs not from the dust,
    Nor sorrow from the ground;
Yet ills on ills, by Heav'n's decree,
    In man's estate are found.

2 As sparks in close succession rise,
    So man, the child of woe,
Is doom'd to endless cares and toils
    Through all his life below.

3 But with my God I leave my cause;
    From him I seek relief;
To him, in confidence of prayer,
    Unbosom all my grief.

4 Unnumber'd are his wondrous works,
    Unsearchable his ways;
'Tis his the mourning soul to cheer,
    The bowed down to raise.

(208)   VIII.   *Dundee.*

1 Few are thy days, and full of woe,
    O man, of woman born!
Thy doom is written, "Dust thou art,
    And shalt to dust return."

2 Behold the emblem of thy state
    In flow'rs that bloom and die,
Or in the shadow's fleeting form,
    That mocks the gazer's eye.

3 Guilty and frail, how shalt thou stand
    Before thy sov'reign Lord?
Can troubled and polluted springs
    A hallow'd stream afford?

4 Determined are the days that fly
    Successive o'er thy head;

PARAPHRASES.

   The number'd hour is on the wing
     That lays thee with the dead.
5 Great God! afflict not in thy wrath
     The short allotted span,
   That bounds the few and weary days
     Of pilgrimage to man.
13 O may the grave become to me
     The bed of peaceful rest,
   Whence I shall gladly rise at length,
     And mingle with the blest!

(209)   IX.   *St. Gregory,*
                                  or *York.*

1 WHO can resist th' Almighty arm
     That made the starry sky?
   Or who elude the certain glance
     Of God's all-seeing eye?
2 From him no cov'ring veils our crimes;
     Hell opens to his sight;
   And all Destruction's secret snares
     Lie full disclosed in light.
3 Firm on the boundless void of space
     He poised the steady pole,
   And in the circle of his clouds
     Bade secret waters roll.
4 While nature's universal frame
     Its Maker's power reveals,
   His throne, remote from mortal eyes,
     An awful cloud conceals.

(210)   XV.   *Melcombe.*

1 As long as life its term extends,
   Hope's blest dominion never ends;
   For while the lamp holds on to burn,
   The greatest sinner may return.

PARAPHRASES.   281

2 Life is the season God hath giv'n
 To fly from hell, and rise to heav'n;
 That day of grace fleets fast away,
 And none its rapid course can stay.

3 The living know that they must die;
 But all the dead forgotten lie:
 Their mem'ry and their name is gone,
 Alike unknowing and unknown.

5 Then what thy thoughts design to do,
 Still let thy hands with might pursue;
 Since no device nor work is found,
 Nor wisdom underneath the ground.

(211)   XVIII.   *Newington.*

1 BEHOLD! the mountain of the Lord
  In latter days shall rise
 On mountain tops above the hills,
  And draw the wond'ring eyes.

2 To this the joyful nations round,
  All tongues and tribes shall flow;
 Up to the hill of God, they'll say,
  And to his house we'll go.

3 The beam that shines from Sion hill
  Shall lighten ev'ry land;
 The King who reigns in Salem's towers
  Shall all the world command.

4 Among the nations he shall judge;
  His judgments truth shall guide;
 His sceptre shall protect the just,
  And quell the sinner's pride.

7 Come then, O house of Jacob! come
  To worship at his shrine;
 And, walking in the light of God,
  With holy beauties shine.

(212) XIX. *Old 68th.*

1 THE race that long in darkness pined
    Have seen a glorious light;
  The people dwell in day, who dwelt
    In death's surrounding night.

2 To hail thy rise, thou better Sun!
    The gath'ring nations come,
  Joyous, as when the reapers bear
    The harvest treasures home.

3 For thou our burden hast removed,
    And quell'd th' oppressor's sway,
  Quick as the slaughter'd squadrons fell
    In Midian's evil day.

4 To us a Child of hope is born;
    To us a Son is giv'n;
  Him shall the tribes of earth obey,
    Him all the hosts of heav'n.

5 His name shall be the Prince of Peace,
    For evermore adored,
  The Wonderful, the Counsellor,
    The great and mighty Lord.

6 His power increasing still shall spread,
    His reign no end shall know;
  Justice shall guard his throne above,
    And peace abound below.

(213) XX. *St. Thomas's.*

1 How glorious Sion's courts appear,
    The city of our God!
  His throne he hath establish'd here,
    Here fix'd his loved abode.

2 Its walls, defended by his grace,
    No power shall e'er o'erthrow,

Salvation is its bulwark sure
 Against th' assailing foe.

3 Lift up the everlasting gates,
 The doors wide open fling;
Enter, ye nations, who obey
 The statutes of our King.

4 Here shall ye taste unmingled joys,
 And dwell in perfect peace,
Ye, who have known JEHOVAH'S name,
 And trusted in his grace.

5 Trust in the Lord, for ever trust,
 And banish all your fears;
Strength in the Lord JEHOVAH dwells
 Eternal as his years.

(214)   XXI.   *York.*

1 ATTEND, ye tribes that dwell remote,
 Ye tribes at hand, give ear;
Th' upright in heart alone have hope,
 The false in heart have fear.

2 The man who walks with God in truth,
 And ev'ry guile disdains;
Who hates to lift oppression's rod,
 And scorns its shameful gains;

3 Whose soul abhors the impious bribe
 That tempts from truth to stray,
And from th' enticing snares of vice
 Who turns his eyes away:

4 His dwelling, 'midst the strength of rocks,
 Shall ever stand secure;
His Father will provide his bread,
 His water shall be sure.

5 For him the kingdom of the just
    Afar doth glorious shine;
   And he the King of kings shall see
    In majesty divine.

(215)　　　　XXIII.　　　*Manchester.*

1 BEHOLD my Servant! see him rise
    Exalted in my might!
   Him have I chosen, and in him
    I place supreme delight.

2 On him, in rich effusion pour'd,
    My Spirit shall descend;
   My truths and judgments he shall shew
    To earth's remotest end.

3 Gentle and still shall be his voice,
    No threats from him proceed;
   The smoking flax he shall not quench,
    Nor break the bruised reed.

4 The feeble spark to flames he'll raise;
    The weak will not despise;
   Judgment he shall bring forth to truth,
    And make the fallen rise.

(216)　　　　XXIII.　　　*St. Gregory.*

12 SING to the Lord in joyful strains!
    Let earth his praise resound,
   Ye who upon the ocean dwell,
    And fill the isles around!

13 O city of the Lord! begin
    The universal song;
   And let the scatter'd villages
    The cheerful notes prolong.

14 Let Kedar's wilderness afar
    Lift up its lonely voice;

        And let the tenants of the rock
           With accents rude rejoice;
15 Till 'midst the streams of distant lands
           The islands sound his praise;
        And all combined, with one accord,
           JEHOVAH'S glories raise.

(217)   XXIV.   *Jackson's.*

2 BEHOLD how gracious is our God!
           Hear the consoling strains,
        In which he cheers our drooping hearts,
           And mitigates our pains.

3 Cease ye, when days of darkness come,
           In sad dismay to mourn,
        As if the Lord could leave his saints
           Forsaken or forlorn.

4 Can the fond mother e'er forget
           The infant whom she bore?
        And can its plaintive cries be heard,
           Nor move compassion more?

5 She may forget: nature may fail
           A parent's heart to move;
        But Sion on my heart shall dwell
           In everlasting love.

(218)   XXV.   *Bromfield.*

7 HIS sacred blood hath wash'd our souls
           From sin's polluted stain;
        His stripes have heal'd us, and his death
           Revived our souls again.

8 We all, like sheep, had gone astray
           In ruin's fatal road:
        On him were our trangressions laid;
           He bore the mighty load.

14 His soul, rejoicing, shall behold
    The purchase of his pain ;
    And all the guilty whom he saved
    Shall bless Messiah's reign.

16 He dy'd to bear the guilt of men,
    That sin might be forgiv'n :
    He lives to bless them and defend,
    And plead their cause in heav'n.

(219)   XXVI.   *Huddersfield.*

7 SEEK ye the Lord while yet his ear
    Is open to your call ;
    While offer'd mercy still is near,
    Before his footstool fall.

8 Let sinners quit their evil ways,
    Their evil thoughts forego :
    And God, when they to him return,
    Returning grace will shew.

9 He pardons with o'erflowing love :
    For, hear the voice divine !
    My nature is not like to yours,
    Nor like your ways are mine :

10 But far as heav'n's resplendent orbs
    Beyond earth's spot extend,
    As far my thoughts, as far my ways,
    Your ways and thoughts transcend.

(220)   XXVII.   *London New.*

1 THUS speaks the high and lofty One ;
    Ye tribes of earth, give ear ;
    The words of your Almighty King
    With sacred rev'rence hear :

2 Amidst the majesty of heav'n
    My throne is fix'd on high ;

And through eternity I hear
    The praises of the sky :

3 Yet, looking down, I visit oft
    The humble hallow'd cell ;
  And with the penitent who mourn
    'Tis my delight to dwell ;

4 The downcast spirit to revive,
    The sad in soul to cheer ;
  And from the bed of dust the man
    Of heart contrite to rear.

5 With me dwells no relentless wrath
    Against the human race ;
  The souls which I have form'd shall find
    A refuge in my grace.

(221)   XXIX.   *St. Paul's.*

1 AMIDST the mighty, where is he
    Who saith, and it is done ?
  Each varying scene of changeful life
    Is from the Lord alone.

2 He gives in gladsome bowers to dwell,
    Or clothes in sorrow's shroud ;
  His hand hath form'd the light, his hand
    Has form'd the dark'ning cloud.

3 Why should a living man complain
    Beneath the chast'ning rod ?
  Our sins afflict us ; and the cross
    Must bring us back to God.

4 O sons of men ! with anxious care
    Your hearts and ways explore ;
  Return from paths of vice to God :
    Return, and sin no more :

(222)   XXX.   *Old* 23*d.*

1 COME, let us to the Lord our God
   With contrite hearts return;
   Our God is gracious, nor will leave
   The desolate to mourn.

2 His voice commands the tempest forth,
   And stills the stormy wave;
   And though his arm be strong to smite,
   'Tis also strong to save.

3 Long hath the night of sorrow reign'd;
   The dawn shall bring us light:
   God shall appear, and we shall rise
   With gladness in his sight.

4 Our hearts, if God we seek to know,
   Shall know him, and rejoice;
   His coming like the morn shall be,
   Like morning songs his voice.

(223)   XXXI.   *Bedford.*

1 THUS speaks the heathen: How shall man
   The Power Supreme adore?
   With what accepted off'rings come
   His mercy to implore?

2 Shall clouds of incense to the skies
   With grateful odour speed?
   Or victims from a thousand hills
   Upon the altar bleed?

5 He what is good hath clearly shewn,
   O favour'd race! to thee;
   And what doth God require of those
   Who bend to him the knee?

6 Thy deeds, let sacred justice rule;
    Thy heart, let mercy fill;
  And, walking humbly with thy God,
    To him resign thy will.

(224)   XXXIII.   *St. Stephen's.*

1 FATHER of all! we bow to thee,
    Who dwell'st in heav'n adored;
  But present still through all thy works,
    The universal Lord.

2 For ever hallow'd be thy name
    By all beneath the skies;
  And may thy kingdom still advance,
    Till grace to glory rise.

3 A grateful homage may we yield,
    With hearts resign'd to thee;
  And, as in heav'n thy will is done,
    On earth so let it be.

4 From day to day we humbly own
    The hand that feeds us still:
  Give us our bread, and teach to rest
    Contented in thy will.

5 Our sins before thee we confess;
    O may they be forgiv'n!
  As we to others mercy shew,
    We mercy beg from Heav'n.

6 Still let thy grace our life direct;
    From evil guard our way;
  And in temptation's fatal path
    Permit us not to stray.

(225)   XXXIV.   *French.*

4 THOU only know'st the Son: from thee
    My kingdom I receive;

And none the Father know but they
   Who in the Son believe.

5 Come then to me, all ye who groan,
   With guilt and fears opprest;
  Resign to me the willing heart,
   And I will give you rest.

6 Take up my yoke, and learn of me
   The meek and lowly mind;
  And thus your weary troubled souls
   Repose and peace shall find.

7 For light and gentle is my yoke;
   The burden I impose
  Shall ease the heart, which groan'd before
   Beneath a load of woes.

(226)   XXXV.   *Communion.*

3 My broken body thus I give
  For you, for all; take, eat, and live;
  And oft the sacred rite renew,
  That brings my wondrous love to view.

4 Then in his hands the cup he raised,
  And God anew he thank'd and praised;
  While kindness in his bosom glow'd,
  And from his lips salvation flow'd.

5 My blood I thus pour forth, he cries,
  To cleanse the soul in sin that lies;
  In this the covenant is seal'd,
  And Heav'n's eternal grace reveal'd.

6 With love to man this cup is fraught,
  Let all partake the sacred draught;
  Through latest ages let it pour,
  In mem'ry of my dying hour.

(227)   XXXIX.   *Tiverton.*

1 HARK, the glad sound, the Saviour comes!
    The Saviour promised long;
  Let ev'ry heart exult with joy,
    And ev'ry voice be song!

3 He comes! the pris'ners to relieve,
    In Satan's bondage held;
  The gates of brass before him burst,
    The iron fetters yield.

4 He comes! from dark'ning scales of vice
    To clear the inward sight;
  And on the eye-balls of the blind
    To pour celestial light.

5 He comes! the broken hearts to bind,
    The bleeding souls to cure;
  And with the treasures of his grace
    T' enrich the humble poor.

6 The sacred year has now revolved,
    Accepted of the Lord,
  When Heav'n's high promise is fulfill'd,
    And Israel is restored.

(228)   XLI.   *St. Magnus.*

1 As when the Hebrew prophet raised
    The brazen serpent high,
  The wounded look'd, and straight were cured,
    The people ceased to die:

2 So from the Saviour on the cross
    A healing virtue flows;
  Who looks to him with lively faith
    Is saved from endless woes.

3 For God gave up his Son to death,
    So gen'rous was his love,

    That all the faithful might enjoy
      Eternal life above.

4 Not to condemn the sons of men
    The Son of God appear'd;
  No weapons in his hand are seen,
    Nor voice of terror heard:

5 He came to raise our fallen state,
    And our lost hopes restore:
  Faith leads us to the mercy-seat,
    And bids us fear no more.

(229)   XLII.   *Dunfermline.*

1 LET not your hearts with anxious thoughts
    Be troubled or dismay'd;
  But trust in Providence divine,
    And trust my gracious aid.

2 I to my Father's house return;
    There num'rous mansions stand,
  And glory manifold abounds
    Through all the happy land.

3 I go your entrance to secure,
    And your abode prepare;
  Regions unknown are safe to you,
    When I, your friend, am there.

4 Thence shall I come, when ages close,
    To take you home with me;
  There we shall meet to part no more,
    And still together be.

5 I am the way, the truth, the life:
    No son of human race,
  But such as I conduct and guide,
    Shall see my Father's face.

(230)   XLIII.   *Greyfriars.*

1 You now must hear my voice no more ;
    My Father calls me home ;
But soon from heav'n the Holy Ghost,
    Your Comforter, shall come.

2 That heavenly Teacher, sent from God,
    Shall your whole soul inspire ;
Your minds shall fill with sacred truth,
    Your hearts with sacred fire.

3 Peace is the gift I leave with you ;
    My peace to you bequeath ;
Peace that shall comfort you through life,
    And cheer your souls in death.

4 I give not as the world bestows,
    With promise false and vain ;
Nor cares, nor fears, shall wound the heart
    In which my words remain.

(231)   XLIV.   *Redemption.*

3 'Tis finish'd—was his latest voice ;
    These sacred accents o'er,
He bow'd his head, gave up the ghost,
    And suffer'd pain no more.

4 'Tis finish'd—the Messiah dies
    For sins, but not his own ;
The great redemption is complete,
    And Satan's power o'erthrown.

5 'Tis finish'd—all his groans are past ;
    His blood, his pain, and toils,
Have fully vanquished our foes,
    And crown'd him with their spoils.

6 'Tis finish'd—legal worship ends,
   And gospel ages run ;
  All old things now are past away,
   And a new world begun.

(232)   XLVI.   *St. David's.*

1 VAIN are the hopes the sons of men
   Upon their works have built ;
  Their hearts by nature are unclean,
   Their actions full of guilt.

2 Silent let Jew and Gentile stand,
   Without one vaunting word ;
  And, humbled low, confess their guilt
   Before heav'n's righteous Lord.

3 No hope can on the law be built
   Of justifying grace ;
  The law, that shows the sinner's guilt,
   Condemns him to his face.

4 Jesus ! how glorious is thy grace !
   When in thy name we trust,
  Our faith receives a righteousness
   That makes the sinner just.

(233)   XLVII.   *Farrant.*

1 AND shall we then go on to sin,
   That grace may more abound ?
  Great God, forbid that such a thought
   Should in our breast be found !

2 When to the sacred font we came,
   Did not the rite proclaim,
  That, wash'd from sin, and all its stains,
   New creatures we became ?

3 With Christ the Lord we died to sin ;
   With him to life we rise,

To life, which now begun on earth,
　Is perfect in the skies.

4 Too long enthrall'd to Satan's sway,
　We now are slaves no more ;
For Christ hath vanquish'd death and sin,
　Our freedom to restore.

(234)　　　　　XLVIII.　　　*Newington.*

1 Let Christian faith and hope dispel
　　The fears of guilt and woe ;
　The Lord Almighty is our friend,
　　And who can prove a foe ?

2 He who his Son, most dear and loved,
　　Gave up for us to die,
　Shall he not all things freely give
　　That goodness can supply ?

3 Behold the best, the greatest gift,
　　Of everlasting love !
　Behold the pledge of peace below,
　　And perfect bliss above !

4 Where is the judge who can condemn,
　　Since God hath justified ?
　Who shall charge those with guilt or crime
　　For whom the Saviour died ?

(235)　　　　　XLVIII.　　　*Manchester.*

5 The Saviour died, but rose again
　　Triumphant from the grave ;
　And pleads our cause at God's right hand,
　　Omnipotent to save.

6 Who then can e'er divide us more
　　From Jesus and his love,
　Or break the sacred chain that binds
　　The earth to heav'n above ?

7 Let troubles rise, and terrors frown,
  And days of darkness fall;
Through him all dangers we 'll defy,
  And more than conquer all.

8 Nor death nor life, nor earth nor hell,
  Nor time's destroying sway,
Can e'er efface us from his heart,
  Or make his love decay.

(236)　　　　　XLIX.　　　*Stroudwater.*

9 LOVE still shall hold an endless reign
  In earth and heav'n above,
When tongues shall cease, and prophets fail,
  And ev'ry gift but love.

12 Now dark and dim, as through a glass,
  Are God and truth beheld;
Then shall we see as face to face,
  And God shall be unveil'd.

13 Faith, Hope, and Love, now dwell on earth,
  And earth by them is blest;
But Faith and Hope must yield to Love,
  Of all the graces best.

14 Hope shall to full fruition rise,
  And Faith be sight above:
These are the means, but this the end;
  For saints for ever love.

(237)　　　　　L.　　　*Durham.*

1 WHEN the last trumpet's awful voice
  This rending earth shall shake,
When opening graves shall yield their charge
  And dust to life awake;

2 Those bodies that corrupted fell
  Shall incorrupted rise,

And mortal forms shall spring to life
    Immortal in the skies.

4 Let Faith exalt her joyful voice,
    And thus begin to sing;
O Grave! where is thy triumph now?
    And where, O Death! thy sting?

6 Our God, whose name be ever bless'd!
    Disarms that foe we dread,
And makes us conquerors when we die,
    Through Christ our living head.

(238)   LI.   *French.*

1 Soon shall this earthly frame, dissolved,
    In death and ruins lie;
But better mansions wait the just,
    Prepared above the sky.

2 An house eternal, built by God,
    Shall lodge the holy mind;
When once those prison walls have fall'n
    By which 'tis now confined.

3 Hence, burden'd with a weight of clay,
    We groan beneath the load,
Waiting the hour which sets us free,
    And brings us home to God.

4 We know, that when the soul, unclothed,
    Shall from this body fly,
'Twill animate a purer frame
    With life that cannot die.

(239)   LI.   *Harrington.*

7 What faith rejoices to believe,
    We long and pant to see;

  We would be absent from the flesh,
   And present, Lord! with thee.
 8 But still, or here, or going hence,
   To this our labours tend,
  That, in his service spent, our life
   May in his favour end.

 9 For, lo! before the Son, as judge,
   Th' assembled world shall stand,
  To take the punishment or prize
   From his unerring hand.

10 Impartial retributions then
   Our diff'rent lives await:
  Our present actions, good or bad,
   Shall fix our future fate.

(240)   LII.   *Bromfield.*

 1 YE who the name of Jesus bear,
   His sacred steps pursue;
  And let that mind which was in him
   Be also found in you.

 2 Though in the form of God he was,
   His only Son declared,
  Nor to be equally adored
   As robb'ry did regard;

 3 His greatness he for us abased,
   For us his glory veil'd;
  In human likeness dwelt on earth,
   His majesty conceal'd:

 4 Nor only as a man appears,
   But stoops a servant low;
  Submits to death, nay, bears the cross,
   In all its shame and woe.

PARAPHRASES.

(241)   LIII.   *St. Andrew's.*

3 As Jesus died, and rose again
    Victorious from the dead ;
So his disciples rise, and reign
    With their triumphant Head.

4 The time draws nigh, when from the clouds
    Christ shall with shouts descend,
And the last trumpet's awful voice
    The heav'ns and earth shall rend.

6 The saints of God, from death set free,
    With joy shall mount on high ;
The heav'nly hosts with praises loud
    Shall meet them in the sky.

7 Together to their Father's house
    With joyful hearts they go ;
And dwell for ever with the Lord,
    Beyond the reach of woe.

8 A few short years of evil past,
    We reach the happy shore,
Where death-divided friends at last
    Shall meet to part no more.

(242)   LIV.   *London New.*

1 I 'M not ashamed to own my Lord,
    Or to defend his cause,
Maintain the glory of his cross,
    And honour all his laws.

2 Jesus, my Lord ! I know his name,
    His name is all my boast ;
Nor will he put my soul to shame,
    Nor let my hope be lost.

3 I know that safe with him remains,
    Protected by his power,

What I've committed to his trust,
Till the decisive hour.
4 Then will he own his servant's name
Before his Father's face,
And in the new Jerusalem
Appoint my soul a place.

(243)   LV.   *Lancaster.*

1 MY race is run; my warfare's o'er,
The solemn hour is nigh,
When offer'd up to God, my soul
Shall-wing its flight on high.

2 With heav'nly weapons I have fought
The battles of the Lord;
Finish'd my course, and kept the faith,
Depending on his word.

3 Henceforth there is laid up for me
A crown which cannot fade :
The righteous Judge at that great day
Shall place it on my head.

4 Nor hath the Sov'reign Lord decreed
This prize for me alone ;
But for all such as love like me
Th' appearance of his Son.

5 From ev'ry snare and evil work
His grace shall me defend,
And to his heav'nly kingdom safe
Shall bring me in the end.

(244)   LVI.   *Huddersfield.*

3 VAIN and presumptuous is the trust
Which in our works we place,
Salvation from a higher source
Flows to the human race.

PARAPHRASES.

4 'Tis from the mercy of our God
   That all our hopes begin ;
 His mercy saved our souls from death,
   And wash'd our souls from sin.

5 His Spirit, through the Saviour shed,
   Its sacred fire imparts,
 Refines our dross, and love divine
   Rekindles in our hearts.

6 Thence raised from death, we live anew ;
   And, justified by grace,
 We hope in glory to appear,
   And see our Father's face.

(245)   LVIII.   *Hamburgh.*

1 WHERE high the heav'nly temple stands,
  The house of God not made with hands,
  A great High Priest our nature wears,
  The guardian of mankind appears.

2 He who for men their surety stood,
  And pour'd on earth his precious blood,
  Pursues in heav'n his mighty plan,
  The Saviour and the friend of man.

3 Though now ascended up on high,
  He bends on earth a brother's eye ;
  Partaker of the human name,
  He knows the frailty of our frame.

4 Our fellow-suff'rer yet retains
  A fellow-feeling of our pains ;
  And still remembers in the skies
  His tears, his agonies, and cries.

5 In ev'ry pang that rends the heart,
  The Man of sorrows had a part ;

He sympathizes with our grief,
And to the suff'rer sends relief.

6 With boldness, therefore, at the throne,
Let us make all our sorrows known;
And ask the aids of heav'nly power
To help us in the evil hour.

(246) LIX. *St. Paul's.*

1 BEHOLD what witnesses unseen
  Encompass us around;
  Men, once like us, with suff'ring tried,
  But now with glory crown'd.

2 Let us, with zeal like theirs inspired,
  Begin the Christian race,
  And, freed from each encumb'ring weight,
  Their holy footsteps trace.

3 Behold a witness nobler still,
  Who trod affliction's path,
  Jesus, at once the finisher
  And author of our faith.

4 He for the joy before him set,
  So gen'rous was his love,
  Endured the cross, despised the shame,
  And now he reigns above.

(247) LIX. *St. Stephen's.*

10 A FATHER'S voice with rev'rence we
   On earth have often heard;
   The Father of our spirits now
   Demands the same regard.

11 Parents may err; but he is wise,
   Nor lifts the rod in vain;
   His chast'nings serve to cure the soul
   By salutary pain.

12 Affliction, when it spreads around,
    May seem a field of woe;
Yet there, at last, the happy fruits
    Of righteousness shall grow.

13 Then let our hearts no more despond,
    Our hands be weak no more;
Still let us trust our Father's love,
    His wisdom still adore.

(248)   LX.   *Santa Maria.*

1 FATHER of peace, and God of love!
    We own thy power to save,
That power by which our Shepherd rose
    Victorious o'er the grave.

2 Him from the dead thou brought'st again,
    When, by his sacred blood,
Confirm'd and seal'd for evermore,
    Th' eternal cov'nant stood.

3 O may thy Spirit seal our souls,
    And mould them to thy will,
That our weak hearts no more may stray,
    But keep thy precepts still;

4 That to perfection's sacred height
    We nearer still may rise,
And all we think, and all we do,
    Be pleasing in thine eyes.

(249)   LXI.   *St. Magnus.*

1 BLESS'D be the everlasting God,
    The Father of our Lord;
Be his abounding mercy praised,
    His majesty adored.

2 When from the dead he raised his Son,
 And call'd him to the sky,
 He gave our souls a lively hope
 That they should never die.

3 To an inheritance divine
 He taught our hearts to rise;
 'Tis uncorrupted, undefiled,
 Unfading in the skies.

4 Saints by the power of God are kept
 Till the salvation come:
 We walk by faith as strangers here;
 But Christ shall call us home.

(250) LXII. *Dunfermline.*

9 STILL all may share his sov'reign grace,
 In ev'ry change secure;
 The meek, the suppliant contrite race,
 Shall find his mercy sure.

10 The contrite race he counts his friends,
 Forbids the suppliant's fall;
 Condemns reluctant, but extends
 The hope of grace to all.

13 Since all this frame of things must end,
 As Heav'n has so decreed,
 How wise our inmost thoughts to guard,
 And watch o'er ev'ry deed;

14 Expecting calm th' appointed hour,
 When, Nature's conflict o'er,
 A new and better world shall rise,
 Where sin is known no more.

(251) LXIII. *Newington.*

1 BEHOLD th' amazing gift of love
 The Father hath bestow'd

On us, the sinful sons of men,
  To call us sons of God!

2 Conceal'd as yet this honour lies,
  By this dark world unknown,
A world that knew not when he came,
  Ev'n God's eternal Son.

3 High is the rank we now possess;
  But higher we shall rise;
Though what we shall hereafter be
  Is hid from mortal eyes:

4 Our souls, we know, when he appears,
  Shall bear his image bright;
For all his glory, full disclosed,
  Shall open to our sight.

5 A hope so great, and so divine,
  May trials well endure;
And purge the soul from sense and sin,
  As Christ himself is pure.

(252)   LXIV.   *Old* 68*th.*

1 To him that loved the souls of men,
  And wash'd us in his blood,
To royal honours raised our head,
  And made us priests to God;

2 To him let ev'ry tongue be praise,
  And ev'ry heart be love!
All grateful honours paid on earth,
  And nobler songs above!

3 Behold, on flying clouds he comes!
  His saints shall bless the day;
While they that pierced him sadly mourn
  In anguish and dismay.

4 I am the First, and I the Last;
   Time centres all in me;
Th' Almighty God, who was, and is,
   And evermore shall be.

(253)   LXV.   *St. Andrew's.*

5 HARK how th' adoring hosts above
   With songs surround the throne!
Ten thousand thousand are their tongues:
   But all their hearts are one.

6 Worthy the Lamb that died, they cry,
   To be exalted thus;
Worthy the Lamb, let us reply,
   For he was slain for us.

7 To him be power divine ascribed,
   And endless blessings paid;
Salvation, glory, joy, remain
   For ever on his head!

8 Thou hast redeem'd us with thy blood,
   And set the pris'ners free;
Thou mad'st us kings and priests to God,
   And we shall reign with thee.

10 Let all that dwell above the sky,
   Or on the earth below,
With fields, and floods, and ocean's shores,
   To thee their homage shew.

11 To Him who sits upon the throne,
   The God whom we adore,
And to the Lamb that once was slain,
   Be glory evermore.

Hymns.

(254)   I.   *Creation.*

1 THE spacious firmament on high,
 With all the blue ethereal sky,
 And spangled heav'ns, a shining frame,
 Their great Original proclaim.

2 Th' unwearied sun, from day to day,
 Does his Creator's power display;
 And publishes to ev'ry land
 The work of an Almighty hand.

3 Soon as the evening shades prevail,
 The moon takes up the wondrous tale,
 And, nightly to the list'ning earth,
 Repeats the story of her birth;

4 While all the stars that round her burn,
 And all the planets in their turn,
 Confirm the tidings as they roll,
 And spread the truth from pole to pole.

(255)   II.   *Bedford.*

1 BLEST morning! whose first dawning rays
   Beheld the Son of God
 Arise triumphant from the grave,
   And leave his dark abode.

2 Wrapt in the silence of the tomb
   The great Redeemer lay,
 Till the revolving skies had brought
   The third, th' appointed day.

3 Hell and the grave combined their force
   To hold our Lord in vain;

Sudden the Conqueror arose,
And burst their feeble chain.

4 To thy great name, Almighty Lord!
We sacred honours pay,
And loud hosannahs shall proclaim
The triumphs of the day.

5 Salvation and immortal praise
To our victorious King!
Let heav'n and earth, and rocks and seas,
With glad hosannahs ring.

6 To Father, Son, and Holy Ghost,
The God whom we adore,
Be glory, as it was, and is,
And shall be evermore.

(256) III. *Norwich.*

1 SUN of the soul! thou Saviour dear,
It is not night if thou appear;
Oh, may no earth-born cloud arise,
To hide thee from thy servants' eyes.

2 When with dear friends sweet talk we hold,
And all the flowers of life unfold,
Let not our hearts within us burn,
Except we thee in all discern.

3 When the soft dews of kindly sleep
Our weary eyelids gently steep,
Be our last thought,—how sweet to rest
For ever on our Saviour's breast.

4 Abide with us from morn to eve,
For without thee we cannot live;
Abide with us when night is nigh,
For without thee we dare not die.

(257)   IV.   *Pascal.*

1 HARK! the herald angels sing
   Glory to the new-born King,
   Peace on earth and mercy mild,
   God and sinners reconciled.

2 Joyful all ye nations rise,
   Join the triumph of the skies;
   With th' angelic host proclaim,—
   Christ is born in Bethlehem.

3 See the everlasting Lord,
   Christ by highest heav'n adored,
   Pleased as man with men to dwell,
   Jesus our Immanuel.

4 Lo! he lays his glory by,
   Born that men no more might die,
   Born to raise the sons of earth,
   Born to give them second birth.

5 Hail, the heav'n-born Prince of peace!
   Hail, the Sun of righteousness!
   Ris'n with healing in his wings,
   Light and life to all he brings.

6 Let us then with angels sing
   Glory to the new-born King!
   Glory in the highest heav'n,
   Peace on earth, and man forgiv'n!

(258)   V.   *Easter Hymn.*

1 CHRIST is risen from the dead,—*Hal.*
   High ascended as our head,—*Hal.*
   Enter'd heaven with his blood,—*Hal.*
   Seated on the throne of God.—*Hal.*

2 Now his work appears complete ;—*Hal.*
For he reigns in glory great ;—*Hal.*
Angels sound his praise aloud ;—*Hal.*
Praise him, all ye saints of God.—*Hal.*

3 God is pleased in Christ his Son—*Hal.*
For the work that he hath done,—*Hal.*
For the glory he hath giv'n—*Hal.*
To the Lord of earth and heav'n.—*Hal.*

4 Justice, now, has met with grace ;—*Hal.*
Peace and righteousness embrace ;—*Hal.*
Hope has lifted up her head :—*Hal.*
Christ is risen from the dead.—*Hal.*

(**259**)　　　　　　VI.　　　　*Haydn's Hymn.*

1 CHRIST is coming ! let creation
　　From her groans and travail cease ;
　Let the glorious proclamation
　　Hope restore, and faith increase :
　　　Christ is coming !
　Come, thou blessed Prince of Peace.

2 Earth can now but tell the story
　　Of thy bitter cross and pain ;
　She shall yet behold thy glory
　　When thou comest back to reign :
　　　Christ is coming !
　Let each heart repeat the strain.

3 Long thine exiles have been pining,
　　Far from rest, and home, and thee ;
　Soon, in heav'nly glory shining,
　　Their Restorer shall they see :
　　　Christ is coming !
　Haste the joyous jubilee !

4 With that blessed hope before us,
 Let no harp remain unstrung;
 Let the mighty advent chorus
  Onward roll in every tongue :
   Christ is coming!
  Come, Lord Jesus, quickly come!

(260)   VII.   *Cowes.*

1 Lo, he comes with clouds descending,
 Once for guilty sinners slain ;
 Thousand thousand saints attending,
  Swell the triumph of his train ;
   Halleluia! halleluia!
  Jesus comes, he comes to reign.

2 Ev'ry eye shall now behold him
 Robed in dreadful majesty ;
 They who set at nought and sold him,
  Pierced and nail'd him to the tree,
   Now, with terror, and with wailing,
  Him, their Judge and Sov'reign see.

3 Blest redemption—long expected!
 All his saints his glory share :
 They, no more despised, rejected,
  Rise to meet him in the air.—
   Halleluia! halleluia!
  Jesus, King of saints, is there.

4 Glorious King! let all adore thee,
 Seated on thy Father's throne.
 Saviour! take the power and glory,—
  Take the kingdom for thine own.
   Thou art worthy! thou art worthy!
  Make thy boundless mercy known.

(261)   VIII.   *Winchester.*

1 THEE, God, we praise, thee, Lord, confess,
Thee, Father everlasting, bless;
The tribes of earth and air and sea,
With wondrous voices worship thee.

2 To thee all angels ceaseless cry,
With all the princes of the sky;
The cherub and the seraph join,
And thus they hymn the praise divine:

3 Thee, holy, holy, holy King,
Lord of Sabaoth, thee we sing;
Both heav'n and earth are full of thee,
Father of boundless majesty.

4 Thee, the apostles' glorious choir,
Thee, prophets with their tongues of fire,
Thee, white-robed hosts of martyrs bright,
Worship and praise day without night.

5 Thee through the earth thy saints confess;
Thee, Father infinite, they bless;
Thy true, divine, and only Son;
Thy Holy Spirit, Three in One.

(262)   IX.   *Calcott.*

1 BE still, my soul! the Lord is on thy side;
Bear patiently the cross of grief and pain;
Leave to thy God to order and provide;
In every change he faithful will remain.

2 Be still, my soul! thy God doth undertake
To guide the future as he hath the past;
Thy hope, thy confidence let nothing shake,
All, now mysterious, shall be clear at last.

3 Be still, my soul! when dearest friends depart,
And all is darken'd in the vale of tears;

Then thou shalt better know his love, his heart,
Who comes to soothe thy sorrow and thy fears.

4 Be still, my soul! the hour is hast'ning on
When thou shalt be for ever with the Lord;
When disappointment, fear, and grief are gone,
Sorrow forgot, love's purest joys restored.

263.   X.   *Theodora.*

1 Jesus, lover of my soul,
 Let me to thy bosom fly,
While the raging billows roll,
 While the tempest still is high.

2 Hide me, O my Saviour, hide,
 Till the storm of life be past;
Safe into the haven guide;
 Oh, receive my soul at last.

3 Other refuge have I none,
 Clings my helpless soul to thee;
Leave, oh, leave me not alone,
 Still support and comfort me.

4 All my trust on thee is stay'd,
 All my help from thee I bring;
Cover my defenceless head
 With the shadow of thy wing.

5 Plenteous grace with thee is found,
 Grace to pardon all my sin;
Let the healing streams abound,
 Make and keep me pure within.

6 Thou of life the fountain art,
 Freely let me take of thee;
Spring thou up within my heart,—
 Ev'n to all eternity.

(264)　　　　　　　XI.　　　　　*Norwood.*

1 GUIDE us, O thou great Jehovah!
　　Pilgrims through this barren land;
　We are weak, but thou art mighty,
　　Hold us with thy powerful hand.

2 Open thou the heav'nly fountain,
　　Whence the healing waters flow;
　Let the fiery, cloudy pillar,
　　Guide us all our journey through.

3 When we tread the verge of Jordan,
　　Bid our spirits fear no more;
　Guard us through the threat'ning billows,
　　Land us safe on Canaan's shore.

(265)　　　　　　　XII.　　　　　*Waterstock.*

1 O FATHER, let me be
　　The object of thy care,
　For daily unto thee
　　I lift my humble prayer:
　Preserve my soul, for I am thine,
　And guide me with thy truth divine.

2 When care and trouble fall
　　On my afflicted soul,
　To thee, O Lord, I call,
　　For thou canst make me whole;
　And thou wilt hear my suppliant cry,
　And bid affection's tear be dry.

3 Teach me thy way, O Lord,
　　That I may walk therein;
　Thy gracious help afford
　　To keep my heart from sin;
　So shall I praise thy glorious name,
　And thy redeeming love proclaim.

(266)   XIII.   *St. Pancras*, or *Evening Hymn.*

1 My God, my Father, while I stray,
Far from my home, on life's rough way,
O teach me from the heart to say—
           Thy will be done!

2 If thou shouldst call me to resign
What most I prize—it ne'er was mine;
I only yield thee what is thine:
           Thy will be done!

3 Renew my will from day to day;
Blend it with thine, and take away
All that now makes it hard to say—
           Thy will be done!

4 Then when on earth I breathe no more
The prayer, oft mix'd with tears before,
I 'll sing upon a happier shore—
           Thy will be done!

(267)   XIV.   *Solomon.*

1 JERUSALEM, my happy home,
   Name ever dear to me,
When shall my labours have an end,
   Thy joys when shall I see?

2 When shall mine eyes thy glorious walls,
   And gates of pearl behold,
Thy bulwarks with salvation strong,
   And streets of purest gold?

3 Apostles, martyrs, prophets, there
   Around my Saviour stand;

And all I love in Christ below
Shall join the glorious band.

4 Jerusalem ! our happy home !
Our souls still long for thee :
Then shall our labours have an end,
When we thy joys shall see.

THE END.

EDINBURGH : T. AND A. CONSTABLE,
PRINTERS TO THE QUEEN, AND TO THE UNIVERSITY.

www.ingramcontent.com/pod-product-compliance
Lightning Source LLC
Chambersburg PA
CBHW030014240426
43672CB00007B/945